The Savannah

Rivers of America Books

ALREADY PUBLISHED ARE:

KENNEBEC by Robert P. Tristram Coffin
UPPER MISSISSIPPI (New Revised Edition, 1944)
by Walter Havighurst
SUWANNEE RIVER by Cecile Hulse Matschat
POWDER RIVER by Struthers Burt
THE JAMES (New Revised Edition, 1945)
by Blair Niles
THE HUDSON by Carl Carmer
THE SACRAMENTO by Julian Dana
THE WABASH by William E. Wilson
THE ARKANSAS by Clyde Brion Davis
THE DELAWARE by Harry Emerson Wildes
THE ILLINOIS by James Gray
THE KAW by Floyd Benjamin Streeter
THE BRANDYWINE by Henry Seidel Canby
THE CHARLES by Arthur Bernon Tourtellot
THE KENTUCKY by T. D. Clark
THE SANGAMON by Edgar Lee Masters
THE ALLEGHENY by Frederick Way, Jr.

RIVERS OF AMERICA

EDITED BY *Hervey Allen* AND *Carl Carmer*

AS PLANNED AND STARTED BY

Constance Lindsay Skinner

ASSOCIATE EDITOR
JEAN CRAWFORD

ART EDITOR
BENJAMIN FEDER

THE SAVANNAH

Thomas L. Stokes

(handwritten: Lunsford)

ILLUSTRATED BY

Lamar Dodd

Rinehart & Co., Inc.

NEW YORK
TORONTO

TO *Hannah, Chip and Layton*

CONTENTS

ix

The Savannah

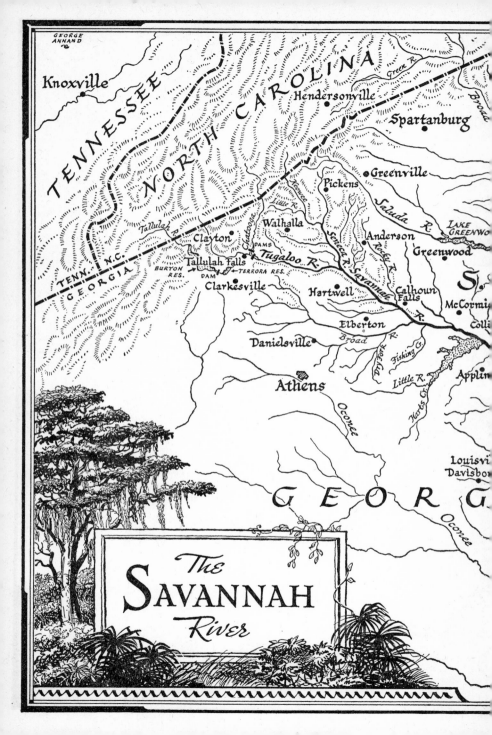

A River Is a Personal Thing

I first knew the Savannah as a young newspaper reporter on the threshold of experience.

I knew it at the city of Savannah as a broad and sluggish stream that crawled by the wharves, full and red with Georgia and Carolina earth sucked from the hills and the plains in its long journey from the Appalachians to the sea. It was like a giant snake lying in the mud and marshes, hardly stirring now, torpid under the sun, sleepy and satiated. It was patient of wind and weather now that its long ordeal was nearly over.

The river was a symbol of permanence as I watched it day by day, hurrying as I must along the waterfront high on the bank above it in search of ephemeral items for the newspapers. Now I saw it between the buildings; now I saw it spread out below me as I sat on the porch of a shipping office and chatted with a friendly sea captain.

But it was at night that I loved it best when it was a mysterious pathway, an open-sesame to young men's dreams. Then I would climb down the stairway that led from the streets and the city above, walk down the ancient cobblestone path around the edge of a dark building, and come upon it.

I liked it best in the moonlight, a radiant highway along which my imagination took flight fancifully to the open sea that I knew lay beyond. But I liked it also when there was no moon, when it was a mystery flowing in and around and behind the ships that lay along the wharves, a dark mystery accentuated by the twinkling lights from the ships that danced fitfully in the mirror of its encompassing black surface. It impressed itself on memory by ships' bells that tolled the half hour to cry out mere man's slavery to time, ironically enough in the presence of a river that is eternal; by the muffled shuffle of footsteps along the decks, hushed it seemed by the quiet omniscience of the river; and by subdued, seemingly secret snatches of talk that penetrated the nightlike voices overheard from another planet.

Sometimes, emboldened by a friendly word from a ship's deck, I would board one of the tramp steamers that had wandered into our harbor, and listen for an idle hour to the tall tales of men who had sailed the seven seas, sharing a pipe and mutual loneliness while the ship strained and creaked and groaned against the dock.

The Savannah was adventure to me in those days, vicarious adventure.

It led through the marshes to the big world of which these men spoke so knowingly and so casually. It was the river that flowed from reality into imagination, from youth to full life, from provincialism to the cosmopolitanism of great cities that hovered in my mind's eye over its horizons.

I was an inlander, born some three hundred miles away in the Georgia Piedmont, and the sea had for me the lure that it has for the inlander. This river, this slow-flowing Savannah that I knew, was the pathway to the sea and to the worlds beyond it; to worlds not only of today, but those long past—of Greece, Rome, and the Renaissance, of Spanish galleons laden with treasure, and the fierce and bewhiskered English sea captains roaming the ocean to capture treasure and loot cities along the Spanish Main. It brought me reminders of a wilder and sweeter England which could cut off the head of a king and listen to the poetry of Marlowe and Shakespeare, a land that sent its hardy children to make their homes in the wildernesses of the New World, to hold them against all comers. For of all this the Savannah was a part. I still see myself standing there as a young man, looking toward the sea down the broad reaches of the Savannah.

But now I can also see other young men, back in those other earlier days, who stood by rivers in foreign lands and gazed longingly toward the sea. They looked to the land on which I stood—to a new and strange land of weird legend and boundless hopeful impossibilities. And, in time, some of them realized their yearnings and came by toil and hardship and wind and hurricane to this New World of America, and in toil and hardship spent all the rest of the days of their lives there, still seeing afar off the land that it might become, and leaving to their sons and their sons' sons a faith in it that endured.

Rivers that lead to the sea are like magnets to those who stand, young and fresh, upon their shores. Rivers of other, far-away lands also are like magnets that attract the adventurous of the world, and so we plant new civilizations along their shores. Bit by bit they arise. First the rude shelter, then the rough home, then the mansion, then the tenement. We build new worlds and sprawl mightily over them, until we crowd ourselves with ourselves, and create poverty and disease and foul smells. Then some of us look from the banks of our rivers to the sea again, to other lands across the sea which may not, perchance, be so crowded, where we may draw a breath and live as free men once more. Thus have we built our worlds, from river to river.

My own river, the Savannah, was once the way to a pristine world. Now it has become a way to understanding. It is a many-paged book of life.

Here, in the lands that border it, in the flatlands and the uplands, in the mountains whence rise its tributary streams, and in its people, poor and rich, raw and cultured, I have read the story of a cycle of man creating a new world by ravishing it

with his impatience and his cupidity. Then, slowly, awaking to his sins, and trying to restore it. And also I have read the story of my own South, a beautiful and tragic story of men who built a way of life upon foundations of sand. For cruelty and jealousy, bravery and high idealism, all are mingled in the story of the Savannah.

Young men who stand along the shores of rivers looking to the sea may indeed learn many things in time.

Prelude

What is there about the Savannah?

There are many answers.

One is universal in the souls of men.

I found it one afternoon in early May, sitting in an automobile beside a deserted wharf along the banks of the river.

The car was parked on the grassy embankment of the levee that protects Augusta from those recurrent floods when the mountains gather up their waters and pour them into the tributaries of the Savannah two and three hundred miles away, and the tributaries pour them into the Savannah, and the Savannah pours them into the sea two hundred miles below where we sat.

"We," I say, for there was someone with me, someone who has lived his life with the river. I found an answer in his heart, although he opened it to me, slowly and timidly, for he was a big, husky fellow, reluctant of emotion. But as we talked together here, beside the river, I found an answer, in his face, too. He was looking down the river that was shining in the sun of late afternoon. It made a serene pathway between the fresh green of the trees on either bank. The trees were a border on one side for pleasant, rolling farm country; on the other for the houses and buildings of the city. The road of the river disappeared around a bend in the distance in its quest for the eventual sea.

There was peace in his face and there was contentment and ultimate satisfaction in his heart. He was at rest now that he was here, with the city and its people and its ways behind him.

I was very conscious of all this. Finally I asked:

"What is there about this river?"

He did not reply. He kept looking at it.

"You love this river, don't you?"

He nodded. "I could just sit here all day and look at it."

He said it simply and very quietly, but it was as if I heard a song in the air. He is not a demonstrative person, the man they know about Augusta as "Reggie" Dales. In those few words, and the way he said them, he had said it all. And I knew that he was a symbol for all the people who love this river. He had spoken for all of them.

As he drove the car up to this vantage point on the levee, he threw his hand in a helpless gesture toward the deserted building that carried across one end in big letters, now fading like an old newspaper, the label "Augusta Municipal Wharf."

"An eyesore," he grunted disdainfully.

Chagrin and despair mingled in his voice. It was a bitter protest.

There was hardly a ripple on the river there below us, and not a boat. He is a man of boats.

He was despondent with river hunger. He wanted a boat, another boat. He wanted to shove it out into the stream again and take it down to Savannah at the mouth, there where the river joins the ocean finally.

But there was the great World War. The government had taken his boat, the *Merry Queen*, a handsome cargo boat that could load a thousand tons and carry it on her back down the Savannah to the sea. It was the last of two boats on the river.

The government had taken the other, too. Both were in service elsewhere. This was in 1943.

His cargo was very common cargo—mostly bricks. But it's not cargo that matters finally, underneath, except as a means.

It's the river, and to him it is a very personal thing, like part of him, and so it becomes for all of us who learn it, its devious ways like a woman, its history like a never-ending book.

For about twenty miles below Augusta it remains the placid highway between comfortable rows of trees as we saw it from the levee, not grand or magnificent or grim trees, just friendly trees—elms, maples, oak, walnut, hickory, ash, pine, magnolia, mimosa—and beyond them, rising gradually toward the horizon, the plowed fields of neat farms.

Then the river changes, becomes a wild and alluring thing, full of mystery and passion. It twists and turns down an avenue of bigger trees, gloomier trees—cypress, giant cedar—which sit knee deep in the marshes behind picket fences of tall canes, and back of them, dark and awesome, is the jungle that extends for four or five miles on each side, a world away from the world, primitive and aloof, with eerie, glassy stretches of water that mirror the forbidding forest.

Here the river is the river that ran through another world, back through the centuries, before the Indian, before the Spaniard, before the Frenchman, before the Englishman. There is about it the dark magic of antiquity. Here and there wharves project from the ends of roads through the wilderness that you are sure lead back to civilization, wharves with strange names— Blue House, Robinson Round, Poor Robin, Hog's Nose Round, Frying Pan, Flat Dish, Cut Finger Cut, Wild Cat, Saucy Boy, Ring Jaw, Devil's Elbow—a wild jumble conjured up by rivermen for two hundred years, with humor, with anxiety, with fear.

Then, toward the city of Savannah, there are the pine barrens where the "poor whites" eternally scratch for a living through the years. Then there is the city, which was settled

over two hundred years ago. Then there is the sea, which is timeless like the river.

"It's the prettiest river in the world," said Reggie Dales.

He added proudly: "And the meanest to navigate."

For it is constantly creating shoals underneath its deceptively guileless surface, and the water becomes too shallow for passage.

"Sometimes you'll get hung up for days, even weeks," he explained. "Then's there's just nothing to do."

He grinned whimsically, like a father recounting the escapades of a mischievous boy.

He has known the river all his life. He was only nine when he had his first boat. He recalled with peculiar delight how, as a youngster, he and a crew of his boyhood companions would float down the river on a flatboat, sometimes on beyond Savannah down the inland channel as far as Brunswick and Fernandino, just idling along, stopping when they felt like it to fish or swim, going naked a good deal of the time.

He began to work regularly on river boats when he was sixteen. In time be began to build his own boats, for he is a boat builder as well as master. As if it were a cherished secret he told how he was picking up the necessaries to build another boat, here and there, despite the shortage of materials, second-hand equipment of all sorts. For he ached for another boat.

As he talked, his mood shifted from a determined optimism about building another boat of his own to deep pessimism about the future of river transportation as a business that would make the river alive as it was once in his knowing. River transportation is too slow in these times.

"People want things, when they want them, in a hurry," he said.

Then there are the railroads. They always seem able to hamstring development of the river. The railroads control the docks at Savannah and make the rates so high for cargo boats to unload there, laying all sorts of charges, that the cost of transportation by river is too high to attract shippers.

"They can always do something to stop us."

In his time, however, he remembered the river as a lively highway. He remembered the passenger boats, too, which once paraded to and fro along the river, like great swans. He remembered the fires along the shore, at the wharves. A fire was lighted when someone wanted the boat to stop. That was the signal. Of a night you could see the fires along the shore from afar. Sometimes, when the river was obstreperous and cranky and the going was slow, or when traffic was heavy and there were many stops, people often had to wait hours for the boat.

What is there about the Savannah?

There is another answer, for the imaginative, in a study of the cold contours of a map, in following with the eye and the mind's eye the fine, spidery lines of the tributaries that begin where the mountains are marked off in those little curlicues over the border in North Carolina and South Carolina, spidery lines that come together later, after you leave the mountains, into one broad line that sweeps on down between Georgia and South Carolina to the sea.

For you become conscious that it is a mighty river. With its tributaries it drains 10,600 square miles, an area with some of the heaviest rainfall in the continent. It was important once in first opening a rich section to exploration, then to settlement, and later on as an avenue of transport and commerce to haul the products of the valley down to the ocean, or take back inland the comforts and conveniences of civilization produced in lands across the sea in the early days, afterward elsewhere in the United States.

It was one of those arteries which helped pump lifeblood into America from the sea.

The Savannah proper begins officially—meaning by authority of reports by the United States Army Engineers—where the Seneca and Tugaloo Rivers join just above an imaginary line drawn from Hartwell, Georgia, across to Anderson, South Carolina. From there to the sea at Savannah it forms the boundary between the two states, just as the Tugaloo forms the boundary from that point northwestward.

Both the Seneca and the Tugaloo have their origins in North Carolina. The Seneca flows from the northeast across a section of South Carolina. The Tugaloo flows from the northwest. Following the Seneca back toward its sources we find that its name is changed to Keowee in its upper reaches, and that the Keowee is formed by the union of Toxaway River and Whitewater River, both of which have their springs in the North Carolina mountains. If we follow the Tugaloo back to its sources, we find that it is formed by a junction of the Chattooga and the Tallulah, both of which likewise have their springs in the North Carolina mountains. The Tallulah flows down across a section of northeast Georgia.

What was the parent tributary, whether the Tugaloo or the Seneca, was a matter of dispute in the early days between Georgia and South Carolina. For a large tract of land was at stake. The Savannah was the boundary between the two states. But the question was: which was the main stream of the Savannah—the Tugaloo-Chattooga tributary or the Seneca-Keowee branch? If the latter were the main stream, then Georgia would get a large slice of what is now South Carolina; contrarily, it would yield this land to South Carolina should the Tugaloo-Chattooga tributary be fixed as the main stream.

A trading point was interjected cleverly by South Carolina. She renewed an ancient claim to the southern part of Georgia dating from early colonial times. In 1785 South Carolina asked the old Confederation Congress to appoint a board of arbitration. Before this was done, however, the two states settled the issue themselves in a conference at Beaufort, South Carolina, where commissioners from the two states met in 1787. The boundary was determined to be the Tugaloo-Chattooga tributary, giving South Carolina the land lying between this branch and the Seneca-Keowee tributary, while South Carolina surrendered its hoary and questionable royal charter claim to southern Georgia.

But this did not end the boundary controversy. The river was the boundary, yes, but where in the waters of the river did the line actually lie? This was in litigation for well over a century, for 135 years to be exact, and finally was settled by a United States Supreme Court decision in 1922 (*Georgia* v. *South Carolina*, 257 U.S. 516). This decreed that the middle of the river was the boundary, except where there were islands. In such places the boundary was fixed midway between the islands and the South Carolina shore. Thus all the islands in the river were granted to Georgia.

There was not always a river here in the valley of the Savannah. Once, eons ago, the sea was here, both in its lower reaches and among the mountains where its tributaries rise. When the glacier belt receded it left a great inland sea from which the peaks of the Appalachians and the Cumberland Mountains in Tennessee beyond them poked up as islands. Toward the south, down in Georgia and South Carolina—or where they are now—there also was the sea. For the Atlantic swept far up toward the highlands in prehistoric ages.

Slowly the land has risen from the sea.

Time and the glacier cap and the sea welling up from below all had their part in making the country and determining the history of the Savannah and the history of the people who have lived in its valley.

The continental icecap, the great glacier of prehistoric times, did not reach beyond the Appalachians into the Piedmont section, or foothills, of the upper Savannah and its tributaries. Consequently, there is not the lush fertility which the icecap bestowed upon the great midlands that sweep down to the Mississippi by grinding its soils and mingling and mixing and pulverizing them.

Mostly, the soil of the upper Piedmont is sand and clay in varying proportions, the result of decayed crystalline rock, largely granite. This accounts for the poor hillside farms and the poor folk who farmed them, and still do. In many ways they constitute a distinct people.

A belt below this Piedmont marl along the river is not much better. Its base is sandstone. It was raised high and then cut by erosion into a region of gentle hills six or seven hundred feet above sea level. The soil here is sandy and poor. The hills are covered with pine trees, the sharecroppers of vegetation, so along the river, too, farming was hard. Here developed a race of small farmers who struggled for a living, and who acquired an ingrown sort of independence tinged with narrow-mindedness. They cared little for the lowlands, because inherently they were jealous of the prosperity and culture of the lowlands with its slaves and high-tone ways. So a war started by the lowland folks to save their slaves and their way of life had no appeal for them.

Farther to the south, above and below Augusta in a broad belt, the Piedmont becomes a rich land. The rock foundation here is younger and forms a clayey soil or a yellow sandy loam. Here flourished the cotton empire.

And below this fertile belt, once a lush kingdom, there are the pine barrens. Poverty lies next to riches on either side. The "slums of the Savannah" was always a poor man's country. "Land of Forgotten Folks" it is called by my friend, Hilary Mangum, of Augusta, who is so familiar with all this country and its people. Here poor white and Negro tenant farmers and sharecroppers eke out a skimpy living. They also are a people apart. They are cut off from civilization by natural conditions and by that accident of birth which perpetuates a pitiful progeny from generation to generation. They have never been quite able to free themselves from a slavery that has existed since the feudal society of pre-Civil War days. Some of them were slaves to their environment before that.

They live on the ridges that rise from the swamps. They get their meager sustenance by raising a few potatoes, a little corn, a patch of vegetables, some stringy chickens, and a few razor back hogs that they trap in the swamps where these animals run wild. In the days when there was a thriving lumber industry along the Savannah they picked up a few dollars by helping with the logging. They have few contacts with outsiders, mostly when outlanders go into their world on hunting and fishing expeditions. They are most primitive folk, inbred, ignorant, and shiftless.

The Savannah runs through a land of checkered careers.

From this "tenement section," it enters again, down toward its mouth, one of its ancestrally civilized centers, for here where it spreads into the bayous and the marshes, and sends its tentacles into the lowlands in myriad streams, was the empire of rice, once a profitable crop that created fortunes so that plantation owners might live in a lordly manner. But that was a long time ago, now.

What is there about the Savannah?

There is the rich history that has been made along its banks, so that, as I look upon it, I see it running across the map as a thick red line, for there is the red-earth blood of the hills and the lowlands in its waters as a symbol of the fertility upon which it draws. And there is human blood in its waters, blood of those who have fought through the centuries for these lands, blood of the Indian, of the Spaniard, and of the Englishman, and the blood of American brothers who fought each other in a latter day, in the day before yesterday.

The Spaniards were the first white men who saw it.

PART 1

Cofitachequi — The Dream

CHAPTER ONE

DE SOTO WAS LOOKING FOR GOLD

Hernando De Soto and his army of six hundred—horsemen, foot soldiers, priests, with an escort of Indian guides, the last perpetually and purposely vague—straggled from the dense pine forests where they had wandered aimlessly for days, footsore and hungry, and came upon a clearing along the Savannah River.

It was May Day, 1540.

Before them, across the stream, they beheld an Indian village, the elusive Cofitachequi, which had hovered in their imaginations for days, until it had become almost an hallucination. The spring sun radiated pleasantly from the water, and the wanderers were uplifted and encouraged. The comfortable sounds of living were borne across the river, little echoes of talk, a baby crying, a squaw calling to one of her young, sharp and clear. Here, surely here, must be found the answer that De Soto had sought since he had landed his men and horses on a Florida beach a year ago, to begin a slow march through forests and swamps and resentful Indians who had a plaguey habit of shooting from ambush and quickly scampering. It had been a tribulation. Here they must know the answer to the riddle:

"Where is the gold?"

Again, and soon, he was to be disappointed. For when the chieftainess of this tribe—the Lady of Cofitachequi, of whom his Indian guides had been talking for days—when she stepped a few minutes later from the canoe that had brought her from the village across the river, he noted—as did his soldiers—that there were no gold bracelets about her dark arms, nor any gold ornaments on the bright garments of feathers and skins that she wore. It had been different among the Indians of Peru. We can imagine that the conquistador's mind darted back, as to an impossible dream, to the gold-bedecked women of that country through which he had traveled, a conqueror, with Pizarro, so long, long ago it seemed now. This, certainly, was a poor country which he had chosen to add to his prestige, with an expedition, now beginning to droop, for which he had paid, himself, from the rich dividends of Peru. But, as the Indian princess came nearer, he did catch the glint of pearls, mellow and soft in the morning light, which she wore in a lavish rope about her neck. That was something. A very comely woman she turned out to be, seemingly about thirty-five years old. She deported herself with dignity and was paid by her attendants the homage due a ruler.

Standing before De Soto, she lifted the rope of pearls over her head and, through an interpreter, said she wanted to present the pearls to the commander. She would not deign directly to make the gift herself. Womanly modesty forbade such a crass performance. But De Soto, ever gallant, insisted. He kneeled before her. About his neck he himself draped the handsome beads. In turn, he took from his finger a signet ring and gave it to her. Graciously she thanked him.

The cacica provided boats for the Spanish army to cross

the river. At her town on the far bank they received a kindly welcome, one that served to remind them that they were at last out of the wilderness, at least for the time being, guests of a civilization, primitive though it might be. For the Indian princess turned over to the Spaniards half the houses in her village, moving out the native inhabitants to accommodate the strangers. She also fed them well, and greedily they made up for the thin rations upon which they had been subsisting for several days in the stretch of sparse country through which they had last come. The prospect was entirely pleasing, so much so that some of the Spanish explorer's followers thought perhaps their leader might decide to settle here, along the banks of this agreeable river. In this clearing so restful and alluring, they might establish a Spanish colony. The sea was not so far away, although farther than they reckoned at the time. The climate seemed healthful. Crops flourished abundantly.

But rest was not for their leader, nor for them.

He must go on and on—and so he told them.

This was pleasing country, yes. But it could not be the fabled land of El Dorado of which he had heard. However, he did not hurry his army away from so beguiling a spot. Men and horses needed a rest. With renewed hope he heard the Indians speak of gold.

The princess ordered her people to bring some to him. But it was only copper. They brought silver, as they called it. But it turned out to be mica and crumbled glittering in his hand. There were, however, pearls. De Soto dropped many hints about them. The Indian princess told him he could find many in their burial place, and that he was welcome to help himself. He visited the mosque, the big death house, where the mummies were kept, and there he found pearls used most extravagantly about the interior in beaded decorations of all sorts. He took his fill, some 350 pounds of them, which he laid aside to be loaded with their goods. He was seldom niggardly in the presence of treasure, even if it meant robbing the resting place of

the dead. They were not very fine pearls. The Indians used fire
in opening the shells of both oysters and mussels. This latter
shellfish abounded at that time in the Savannah and in other
streams in what is now Georgia, even as far from the ocean
as Cofitachequi, which presumably was located about 125 miles
from the mouth of the river. Also some of the pearls were punched
with holes, for stringing, which had been done by using a red-hot
spindle which singed them. Some, however, were whole and
apparently of value.

The princess, conscious of the acquisitive glint in the Spanish eye, and hopeful of ridding her people of the avaricious
white strangers with as little harm as possible, willingly resorted
to bribery. She told De Soto of another village, Talimeco, a few
miles away, where there was a temple and more pearls. He
protested. He had all his army could carry. But, on second
thought, he decided to visit the place. He was well rewarded
as a sightseer. For the temple was spacious and well worth a
trip. Before it stood huge carved figures, one twelve feet high.
These figures wore a most grim and ferocious aspect and for a
long time the commander and his men stood and looked on,
wrapped in wonder. Here was primitive artistry. Inside, they
were further delighted. From the roof hung festoons of plumes
and pearls. About the walls were more large figures, both male
and female. The men were carved as warriors, ready for battle,
weapons in their upraised hands. Within the temple were all
sorts of weapons, some of copper, some of stone. Also there
were shields of buffalo skins which must have come from far
away.

De Soto came here only in the role of a tourist to see and
wonder. He took no pearls.

Again, with the view of this temple, another aspect of
primitive Indian civilization, and with the thought of the kindness and hospitality of these red people came the hope among
the Spaniards that they might settle here, at least some of them,
and establish a colony. The whole history of the American con-

tinent might have been changed hereby—though of course they could not know this—for an outpost here along the Savannah might have become a bulwark against the later invasion by the English. De Soto could not look that far ahead. All he could see was the tangled wilderness that closed in on every side like a forbidding wall, and no gold. He was looking for treasure that was real, that you could see with your eyes and feel with your hands, treasure for the ships, now waiting far away on the Gulf coast for his return, to transport back to Spain to show before a startled king and jealous courtiers. That was what he wanted. He could not rest here. So, with the army fed and fully rested, he gave the command to go forward.

He performed now one of those capriciously mean acts for which the conquering race became famous when it found itself in the wilderness, which has left a stigma upon its name down to this day. He insisted upon taking the princess along for a hostage as a guarantee that the Indian bearers she had very agreeably furnished would serve him faithfully. Even the diarists of the expedition, to whom we are indebted for the story of the amazing adventure from first to last, were harsh in writing about this incident. For the cacica had been so hospitable.

She went along, with her female attendants, as a part of the expedition that moved forward from day to day beside the Savannah, a world known to her but strange and continually new to the visitors from across the ocean. After several days, however, she escaped. She gave the Spaniards the slip very neatly, exercising a female prerogative. She asked one day that she and her ladies might be excused into the woods for a moment, and the request was granted. They never saw her again. But she had her little revenge. She took the choicest of the pearls that she had given to De Soto, a whole basketful of them.

The Indians who lived about Cofitachequi, the tribe ruled by the Indian princess in a matriarchy rare among the race, were

Creeks. They had known the white man before. For, in the death house where De Soto had garnered his loot of pearls, he had found Biscayan axes and rosaries which had belonged to men in the expedition of Vásquez de Ayllón, who had explored the North Carolina coast and established a colony in the Cape Fear district. The colony had survived only a year, and Ayllón had died there. Thus there had been some contact between these Creeks along the Savannah and that short-lived Spanish colony.

But as De Soto and his army marched northwestward along the Savannah they traveled among Indians who actually saw white men for the first time, that is, so far as we know.

De Soto's route, here as elsewhere, is a subject of controversy among historians, and has been for over two centuries. Books have been written to prove that he went this way or that. A twelfth version was added to the eleven others by a special commission created by Congress, and we have what amounts to an "official" route. The variations are due to obvious factors, among them the differences as to distances traveled between various points in the four accounts of the expedition that have come down to us; the difficulty of locating, years afterward, the places described, because of the disappearance of Indian villages and landmarks of all sorts, all accentuated by slightly divergent descriptions of the same places where there were notations, including rivers that were crossed. The four chroniclers were: the writer known to us only as the Gentleman of Elvas, Biedma, Ranjel, who was De Soto's private secretary (all of whom were members of the expedition), and Garcilaso de la Vega, who did not come to America but compiled an account from interviews with survivors.

For quite a while, the expedition crawled along the Savannah, the only question being whether it proceeded along the south or north bank. The preponderance of authority favors the north bank. The course probably lay through what is today northwestern South Carolina. In time the Spaniards came upon a fortified town in the foothills along the Keowee, one of the tributary streams of the Savannah, the town of Xuala, as it is called. This is now generally thought to have been situated just south of the present North Carolina border. There they met the chief, rich as Indian wealth was counted, and a red man very hospitably inclined. He stocked the Spaniards with provisions of all kinds and furnished them with burden bearers for their journey. These Indians probably were Cheraws, a South Carolina tribe that moved about from place to place through recorded history.

From there the Spaniards ascended into the North Carolina mountains, and here they traveled among the Cherokees who had come into these mountains not so long before from the north.

Here we must leave them, watch them disappear into the mists of history. They march out of our sight, and struggle valiantly westward to the great Mississippi into which the fever-ridden body of De Soto, the great commander and explorer, was lowered, deep in the night, weighted with rocks so that it would sink to the bottom safe from the heathen hands of the marauding Indians, who were snapping constantly, like a pack of angry dogs, at the desperate and harried expedition, now thinned by incessant hardships.

CHAPTER TWO

THE FRENCH CAME EARLY, TOO

The French also knew the Savannah at an early date, but only at its mouth. They never explored its waters. Their corsairs roved the South Atlantic coast, playing havoc occasionally with Spanish galleons in the Caribbean and raiding Spanish ports. Once, too, some French Huguenots had established abortive settlements at Port Royal, in what later became South Carolina, and at the mouth of the St. Johns River in present Florida, but they had been exterminated ruthlessly by the Spanish in the madness of religious frenzy.

Late in the sixteenth century and early in the seventeenth the French were frequently about the mouth of the Savannah to trade with the Indians for the sassafras that put out its yellow blossoms and small dark-blue berries in the spring of the year. The sassafras trade was the first commerce of the Savannah in which Europeans engaged.

Sassafras tea, thanks to these early French traders, was having quite a fashion in Europe as a medicinal beverage. It swept through the smart circles of Europe, as such fads did, and the business was quite profitable. The French discovered that among the Indians sassafras not only was a medicine, but also was used as a test of fitness of their warriors, or so we are told by Jacques Le Moyne, the artist who accompanied René Laudonnière when he established the colony at St. Johns, which held on to the semitropical coast so briefly.

Sassafras tea, he wrote, "has the quality of at once throwing into a sweat whoever drinks it. On this account those who can

not keep it down, but whose stomach rejects it, are not en-
trusted with any difficult commission or any military responsibility, being considered unfit, for they often have to go three or
four days without food; but one who can drink this liquor can
go for 24 hours afterward without eating or drinking."

Here, at the mouth of the Savannah, in pursuit of the
sassafras trade, the French engaged with the Spanish in the
first naval battle ever to occur in the waters of the Savannah.
This was in 1603.

The French made no secret of their presence along the coast on this particular venture. The Spaniards discovered the visitation by foreigners when a small boat was seen taking soundings at the entrance of St. Augustine harbor. It disappeared and was forgotton. But a few days later word came back from the priest at San Pedro Mission on Cumberland Island of a boat taking soundings there. He reported eight Frenchmen in a small boat which belonged, he said, to a French cruiser. So the signal was passed back to St. Augustine as the French, unwary, proceeded up the coast. A loyal and resourceful Indian chief on Santa Catalina Island (St. Catherine's), a few miles below the mouth of the Savannah, captured four Frenchmen when the small boat put off there and, at the same time, hurried the alarm back to St. Augustine. Governor Ybarra dispatched one boat after another up the coast in pursuit, so that eventually a small fleet of three vessels was on the tail of the French cruiser, under command of Captain Francisco de Ejica, an experienced pilot whose name appears frequently in the Spanish annals of those days. He was often up and down the coast on such errands.

They caught up with the French cruiser in the mouth of the Savannah, coming upon a peaceful scene of primitive commerce. Indian canoes were paddling back and forth in the river between the shore and the warship, and the French were bargaining for sassafras and other articles of trade. The alarm was given, but too late, when the Spanish fleet came into sight. The fight was soon over. The French were outmaneuvered and outnumbered. Several were killed in the hand-to-hand fighting as Captain de Ejica's boat, in the van, tied on and his men streamed onto the French ship. The doughty captain got a heavy blow in the fighting, but it was not serious. The French set fire to their vessel to keep it from the Spaniards, but the other two Spanish boats came alongside and the blaze was checked in time. The Spanish captain took possession of the prize, and the four vessels turned southward. They sailed into

St. Augustine in triumph, for the French prize was a comely and useful vessel, carrying nine pieces of artillery.

Captain de Ejica sat down later to report on his experience, and he gives us the first word picture of the mouth of the Savannah, which was called by the Spanish Rio Dulce, sweet river, soft river, while the French called it Grande.

"The Bay of Los Bajos," he wrote, "is a deep bay; and the entrance to the harbor is northwest-southwest; the bar has in the deepest part of the channel three fathoms of water; it is a very wide harbor, and it is possible to beat to windward within it. A fresh-water river empties into it, and the channel of the bar is on the south side close to a wooded point, below which there is another point, sandy. Within the bay, there is an island over two leagues wide."

Thus he wrote of Tybee Roads and Tybee Island, and the fresh-water river, the Savannah.

It was a lonely world then, a dream world.

CHAPTER THREE

A DOCTOR FINDS A RIVER AND STARTS AN EMPIRE

Through all the forest was the sound of the rain. It rattled on the roof of branches and leaves overhead. It dropped, in noisy, irregular spatters, on the leaves and branches lower down, and off to the ground to run helter-skelter in crazy rivulets. It was a chill, autumn rain, not at all cozy and friendly here in the midst of the wilderness. So meditated the young white man who trudged along with his Indian guides. The clammy fingers of the underbrush switched venomously at their faces and tired bodies. The soggy carpet of dead leaves and saturated earth clutched at their feet, pulled heavily on weary legs.

This was Carolina, in the rain, in late October, in the year 1674.

Young Dr. Henry Woodward, the rugged, thickset adventurer from Charleston—now miles and miles back along the Atlantic coast—plodded along philosophically. In his face was the fresh feel of the rain and in his nostrils was the damp smell of the woods. His expression was a contrast in its piquant eagerness to the solemn masks of his Indian companions. They were dour, silent fellows, not much company, and yet it was comforting the way they followed the hardly discernible trail through these wilds. Indians were no strangers to young Dr. Woodward. He had learned their ways a long time ago. So patiently and without fear he followed them through the dripping waste of woods. For seven days they had walked in the rain. It had been raining when they left Charleston.

Suddenly his guides halted and stared ahead, motionless. They were tense with the awareness of danger. Poised like pointers, they waited. Through the wet wall of the forest appeared two figures, two other Indians. Immediately Dr. Woodward's companions relaxed. It all happened in a flash. The two other Indians were of their own tribe, Westoes. The chatter of recognition was followed by the warm and comfortable babble of friends. The newcomers had come to meet the wanderers. The leader of the Indian guides had sent ahead four of his men a few days before to advise of the approach of the white man. These two were the messengers of welcome, stoical though they seemed for such a mission.

The party came to a camp in a clearing beside the Savannah River, as it came to be called some years later. There before him the white man saw the wide and sluggish body of water which, in the coming years, was to become so familiar a friend of the wilderness, a pathway to a strange new world and the road that led home to Charleston. There came over him suddenly—as he emerged from the woods that so hemmed one in, body and soul, and walked into the open to the river—an expanding feeling of spaciousness. There was an overwhelming vacancy. Sounds were sharp and clear, and no longer muffled and shrouded.

This was another world, all this and the river.

An Indian "captain," as he calls him in his memoirs, received the young Englishman. A veritable banquet of native food was spread before him. The stranger was so unfamiliar with the geography of this country that he thought the river was the River May. So he identified it. That was the French name for the St. Johns River farther south shown on early maps available to him. After he had finished his meal, the party took to canoes and the doctor was rowed up the stream, a "spatious river," he described it. They paddled for about six miles when the young man saw a sizable Indian settlement on a promontory ahead on the right, or east, bank of the river. Many Indians were gathered along the bluff. He fired his gun into the air in salute. The river echoed and re-echoed with a responding volley from fifty or sixty others on the bluff. The canoes were beached at the foot of the high bank where, piled about on the sand, he counted nearly a hundred other boats and was conscious of the activity of this tribe and the extent of their traffic along the river. He was escorted to the assembled Indians and was received with considerable commotion. They led him to the chief's house, young and old scurrying about him, looking him over. The warriors of the tribe were decked out in paint and feathers to let the white man know what caliber of Indian folk they were who lived here along the river. Undoubtedly the doctor was properly impressed.

Later he stood in the middle of the chief's house, a roomy, round structure. The Indians pressed about him, still curious of his every move. He became more keenly aware of the dramatic part he was playing when he looked up to see young boys—"the small fry," as he termed them—taking off sections of the roof the better to see him and join in the spirit of this festive occasion.

There in the chief's house, one white man among so many red, he listened to a long speech by the headman of the tribe. He gathered from the gestures of the chief and the solemn nods from the serious faces about him that he was being told about the prowess of the Westoes and their desire for friendship with the English. For him they afterward performed all the ceremonies of welcome. They oiled his eyes and "joynts" with bear's grease. They presented him with a parcel of deerskins. They set before him enough food, so he related, for half a dozen people. And that night, weary from his long journey and the incessant hospitality, he slept peacefully among these Indians who were to become his friends and particular charges and with whom the next few very eventful years and his fortunes and those of the infant colony at Charleston were to be so closely entwined.

The next morning, refreshed from his rest, he looked about the village. Hanging from long poles rising above the roofs of their houses were scalps of their Indian enemies, a grisly sight which was sufficient evidence of the fierce reputation of this tribe among the coastal Indians about Charleston. They called the Westoes "man-eaters." There is no proof that they were cannibals. It was probably a fearful figure of speech. Their houses were long and their sides and tops were constructed of bark woven together. He learned that the Westoes traded with white settlers to the north in Virginia, whence they had come, in deerskins and furs and "young Indian slaves" for which, in exchange, they got guns and ammunition and cloth. They were the only Indians who had guns at this early date in the South. The Spaniards, who had had relations with other Indians in this region for over a century, did not supply their savage allies with guns.

Dr. Woodward spent several days among the Westoes. He arranged for the English to trade them guns and cloth for deerskins and furs. The Westoes would become allies of the English against the Spaniards and against Indian tribes leagued with the Spanish, to protect the Charleston colony. In contriving this frontier alliance he was acting on behalf of the Proprietors of the colony back in England headed by the designing and clever Earl of Shaftesbury. The Earl had high hopes of eventual profits from this venture and was relying upon this resourceful young man as an instrument of his schemes.

The earl's choice was a sound one, for Dr. Henry Woodward was the pioneer in making the Savannah an English river, though it was just one of those happy chances, for the two had never seen each other and they did not meet until some years later in England.

Dr. Woodward, at twenty-eight, was a much younger man when he arrived on the middle Savannah on his mission of British Empire than was De Soto when he had led his small army to the same place exactly sixty-four years before. The Englishman already was a veteran of the New World and could look back upon a career of amazing adventure such as is seldom the lot of one of his years, even at that eerie hour of the dawn of a new continent.

Nearly nine years before, he had come out from England to the already large and prosperous settlement of Barbados in the British West Indies, deep in southern tropical waters, a young man seeking the rainbow that seems to hang above the islands of the western seas. In London he had been a medical student, training as a surgeon. It is probable that his education in this line was by no means complete, though he was continually striving to broaden his knowledge of the crude medical science of the day, and to that end constantly collected plants and herbs to experiment with for their health-restoring qualities wherever he went. He was blessed with a curiosity about all things.

He found Barbados crowded already, a land of sugar plantations owned by a few wealthy men, with but slight opportunity for a young fellow seeking more daring adventure in less sheltered places, and a quicker fortune. At the first chance he shipped with an expedition that was bound for the newly founded colony along the Cape Fear River. Even more alluring prospects glimmered in this venture, for Sir John Yeamans, governor of Barbados, who commanded this expedition, also had plans for exploring farther south along the Carolina coast for possible settlement.

It was not until after he had spent several months at the Cape Fear colony, which was faring but meagerly, that he got his opportunity for more adventure. This was the great adventure of his life, though he did not know how much was ahead of him when he sailed, one of a party of twenty-one aboard a ketch, for exploration down the coast. In command of this expedition was Captain Robert Sandford. As they wandered down the coast they explored the inlets and bays and rivers, and were delighted with what they saw. In his report of the journey, Captain Sandford described the vast expanse of green marsh stretching away on every side, resembling a rich prairie, with the broad and noble arms of the sea, the rivers and innumerable creeks, fringed with oak, cedar, jasmine and myrtle.

Eventually they entered the wide harbor at Port Royal, where the French once had set up a colony that ended so disastrously and where later the Spanish had kept a mission and a garrison, until driven off by Sir Francis Drake's sea raiders. Here Captain Sandford decided to stop and take a look. Among the natives who came to see the strange ship and the white visitors was a figure familiar to some on board, an Indian by the name of Shadoo. He had met the expedition of the English along these shores three years before under Captain Hilton and had gone back with Captain Hilton for a time to Barbados. The charts of Captain Hilton were the only guides to these waters possessed by Captain Sandford, and already they had identified the sentinel bluff named Hilton Head after the earlier explorer.

Shadoo invited Captain Sandford to send a party ashore

to visit the Indian village nearby. Dr. Woodward was selected as one of a party of volunteers. They met the cacique of Port Royal, who was most hospitable, and spent the night among the Indians at the village. In front of the big round house in the center of the village, the town house or council chamber, the English visitors were surprised to see still standing "a fair wooden cross," which they learned was a relic of the Spanish settlement there years before. All about the village were fields of corn and the landscape was fruitful with peach trees and fig trees and grapevines. They carried a glowing report back to the ship the next morning, as to both the hospitality of the Indians and the fertility of the country.

The cacique of Port Royal visited the English ship the next day, and brought with him his young nephew—for a purpose, we learn as the story unfolds. He was very anxious for the English to settle here, selfishly, for he wanted protection for his people against the wild inland Indian tribes, including the "man-eating" Westoes. He inquired when the English expected to return. He asked, hopefully, if it would be in three months, pointing to the moon and making a gesture to indicate three orbits. Sandford told him it would be ten moons. The cacique, bargaining, suggested five moons. But Sandford shook his head. No, ten. Then, as a pledge for the much-desired return of the English to settle, the Indian chief insisted on turning his nephew over to the Englishman as a hostage to be brought back when the English came to settle. When the cacique learned that Captain Sandford was planning to sail that night he begged him to stay over until the next day so that he could prepare a feast of venison for the visitors. The Englishman relented.

And now Henry Woodward found himself caught up suddenly in the procession of empire. Perhaps before he realized what he had done, or how it had happened, he found that he had volunteered to stay behind here among the Indians "in the room" of the cacique's nephew, as it was put in Indian symbolism, as a hostage, yes, but a hostage to empire, to certify the claim, in himself, one Englishman, of his nation to all this land. This would be more binding than the formal claim already made by Sandford, when he had first arrived at Port Royal and took possession, with the ancient ceremonial of turf and twig, to the whole country from Latitude 36 North to 29 South and west to the South Seas. Sandford named this newly claimed possession Carolina for his king, Charles II.

The next day Henry Woodward discovered that his decision, whether by sudden impulse or not, was now beyond all recall. For it was sealed with solemn formality when he went along with Captain Sandford and his companions to the Indian village for the feast. The two young men, the Englishman and the Indian nephew of the chief, stood up together beside Captain Sandford and the uncle in the presence of all the assembled Indians. The captain asked the relatives of the Indian whether they were willing for the boy to go with him. They all assented. Then he delivered Henry formally to the cacique, and told the Indians he would require him at their hands when he returned.

The young Englishman now was pushed to the center of the day's events. The cacique escorted him to his own high seat in the council house and sat him down there before the Indians and the English visitors. Then he led him outside and pointed out the field of corn that had been allotted to him. And there were other emoluments, embodied in a woman, with what graces we know not. For the chief brought to him his niece, the sister of his hostage nephew, and presented her to him as a handmaiden, to tend and dress his food, to take care of him, to teach him the Indian language.

Captain Sandford completed this ceremony, which was the beginning of great events, for England, for the nation that succeeded England here, a ceremony whose import none who stood there that day could possibly foresee. He gave Henry Woodward formal possession of this whole country to hold for the Lord Proprietors.

Captain Sandford wasted no further time, now that he had accomplished his mission. He led his crew back to the ship, and before long they had cast off.

That was in 1666. Henry Woodward was twenty years old.

Month after month passed while he waited for the return of the promised English settlers. But the Spaniards came first.

To distant St. Augustine the word had passed of the young doctor's presence and of English intentions to stake out for their own this territory which, in the Spanish mind, was clearly Spanish. The Spaniards arrived, not in a seagoing vessel, but in those large canoes, *periaguas*. They came up the inland channel, between the mainland and the Golden Isles along the Florida and Georgia and Carolina coast, and back the same way they took their captive to St. Augustine, their capital.

Now, day by day, another wonderland opened before him as stout Indian galley slaves paddled the big flatboats southward. It was well he could feast his eyes and enjoy the beauty all about him, for he could not converse with his captors, as he knew no Spanish, and the language spoken by the Indians was different from the dialect he had been learning so laboriously during his months along the Carolina coast. He was made perfectly comfortable, though closely guarded.

Below the Savannah they put in for the night at numerous islands, and Henry Woodward came to know the settled state of Spanish empire which stretched along the coast, island after inhabited island. The mission bells tolled with the confident regularity that comes from a century of ringing, and the soft tones spoke across the waters as if they were telling of an eternity that was and an eternity that was to come. The priests pottered about with their chores, seeking the spiritual salvation of their Indian charges who followed blindly the perpetual motions of a religion of fixed forms, looking after the earthly needs of their converts. The soldiers of the garrisons, found on each island side by side with the mission, went through their daily routine, their drills, the policing of their camp and

quarters, the changing of the guard, as if this had gone on forever.

All this opened his eyes to the task England had set herself in the New World. Houses and missions had the look of
long habitation. He discovered, too, the power and influence
in the Spanish empire of the simple priest with his zeal for
his faith. The priest was the temporal as well as spiritual leader
in this Spanish regime which had, it is true, its faults as well as
its virtues. The priest's days were filled with a ceaseless round
of small duties—teaching the young, saying masses, marrying,
baptizing, doctoring, burying. He, too, was the diplomat, the
personal representative of the king in affairs of state, as well
as guardian of the interests of Mother Church. His nights
were devoted to writing, in a fine-flowing hand, the daily record
of the community in the mission book. He must report to his
religious superiors. He must report, too, to the governor of St.
Augustine of matters that concerned the state. He was the outpost of empire.

Not all of this did Henry Woodward learn on this single,
rather hurried journey down the inland passage, but he got his
first strong impressions of Spanish character, purpose and
method which were later filled out, with more detail, in the
months he spent in St. Augustine. He did get, however, sufficient glimpse of the apparent solidity of Spanish empire in the
islands along the coast to realize that Spain would resist with
vigor any attempt to dislodge her, knowing, as he did, of the
strength upon which she leaned farther south in the isles of
the Caribbean and in Mexico and South America. She had
pushed her tentacles far, and was grasping and clever still.

It was a long time before he saw much of St. Augustine,
for they threw him in a damp and dark prison as soon as they
got him there. When he was freed eventually he was allowed
much liberty in his role of physician and healer. He kept his
observing eyes open and learned much of Spanish empire, its
strength and its weaknesses, as he went about the lovely little

capital city on Matanzas Bay, which had been founded in 1565 and had by now grown confident of itself and of its mission in "Florida," as the Spaniards called the whole southeastern section of the North American continent.

On a slight rise along Matanzas Bay stood the walled fortress that was besieged often in the years to come but never taken, though the enemy did infest the city itself. In the background were the governor's palace, where there was much scheming about empire, and a monastery, where the Franciscan monks moved about softly in their brown robes and wide hats.

St. Augustine was the center and symbol of Spain in southeastern North America. St. Augustine! The very name meant Spanish power. It meant Spain. It created a definite and forbidding image of all Spain stood for when it was uttered fearfully by the Indian, thoughtfully by the Englishman, impressively and arrogantly by the Spaniard. This was true in the backwoods of Georgia, and all up and down the Savannah, in those days. It hovered there in the background always. The image is a definite fact in the story of the Savannah.

To Dr. Woodward, in all the years afterward, it had potency and, too, a seductive kind of charm. He had about resigned himself to its loosely hung bonds. The ease of his life here, the delicious warmth of the sun, which slowly eats away the will to be briskly about the world's business—all these made him content. Then, suddenly, he was taken up and whisked away, just as surprisingly as he had been lifted out of Carolina and deposited here. An English privateer preying upon the Spanish settlements descended one night upon St. Augustine and he escaped to the English ship, which was a simple feat in all the confusion and looting. The vessel, under command of the doughty Captain Robert Searles, was quickly away with its treasure and wandered about the tropical seas taking prizes without benefit of any authority but that of Captain Searles. Dr. Woodward saw a good deal of the pirate's life for several months, as Captain Searles sailed about the Windward and

Leeward Islands. A hurricane cut short this precarious roving, one of those furies bred of the tropical seas, and almost ended the career of the English doctor. It picked up the sturdy vessel and tore it apart as if it were a child's paper boat on a surging wave. Miraculously Dr. Woodward was saved, washed ashore with a few of the crew on the island of Nevis in the Leeward group.

Luck followed him. Here at Nevis after many weeks there arrived an English ship which turned out to be the *Carolina,* bound for the spot where he had once been a hostage with the first contingent of settlers for whom he had waited in vain four years before. He discovered old friends and right happily he joined the party and at last returned to the scene of his lonely vigil, a full-blown colonist to live and work with his own kind for the glory of England.

That was in the year 1670.

We have seen him, four years later, an emissary of empire along the Savannah. He took the Westo alliance back to Charleston as a shining token, but it did not sit happily there. The settlers had an unholy fear of these wild Indians, which spread like a contagion from the panic among the settlement Indians whenever even the name Westo was mentioned. Their relations and their trade were with the nearby tribes, and they were irked at the Proprietors for tying up with this distant and fearsome band of Indians. Dr. Woodward became an object of envy because he got his percentages for this trade and the Proprietors got the rest; in other words, he was definitely tied up with the powers that were in England. This tended to set him apart. Furthermore, Dr. Woodward in behalf of the Proprietors opposed the Indian slave trade in which even some of the leading men of the colony engaged. Though fearful of the Westoes, they did not hesitate to trade surreptitiously with them for slaves which the Westoes had captured from some of the supposed friendly tribes nearer Charleston. This, in turn, irritated these other Indians and they marked their resentment by stealing and pillaging from the outlying settlements.

Dr. Woodward's enemies finally caught him off guard. His own impulsiveness led him into a trap. He discovered that two of the leading men in the colony, slave traders, were off on a mission to the Westoes and suspecting their designs, perhaps wrongly, he warned his Indian friends that, if they did not look out, they might find themselves sold into slavery across the sea. Innocently their aged chieftain talked freely of their protector's warning. This was the opportunity for which his enemies had waited. They accused the doctor of plotting with the Indians against the interests of the colony. He was stripped of his office of Indian agent for the Proprietors and put under bond against any further dealings with them. All at once he was an outcast.

Without his guiding hand the alliance with the Westoes languished and friction increased. Soon it broke into open war. But the colonists did not fight this war. They induced a tribe newly settled along the Savannah to do their fighting for them, and so well did the newcomers carry out their bloody commission that only some fifty Westoes survived the slaughter by the Savannahs, which was the name by which the victorious Indians were known. The once-proud Westoes for whom Dr. Woodward had such admiration were driven from the Savannah.

Briefly, the river of our chronicle had taken its name from the Westoes, being known as Westobou, or River of the Westoes. Now, about 1682, when the Westoes left, its name suddenly was changed.

Now it was given the name by which we know it today, the Savannah. The Savannah Indians, who now succeeded the Westoes along the river as a buffer for the English about Charleston, were a branch of the Shawnees. The other branch of that noted tribe had settled about the Cumberland River in Tennessee when the tribe had migrated from the northeast.

The Shawnees were distinctly a nomadic race, more so than most other Indians, all of whom moved about, through history, here and there. Back and forth across the map the Shawnees roamed, often in small bands which now and again came together for a time in an approach to tribal solidarity. It is hard to trace their comings and goings. Early in the eighteenth century some of the Savannahs began to drift back north. They did not prove a satisfactory buffer for the English, for they would not adapt themselves to a settled life. Twice the Charleston colony sent missions posthaste after parties of them which left their homes along the Savannah for the north. In vain. The Shawnees would not return. In a few years all but a handful had disappeared from the Savannah. In 1725 colonial records reveal precisely eight men, a dozen women, and ten children in the dwindling Shawnee settlement along the Savannah. The two branches, the Cumberland Shawnees and the Savannah Shawnees, were united again along the Scioto in Ohio by 1765, ready for their messiah to appear among them.

For the great Tecumseh was a Shawnee, the masterpiece of this somewhat remarkable tribe. His parents had lived along the Cumberland. They migrated back north about 1750, settling eventually along the Scioto, where, in a rude hut of saplings chinked with sticks and clay, the future Indian leader was born in 1768 and given the name that means Meteor or Falling Star—and how prophetically! The great Indian statesman and warrior appeared later, as a young man seeing the world and the old home of his people, in the southern mountains among the Cherokees, a brooding young spirit of revolt. Some of his own people drifted south again and joined their Cherokee allies about the headwaters of the Savannah just before and after the American Revolution in a series of uprisings that kept the hill country in constant ferment in those years.

Those early Shawnees along the Savannah might have learned what Tecumseh, himself, learned before he fell in the swamp along the Thames River over a century later, might have learned about the white man and his purposes and how the Indian was useful only as a means to an end, had they been able to read a communication which the Proprietors sent to the Charleston colony when they received the word in England that the Shawnees had exterminated the Westoes along the Savannah, to wit:

> The trade that we have hitherto had with ye Westoes hath not been merely out of a design of gaine, but with the further consideration, that by furnishing a bold and warlike people with Arms and Ammunition and other things useful to them which they could not fetch from New England, New Yorke or Canider without great labor and hazard, we tyed them to soe strich a dependence upon us that we thereby kept all the other Indians in aw. . . . Wherefore we desire you seriously to consider whether it will not be extreamly useful for the quyet and peace of our colony to sett up some other Nation in the Room of ye Westoes (whom we deeme ruined) and whose Government is less Anarchical than theirs that shall be furnished by us with arms and ammunition, but with restrictions to them not to furnish any other nations.

This suggestion was found "extremely useful" and the Savannahs consequently were elected to occupy the room of the Westoes.

In those days fortunes fell quickly and arose again as quickly. Dr. Woodward was not down for long after his unfortunate experience with the Westoes. A resourceful gentleman, self-confident, he decided to take direct measures to recoup himself. He took a boat for England and went direct to his former patron, the crafty little Earl of Shaftesbury. He was most persuasive in his own behalf and returned home, many months later, with a commission from the Proprietors to venture westward beyond the Savannah into the land of the Creeks and open up trade with those Indians. This was a daring enterprise, for the Spaniards had established themselves with the Creeks; but that did not daunt the pioneering doctor, who was so sure of his influence with the Indians.

Now, too, he had reason for proving himself anew and becoming a man of affairs again in Carolina. He was a man of family. A few years earlier he had married, and into the upper circles of the colony. He took for his wife a widow, Mary Browne, the daughter of Colonel John Godfrey, who had been a figure of consequence in Barbados before he had migrated to Carolina and now was one of the leading men in the fledgling settlement.

When they said their farewells, they could not know that this was the last great adventure of his life. It was somehow fitting that it should be played out against the background of the Savannah, the river that had come to mean so much for England and England's empire through him.

The journey started inauspiciously. He, and his small party, made their way in a fleet of canoes down the inland passage from Charleston, but hardly had turned into the mouth of the Savannah for the upward trip when they were stopped at Yamacraw, a village of Yamacraw Indians on the bluff, by a patrol of Scotsmen who arrested the doctor. Recently the Scots, under Lord Cardross, had set up a colony at Stuart's Town on Port Royal Island and were asserting a claim to the coast from there southward, even beyond the mouth of the Savannah to include some of the northernmost islands from which the Spaniards were beginning to withdraw because of English and Indian raids. No Englishman, they said, had a right to take a trading expedition through these waters. The doctor was indignant at this effrontery, but he could do nothing about it until the whole dispute was taken back to Charleston. He was freed, of course, to pursue his way, but it was a bad start.

And, when he had left his boats and the Savannah and had begun his slow march overland to the land of the Creeks, he discovered that the Spaniards were ready to challenge his advance. They had sent an army of 250 men to capture him under command of Lieutenant Antonio Matheo, who had a reputation as a military man. Far outnumbered, Dr. Woodward and his handful had to choose the part of hare in a game of hare and hounds, and he eluded his pursuer among the hills, not, however, without leaving behind him a saucy reminder of English nerve in a note he pinned to a tree:

"I am sorry that I came with so small a following that I can not wait for your arrival. Be informed that I came to get better acquainted with the country, its mountains, the seacoast and Apalachee. I trust in God that I shall meet you gentlemen later when I have a larger following. September 2, 1685. Vale."

The Spanish lieutenant found the English hare too clever for him, and gave up the chase and went back to St. Augustine. Hardly had this annoyance vanished, however, before another appeared. Dr. Woodward fell ill of chills and fever. For days he was delirious. He grew weak and haggard. Between spells, however, he talked business with the Creeks, who found him as charming and persuasive as had the Westoes a decade before. They were hospitable and looked after his wants and were favorably inclined to do business with him and the English.

Then, alas, the Spaniards returned, the same Lieutenant Matheo, but with reinforcements, with a larger army this time, and with positive orders to take the doctor and make him a prisoner, to put a stop to these trade negotiations with the Indians, their Indians. The Spaniards, after all, had been in these parts for a long time. Their explorers had searched out this country on a quest for gold, their traders had been busy here for years. So, away with this cocky English intruder. This was the property of Spain.

The Spanish lieutenant was prepared to take drastic measures. He threatened the Creeks with destruction if they did not give up the Englishman and his party. With a few faithful Indians who stood loyally by him, the doctor got away to the hills again, but now he had become so filled with fever, so weak, that they had to carry him on a makeshift litter. He was almost a hopeless invalid. Behind him he left fire and death for the Indians who had dared to befriend him, for the Spaniards burned to the ground four villages which refused to yield. Several other villages saved themselves by making peace with the Spanish lieutenant.

Again, though, the Spaniard lost his quarry. The fugitive party of Englishmen slipped out of the land of the Creeks, with their leader—now just a gaunt ghost of a man—and with a goodly stock of deerskins for Charleston. In his occasional moments of consciousness, the stricken leader could look at the packs of deerskins upon the backs of a hundred and fifty Indian burden bearers with grim satisfaction. He was not going home empty-handed, despite the Spaniards.

Through the wilderness he had loved so well, now bleak with winter, the physician who could not help himself was borne day by day toward the Savannah. The journey was a continuous nightmare of bare trees and red bodies that slid along beside him like so many mechanical figures. Finally they reached the Savannah. The jostling ordeal was over and now his bed was carried along on the smooth waters of the river. He woke occasionally to the dreary reality of the dark forests groaning in the winter wind on either side of the watery highway that seemed to lead into a dread eternity.

He learned, when they reached the inland passage, of the destruction of Stuart's Town by a Spanish expedition that had swept furiously up the coast while he had been away in the land of the Creeks. But Charleston still stood.

Still the Spaniard, the eternal foe.

They yet rose up athwart his path, athwart the path of England. He did not live to see the Spaniard routed and dispersed. We do not know exactly when he died, but it was some time between 1686 and 1690. It was in early 1686 that he came back down the Savannah. The desperate illness left its heavy mark upon him. It is possible that he never left his bed of this devastating illness.

PART 2

Blood Flows in the Savannah

CHAPTER ONE

A FRENCHMAN TEACHES THE ENGLISH

Down the trail from over the mountains, through the land of
the Cherokees, there came wandering about the dawn of the
eighteenth century a vivacious Frenchman bringing tales of
bright adventure far away. Immediately Savannah Town, an
upriver trading post where the city of Augusta was later
located, did not seem so drab, at least to those who listened to
the broken English of Jean Couture. He was a man of wit, a
genial fellow given to what the Indians called "big talk," full of
promises and dreams, and magically he brushed away, for
the moment, the ruffled clay streets of this frontier trading post
and the somber warehouses across the river where the deerskins
were piled to await the pack train or the boat, and created new
empires here and far away for English imaginations.

They wondered how this engaging newcomer had made his way from the great Mississippi so many weary miles to the west. He was eager to tell them. He had followed the Tennessee River to its sources in the mountains and then had traveled along the water courses which, there at the divide, began their long journey to the oceans. He had come down one of the tributaries of the Savannah, and then had picked up the main trail which followed that river on either side down to Savannah Town which, itself, spread on both sides of the river, and now was quite a lively, bustling place, and no longer a mere clearing in the wilderness as Dr. Henry Woodward had seen it a quarter of a century before.

Jean Couture brought late impressions of the mountain Indians, the Cherokees, and the gossip of the Indians and white traders he had met along the trail. He had passed through the villages of the Overhill Cherokees, who lived in the valley of the Tennessee and the Cumberland beyond the Blue Ridge of the Appalachian chain, and through the habitations of the Lower Cherokees who lived in the valleys along the headwaters of the Savannah on this side of the divide. The Frenchman found them a courteous and hospitable folk still, despite the gradual, almost stealthy, inroads of the white man, who was seen more and more along the trails that the Indians had cut for themselves years ago through the mountains. The farther south he came the more conscious he was of how busy the Englishman was getting here in the interest of trade for the empire.

In Savannah Town he found rich evidence. Here, indeed, was a roistering rendezvous, full of the life and color and sound of the hustling frontier, coarse and rude, and ready to enjoy the lighter manners and the quaint speech of a Frenchman who was also a woodsman and ripe with the experience by which a man was measured in those parts. He watched with a practiced eye the movements of trade. He saw the pack horses drag into the town, wearily, blowing from the long hard journey,

their backs warm and chafing from the goods borne from
Charleston 140 miles away through the forests.

There were guns and ammunition for the Indians with
which to keep away the Spaniards and the French and other
Indians covetous of this country. There were practical agricultural implements to till the soil and transform the Indians from
hunters to a farm people content with their river bottoms, until
the English themselves should be ready to take over these lands.
There were many handy things to make life easier and more
pleasant for their squaws—kettles and calico and scissors and
beads, threads and needles—and, to tickle the vanity of the warrior—linen shirts and fancy coats and looking glasses. All these
things he saw transshipped on the backs of other horses toward
the north, east and west, along other trails, under direction of
Indian traders who roamed the forests. Here, too, he watched
the pack trains set off south, back across the trails to Charleston, the horses heavy with mountains of deerskins, for which
English goods were traded to the Indians. He watched the flatboats start off down the river, piled high with deerskins, for the
four-or five-day ride down the Savannah, between the tall trees,
to its mouth and around the inland channel to Charleston for
shipment to England.

The white men who supervised this cargo and the Indians
who guided the boats pushed off right cheerfully, for this was
the easy trick on this route, running with the river, and Charleston was at journey's end, with taverns where a man could sit
down to a drink in some comfort, deep in talk with good company which would include sailors just in from London with
news of the capital. At the crude wharf, also, Jean Couture
watched the incoming boats. The white men and the Indian
polers, weary from the twenty-day push up the river from
Charleston, scrambled ashore with relief, off to a draught of
rum at the bar, and a breathing spell of chatter about the go-
ings-on down in the city.

He noted the avid propensity of the Indians for strong

liquor, readily supplied by the English, and could see how this would serve the greedy purposes of empire building by weakening the fiber of the primitives, softening them up. The bright and gaudy goods they swapped to the Indians for an inordinate amount of the valuable deerskins also had the same effect, creating wants which, when withheld, would bend the red men to their will. Already among the complaints of the Indians echoed here at Savannah Town were too high prices for English goods and the fretful charge that too much water was mixed with the rum. The Indians wanted their liquor stronger and stronger, once they had developed the craving.

Wages, too, for Indians were low. Some who worked on the boats going up and down the river were slaves, but only a few. Some of the helpers of the boatmen and assistants of the pack-horsemen who had charge of the overland trains were white indentured servants. A few Negro slaves also had begun to appear on the river and the trails. In the early days Indian burden bearers who could load about thirty skins apiece on their backs were used, but at the time of Couture's appearance on the Savannah only a few of these toilers of the forest could be seen. For a knickknack or two they would make the trip to Charleston and back. The journal of the Indian Board carries an order to pay "two yards of blew duffields to each man, for their labors and travel to Charleston and home again."

Jean Couture, himself a fur trader, had an eye for the business. Coming through the forests he had observed the abundant source of this trade, the multitude of deer that infested the Cherokee mountains, a sight which had brought from an English traveler several years earlier the comment, "There is such infinite Herds that the whole country seems but one continued park." The Frenchman must have picked up some of the statistics of this lucrative trade, the first extensive commerce of the Savannah. In those days the annual shipment to England down the Savannah and from Charleston averaged 50,000 skins. Later this trade grew even bigger, until it came finally to an end, just before the American Revolution, for the deer finally were nearly exterminated.

Jean Couture did not come to Carolina as a spy. He was a businessman of the promoter type, not an agent of France. He wore lightly the restraints of patriotism, as so many others with minds more on the louis and the pound had done before, and have done in the years since. He was here, a renegade Frenchman, because he refused to be bound by the law of France compelling the sale of furs only in the Montreal market controlled by France. He wanted to use the Savannah as an outlet and move his furs from the interior through the Charleston market, and later he and some of his companions of like mind did open a business down the Savannah.

But such prosaic business as fur trading could not hold the imaginative Frenchman. He was a man of big ideas. His mind glittered with grandiose plans for exploiting the mineral resources which he was sure lay concealed in the streams and mountains of this fair country about the Savannah and its headwaters. The legends that had lured the Spaniards on to death and destruction still sparkled in the talk over the bottle when the hour grew late. The same stories which the Indians year after year had repeated to the Spaniards had grown, perhaps, from the nuggets washed up by the swift and fugitive streams in the Cherokee mountains. These bits of gold had passed from hand to hand through Indian tribes clear down to those whom De Soto first had met when he began his luckless cavalcade in Florida. There was gold. There are even hints, in the pale unwritten footnotes of history, that the Spaniards themselves had at one time opened mines in what became northern Georgia. Jean Couture was confident that the nuggets were the grains of a miraculous reality and perhaps the germs of fortune.

His first enterprise was to get silver from the Savannah River. He joined with a group of prospectors who, like himself, knew the trans-Appalachian country and were extravagant with tales of its riches. The silver venture fell through. Then he turned to gold. He proposed to develop gold mines in the Cherokee mountains. The project got all the way to England through the pleas of two prospectors who were sent over to talk the Board of Trade into it. But the board could not quite see it. They had heard so much talk of gold that had come to nothing. They were more interested in the obvious and proved profits from the Indian trade in deerskins. So this bubble burst. Jean Couture did not develop any mines. It probably was just as well.

For the English he did better, however, in showing them the way to the west, and awaking their imaginations to its possibilities. He acted as a guide to the country beyond the mountains and pointed out to the English the best routes to that expansive and fertile inland empire. He regaled audiences at Savannah Town and in Charleston with stories of his own adventures in that vast territory, told them of the explorations of La Salle and Tonti which he had shared, of the great river that rolled down through the middle of the continent and the endless plains that swept away from it toward the sunset.

He threw the dust of dreams into English eyes, so that they began to covet the French empire just beginning to expand in the west. At the same time he opened their eyes to the threat of the French to their own holdings along the Atlantic. Men like Couture and the heroes of whom he spoke were men who were not easily denied. The English knew that.

They learned of Pierre Le Moyne Iberville who had founded the colony of Louisiana at the mouth of the Mississippi and they saw the cloud that might rise ominously over their own heads. Iberville, they knew, had pushed east along the Gulf coast and established the post of Mobile. Rumors drifted back of this Frenchman's bold plan for a giant squeeze play that would encircle the English in the Carolina colony, in alliance with the Spaniards. The Spaniards would move up from St. Augustine and the French would creep slowly up from Mobile, and they would drive the English literally into the Atlantic Ocean. Or at least that was the plan hatched in the mind of Iberville. It was even worked out in such detail as the shipment of English settlers back to England and transfer of the French Huguenots at Charleston to Mobile for conversion back into the Catholic faith. To further this elaborate project Iberville set out to pacify the Indians who inhabited the lands between Mobile and the upper reaches of the Savannah, to win them over as allies to open a path for the French. He sent his agents among the Choctaws and Chickasaws, who were nearest in Alabama and Mississippi, and among the Creeks and Cherokees in Alabama and Georgia.

CHAPTER TWO

THE TOMAHAWK TALKS BACK

From the trade in deerskins, which, as we have seen, turned the Savannah into a busy artery of commerce, there emerged an intriguing figure—the white Indian agent who bartered with the natives in this flourishing business.

He played a leading role in the creation of English empire in the southeast, in opening up the back country for future settlement, and in defending the frontier thus established. Unfortunately, at one critical period, he brought down the vengeance of the Indians upon the whole valley of the Savannah by tactless and cruel exploitation of the Indians in his zealous pursuit of business. He indulged in the arrogant excesses that come from the easy conquests of commerce with a primitive people avid for the products of civilization.

This red hurricane, for the Yamassee War of 1715 was all of that, nearly swept white men off that section of the map which included the Charleston settlement and the valley of the Savannah. This near escape from oblivion brought the lesson that such holocausts always have down through history, for it led to the erection of a bulwark at the mouth of the river, the colony founded by James Edward Oglethorpe which became the city of Savannah.

The Indian trader was a rough and sometimes uncouth fellow, part businessman, part diplomat, part soldier, part spy. He was an adventurer of the Savannah River and the forests and Indian trails. He knew the secrets of the woods and the psychology of the people who lived there. He was as varied, of course, as is humankind, a curious mixture, part rogue, part hero. There were dissolute men among the traders, quarrelsome fellows, with little respect for man-made law. There were those who did not hesitate to capitalize the ignorance of the Indians in the matters of weights and measures.

Yet, on the other hand, the Indian trader was resourceful and brave. He taught the Indians the use of firearms and European tactics of warfare. Often he led Indian tribes personally in battle. He unraveled the fringes of diplomacy and, in every way possible, sought to promote the interests of England. He was afraid of nothing, not even of losing his own soul.

Withal, though, despite his importance in the wilderness where he often was king and dictator of a little domain, he was in fact merely the pawn in a great game which was plotted and directed from council chambers in cities far away across the seas, far from the woods where he plied his trade and lived his simple life. He made money and provided luxuries for others. His employer was the merchant and planter who lived in style and splendor in the lowlands about Charleston. He was the day laborer working for a pittance. He was close to poverty always, but in recompense had the appealing life of adventure in deep woods and along quiet streams for which so many others, before and since, have paid the same price.

Occasionally he would involve himself so deeply in debt to the principal by whom he was employed that he would not dare venture into Charleston, which was a rendezvous for his kind every spring. When it was absolutely necessary for the principal to confer with such a derelict agent, or when some crisis occurred in the Indian country that drove the agent to the refuge of the city, a moratorium had to be proclaimed for these debt-ridden souls.

Back to the wilderness, along the trails shaded by the tall and friendly trees, the Indian traders would go, after their sojourn in Charleston. They returned to the comforts of such homes as they had in the wilderness, and these were not, in all cases, so crude as we might imagine. The frontier trader along the Savannah usually lived with the Indian tribe with which he did business. He had a home of his own and a squaw for his wilderness wife. From such unions came those half-breeds who, in later years, furnished occasional leaders of an unusual and talented sort, and occasional scamps who shamed both their white and their red blood. The shrewder among the traders became advisers to the chief in statecraft and war. They were the bankers, too, providing credit for the Indian huntsman who brought in the deerskins. The trader's house usually was a grade better than those in which the Indians lived, and might be most commodious, considering the wilderness standards, depending upon taste and ingenuity. It would have a chimney to keep it free of smoke. It was an arsenal as well as a store. There would be about it a garden cultivated by Indian servants under the direction of the squaw. There were cows for milk; chickens, melon patches, peach trees, vegetables, hogs for pork, sheep for woolen clothing.

Life was simple, but it was good.

In the early eighteenth century there were some two hundred of these Indian traders employed by the big houses in Charleston. Their numbers increased gradually, so that there were as many as three hundred of their kind twenty or thirty years later. The names of only about a hundred are to be found in the records of these years, and many of these names are recorded merely for infringement of some regulation or violation of some law, like the hangman's list. Among them, however, were a few who got their names in the history books, a few who settled down, after a time, in civilized pursuits and acquired a competence for themselves.

Such a one was Thomas Nairne, the Scotsman. He had started life as an Indian agent and rose to eminence in the Carolina colony, master of an estate on St. Helena Island. He supervised trade with the Indians as an official of the colony. In this capacity he was the overseer of all Indian traders who traveled the circuit up and down the Savannah River and in the wilderness on either side and to the north among the headwaters. In vain he tried to smooth out the increasing irritations between the Indians and the traders and to avert the impending conflict, and in this lies the ironic tragedy of his long and well-spent life.

He was a soldier, a dreamer, and a philosopher. In his life is mirrored the era in which he lived.

Tom Nairne had followed Governor James Moore in that expedition in 1702 which swept up to the very gates of St. Augustine, but which failed to capture the sturdy citadel, the stout and squat stone fort. The Carolinians withdrew after a long siege, with rich booty, silver plate from the churches, and Indian slaves. The Spaniards struck back four years later, in alliance with the French, in a foray against Charleston, but were beaten off, even though Charleston at the time was under siege from another plague, yellow fever.

Tom Nairne was along also on Governor Moore's expedition into Apalachee which embraced what is now northern and western Florida. This raid uprooted every one of the chain of Spanish missions that stretched westward from St. Augustine up to and slightly beyond the junction of the Chattahoochee and Flint rivers.

The English, French and Spanish were at grips in Queen Anne's War, in America as in Europe, and, in truth, Governor Moore started this war in southeast America, on his own account, on the receipt merely of unofficial advices from England. He did not wait for a formal declaration of war, but struck first, and at St. Augustine. The Carolina colony was constantly on the alert for new attacks from the French and Spanish alliance. Scout boats sailed up and down the Carolina and Georgia coasts past the mouth of the Savannah on regular patrol. Tom Nairne set up warning guns on his plantation on St. Helena Island, and other plantation owners did the same.

The Scotsman saw this struggle for what it was, the fight for the whole southeastern part of the North American continent. The nation that controlled this sector also would control the outlets of trade through the Caribbean, hitherto in the hands of Spain, guarded by St. Augustine and her outposts in Cuba and the other islands. Through the Gulf of Mexico sailed her ships heavy with their rich cargoes from Mexico.

Tom Nairne was a man of big ideas. He consorted with Thomas Welch, an experienced trader among the Chickasaws, a tribe living in Alabama and constantly being courted by the French. Together they devised a scheme to strike directly at the French at Mobile and oust them from that fortress as a first step in a westward movement. They took this project before the colonial assembly at Charleston and it was readily approved. At the same time, the assembly appointed Nairne as sole Indian commissioner and revised trade regulations with the Indians along lines he proposed.

But the enterprise never got under way. It was dropped in the face of precautions by the French and new reports of another big expedition against Charleston, which, however, did not materialize. Jean Baptiste Le Moyne, in command at Mobile, enlarged his stockade as a refuge for neighboring Indian tribes and sent emissaries among the Indians, who got guarantees that they would not join the English in an attack upon Mobile.

Nairne, himself, got into personal difficulties. Governor Robert Johnson of Carolina had opposed his appointment as Indian commissioner. There had been bad blood between the two for some time. The governor had the Indian commissioner arrested on charges of a plot against Queen Anne, seemingly without any foundation whatever, and Nairne was thrown into jail. There he spent several months. He was released at length without ever being tried, and, like Henry Woodward before him, went to England and straightened out his personal problems with the Proprietors, who, meanwhile, had deposed Governor Johnson. Nairne lost out as Indian commissioner, but later he was made head of an Indian board with the same general authority.

Prison could not confine his soaring imagination. While in jail he drafted a grandiose plan. This he submitted to the secretary of state in England. It embraced measures not only for western conquest, but for English dominion over the whole continent, a breath-taking scheme that went too far beyond the thinking of his contemporaries, though its design for strengthening the immediate territory saw fruition in the Savannah colony of a few years later.

The Carolina colony, he argued, must be fortified as the base of attack to drive the French from the south and the Spanish from the southwest where they still had a flourishing empire about Santa Fe and down into Mexico. He would establish posts along the Tennessee, a colony in Apalachee, from which the Spanish now had been driven, possibly another across the Mississippi for an eventual base against the Spanish. He also implored the secretary of state to insist in the peace negotiations at the end of Queen Anne's War upon English control of Mobile. Reaching beyond the south, he urged that the governors of

Maryland and New York make overtures to the Iroquois to enlist them securely on the side of the English and, with farsighted vision, he said:

"All parts of the English dominions ought mutually to espouse one another's interest in Everything that relates to the Common defense against the French and their party."

So spoke Tom Nairne, a man ahead of his time.

At the same time, too, he was a shrewd and practical observer of affairs immediately about him, and from him we have some observations which reveal, in a brief flash, the secrets of English success and the rationalizations natural to a spreading empire.

This, for instance:

"The English trade for cloath always attracts and maintains the obedience and friendship of the Indians, they Effect most who sell best cheap."

Never was it more succinctly put.

He salved his own and English consciences about Indian slavery in this fashion:

"Some men think that it both serves to Lessen their numbers before the French can arm them, and it is a more Effectual way of Civilizing and Instructing than all the Efforts used by the French missionaries."

Honest pride in the success of the Carolina colony with the Indians, in which he had a part, speaks from his observation: "Everybody knows that wee have the greatest number of Indians Subject to this Government of any in all America, and almost as many as all other English Governments put together."

Therefore, it was perhaps with confidence that he undertook the last mission of his life.

This found him, on April 14, 1715, Good Friday Eve, at Pocataligo in Carolina, not many miles from the Savannah River. Here he had come, in line of duty, to look into disquieting reports of imminent trouble from the Yamassee Indians, who were among his charges as head of the Indian Board. The complaints had to do with outrages perpetrated by Indian trading agents. Nairne had been trying to check them. The reports of an impending uprising came from two widely separated areas, taking an alarming turn sufficient to command the intercession of the director of Indian affairs, himself.

A well-known figure in Charleston, William Bray, while hunting runaway Indian slaves in the vicinity of St. Augustine, heard from a friendly Yoa Indian that the Creeks were getting ready to take the war path. The Yoas were related to the Yamassees. This Indian informer, Cuffy by name, said the Creeks planned to strike first at Indian trading agents and then fall upon the settlements. The attack was described by Cuffy as very near. Bray hurried off to Charleston. A second warning was brought by Samuel Warner, who came dashing into Charleston from Palachicola, an Indian settlement on the banks of the Savannah not so far from its mouth, to repeat a rumor among the Indians there that the Creeks, disgusted with the white trading agents, were ready, at one more affront, to "down with them and so go on with it." Bray and Warner arrived in Charleston the same day and told their stories to Governor Craven and the Indian Board. The governor immediately ordered Warner to the Palachicola and Yamassee towns to summon the Indians to a conference at Savannah Town. Nairne went to Pocataligo, and there was joined by Warner and Bray and several Indian traders. Nairne called a conference of the headmen of the Yamassees.

The Yamassee Indians were another of the buffer tribes between the English colony and the outlying Indians and Spaniards which succeeded one another along the Savannah. They had lived somewhat to the south, below the Savannah in Georgia, which the Spaniards called Guale. At this time they occupied several towns north and south of the Savannah. The southern boundary of their settlements was the Altamaha River and they lived as far north as Pocataligo.

They were useful to the English for raids southward upon the Spaniards in the Georgia islands and St. Augustine. Their first marauding expedition southward was at the instigation of the Scotch who had settled at Stuart's Town on Port Royal Island. Spanish retaliation threw them into the arms of the English, and they began to move northward across the Savannah to be closer to the protecting influence of the Charleston colony. Many had settled in the fertile lands between the Savannah and the Combachee River and to the west along the Savannah in a fairly sizable strip of land. They were more docile than the Westoes and the Shawnees, their predecessors in the buffer role, yielding more easily to the blandishments of civilization. For a time they had lived peaceably, for the most part, among the English, their loyalty periodically freshened by gifts.

In the so-called "Indian Land" in which they had settled, which was so called years after they had disappeared, the English also were expanding at the beginning of the eighteenth century. The English were settling on Port Royal Island, and also took over large tracts of land to the north along the Savannah. Here, in the course of time, rice plantations flourished about the mouth of the Savannah and farther north and west large acreage was developed in cattle ranches. Consequently, the Indians found themselves crowded by the forward surge of white settlement. From time to time the colonial authorities had to oust squatters from parts of this rich land that had been recognized as Indian lands. For they were most anxious to keep this buffer tribe satisfied so that it would continue to annoy the Spaniards and check any threatened invasion from the south. There was some friction over land, but this was not the major source of the resentment that finally broke, like the flash of an ominous thundercloud, in the Yamassee War.

The basic cause was the exploitation of the inferior race by unprincipled white trading agents. There were cruelties and brutalities beyond such minor annoyances as stealing of Indian canoes and other property. Indian women were ravished and

carried away. Constantly the trading agents literally forced
their goods upon the susceptible Indians, plied the weaker red
men with liquor, and, in this state, loaded them with goods for
which they could not possibly pay. Then they would try to hold
relatives responsible for these debts.

Finally the cup of Indian endurance was full to overflow-
ing.

This posed a delicate task for the diplomatic Nairne. Yet he
found such a cordial reception when he talked with the Yamassee chiefs, despite the threatening reports that had come to
him, that he worked out an adjustment of their complaints
which seemed satisfactory. The Indians prepared a feast, and
Nairne and his companions sat down with them, eating and
drinking, until well into the night. It was altogether a joyous
occasion. The English visitors were provided with sleeping
quarters in the town house. Tom Nairne lay down to sleep, content with his negotiations. The night was peaceful with the
sweet smells and sounds of spring.

It was broken, with frenzied shrieks and howls, just before
dawn, and the white men awoke from their sleep to a nightmare
of horrible reality. In the eerie light outside they beheld, with
cold terror, a wild band of Indian madmen, ghastly in red and
black paint, dancing like "demons risen from Hell." The knife
and the hatchet fell quickly. Some were slaughtered in cold
blood. Nairne was saved for the supreme savage sacrifice. He
was burned at the stake, "a petit feu," as the French called this
fiendish revenge, his body pricked with hundreds of lightwood
splinters which slowly seared his flesh. For several days he was
tortured until he died in agony.

This was the price of empire of which he dreamed. Others
had paid it. Others would pay it.

Some ninety persons, traders, planters and their families,
were slain on that dreadful night. Only two white men escaped
the slaughter at Pocataligo and the vicinity. One was a Captain

Burroughs, a seaman, who beat his pursuers to the river. Despite severe and painful wounds about his neck and chest, he swam the stream and raced all the way to the plantation of John Barnwell on Port Royal Island to give the alarm. The other who escaped was a trader, nameless to history, who hid in a marsh near the town all day long, watching the torturing of his friends, helpless. He came out from hiding at night, stripped down naked to look like an Indian, and walked unmolested through the town, unnoticed by the hilarious savages who were reveling in their bloody triumph.

Luckily for some four hundred persons at Port Royal there was a captured smuggling boat in the river in which they took refuge. One of the first attacks had struck at Port Royal. The Indians came to the edge of the water and fired at the boat loaded with its terrified cargo of refugees, but it was too far offshore for any damage. Many in Port Royal, however, had not reached the boat and were massacred.

Governor Craven had learned about the massacre at Port Royal on his way to Savannah Town for the conference he had called. He did not return to Charleston, but called out the militia of Colleton County, rounded up a little army which immediately took the field, and declared martial law. Governor Craven was a man of action, a godsend to the beleaguered colony. He threw up a temporary fort, repulsed one band of Indians who attacked, sent off other forces to assault Pocataligo, and a few days later routed a force of Indians about twice the size of his little army of two hundred and forty white men and a few allies of loyal settlement Indians.

All up and down the Savannah and far in the back country the Indians fell first upon the traders who were living among them. The war broke simultaneously at widely separated points, and from several tribes, from the Yamassee close to the colony to the Creeks in Georgia and Alabama, and including the Yuchi who also lived along the middle Savannah, the remnant of Shawnees still there, the Apalachee, the Catawbas to the north in

South Carolina, and minor tribes in the Piedmont section and along the coast, Saraws, Waccamaws, Santee, Cape Fears. The Choctaws in Alabama also turned against the English and again were leagued with the French at Mobile, though the Chickasaws remained peaceful. The directing genius of this terrible onslaught was the Emperor Brim of the Creeks, who turned the flood loose from his home in the hills.

Refugees began to pour into Charleston from the outlying sections, and the town was pallid with the atmosphere of siege. As reports trickled in from distant points, it seemed as if all the Indians in this part of the continent had risen up against the English to destroy them completely. The line of battle drew close to Charleston. Then it receded, only to draw closer again, as the little armies pushed back the Indian invasion, then were compelled to withdraw toward the city by the overwhelming Indian forces. Several "armies" were in the field, mere handfuls of white men and friendly Indian allies in reality.

Governor Craven took command of all the fighting forces under powers granted by the assembly. He dispatched envoys to Virginia to get help, and some two hundred soldiers finally came from that colony, though the two colonies haggled for years afterward over what pay these soldiers should have received, symptomatic of the divided state of the English colonies in America at the time. The governor sent purchasing agents to Massachusetts to buy guns. Negro slaves were quickly inducted into service and hurried into the field under command of white officers. A ring of garrisons was thrown about Charleston and on nearby plantations to check the invaders. Organization and persistence finally won, though not until the colony had gone through dark and desperate days with frequent reverses. For months the war crackled along a lengthy front.

The coup that finally ended the war was one of the boldest exploits of early American annals, a march of three hundred English under command of Captain Maurice Moore, a veteran Indian fighter, along the Savannah River right into the mountains at its headwaters, literally infested with Cherokee and Creek warriors. Some of the colonial guerrillas, in the early days of the war, thought they had recognized Cherokees among the Indians whom they were fighting. This caused much anxiety, for the Cherokees hitherto had been friendly to the English. If they remained friendly they would form a bulwark for the English to hold back the Creeks and other tribes along the line of the Savannah. If they joined the Creeks, however, in the war on the English, this would create an invading inundation that might well sweep the colony and its outlying settlements to destruction.

Inquiry disclosed that the Cherokees still had not joined the war against the English. The strategy, then, was to swing the Cherokees definitely into an alliance with the English against the Creeks, to hold the line along the Savannah. Two Indian agents who escaped the slaughter of so many of their kind, Eleazar Wiggin and Robert Gilchrist, volunteered to act as emissaries to the Cherokee in the interest of an alliance. Their mission was financed by the colonial government and they were promised a bounty of £500 each, quite a nice sum, if they could hold the Cherokees to the English. Triumphantly they returned to Savannah Town from their dangerous excursion, not only whole of body but with a large and influential delegation of Cherokee chieftains in tow, among them the famous Caesar who presided in the Cherokee capital of Echota and was not only a most belligerent Creek-hater but occupied a strategic frontier position at Echota which faced the Creeks along the Chattahoochee. The upshot of the conference was that the Cherokees would join the English in war upon the Creeks. So the chiefs had agreed.

Colonel Moore led an army of three hundred to Savannah Town. But the Cherokees did not show up with the allies they had promised. He waited for several days. Still no Cherokees appeared. The colonel then resolved upon his bold coup. He would march his three hundred right into the land of Cherokees and make a show of force. He gambled that this would rally the Cherokees to his side. So, up the old trading path along the left bank of the Savannah, he directed his expeditionary force toward the hills.

The path was well marked here, but, while the familiar river flowed peacefully down toward the sea on their right, they looked constantly on their left into the forbidding wall of forest wilderness. It concealed a number of Creek scouts sent by the Emperor Brim to spy upon the army and report its progress back to him at his headquarters at Echota. But they did not find that out until later, which was, perhaps, just as well. Colonel Moore led his troops beyond the spot where the Tugaloo joins the Seneca to form the mainstream thereafter called the Savannah. Pushing up the Tugaloo, they marched as far as the Indian town of Tugaloo at the junction of the Tugaloo and the Toccoa. The intrepid leader and his followers now were deep in enemy territory, among the secret and hidden places of the hills where, they knew, they might be trapped any time if the Indians chose to fall upon them. Not until later did they learn how really perilous was their position.

Colonel Moore promptly called the Cherokee leaders together and they sat about the large council house at Tugaloo and talked. Now he discovered a division among the Cherokees, those individualists among Indians, about which he had not been advised. He had counted upon solidarity. He found it did not exist. The Lower Cherokees, the branch of the tribe that lived in the mountains of what is now northeastern Georgia, had friends among some of the Indians now joined in war against the English, and they did not care to enlist in war against them. They had no quarrel with the Shawnees, or the Yuchi and Apalachee who lived to the south, some along the Savannah River, nor could they blame the Catawbas who lived in Piedmont Carolina for their hostility to the English. As for the Creeks, they told the colonial leader that this tribe was sending representatives to confer with him. In short, they did not want to go to war except on a pick-the-enemy basis, which was not exactly helpful to the English, who were beyond the point of choosing. There seemed nothing for Colonel Moore to do except to await the coming of the Creek chieftains, for if he could patch up a peace that would check possible invasion from the hills, so much the better.

There was only one flaw in this plan. The Overhill Cherokees, who lived along the northern Georgia border about Echota and in Tennessee, had been fired by Caesar, their hotheaded chieftain, who was bent on war against the Creeks and saw a rich opportunity in an alliance with the English. Colonel Moore had to soothe the war spirit aroused by Caesar among his people, and sent agents to pacify them. This proved a difficult mission. Caesar continued to shout loudly for war in the conferences. But finally the agents won the confidence of older heads in the tribe, and the war was postponed temporarily. But the Creeks still delayed. Weeks passed, and their representatives failed to appear at Tugaloo. Caesar was restless and could hardly be restrained. He became very irritated with the English for holding him off. Only by wars against the Creeks, he argued with practical Indian logic, had the Cherokees been able to take prisoners of war whom they could sell into slavery to the English in exchange for arms and ammunition. This was a coldly commercial argument, revealing a rather canny insight into the white people with whom he was dealing.

Finally, before Caesar ordered his warriors into action against the Creeks, the spokesmen for that great confederacy turned up and went into secret conclave with the Cherokee leaders at Tugaloo. Colonel Moore sat by anxiously, with his army ready for any emergency, ignorant of what was going on in the secret meeting. Suddenly one day it all came out, and with war whoops which immediately shocked the English army into readiness. But their arms were not needed. The Cherokees handled this emergency themselves. They slaughtered the Creek agents in cold blood and also killed representatives of the Yamassees and other tribes who had gathered for the conferences. This strange and bloody turn of events was explained for the English when it was disclosed that the Creek agents, instead of talking peace, had sought to persuade the Cherokees to join them in war against the English, and, for a time, they seemed to be winning converts. Wiser heads among the Cherokees prevailed and, sensing the danger, decided to strike and strike quickly. Before the English knew what was happening, the deed had been done. The English then discovered, to their consternation, that a large force of Creeks, reported to number from two hundred to five hundred warriors, was hiding in the forest nearby all the time, ready, once the Cherokees consented, to pounce upon the colonial army and exterminate it. Colonel Moore gathered his army and a force of Cherokees to move quickly against the Creeks, hoping to catch them by surprise before they learned that negotiations had broken down, but the Creeks slipped away in safety through the forests they knew so well.

It was a narrow escape, and a lucky one. Colonel Moore knew where he stood now. The Cherokees were his friends. The Creeks definitely were not. But the Cherokees would form a bulwark against the Creeks to stem an invasion from that quarter. Meanwhile he got reports that the Chickasaws, who lived beyond the Creeks in Alabama, also were loyal to the English and would likewise form a protective wall against any attempted advance by the French from Mobile.

Thus, happily, ended a perilous adventure that might have turned out so disastrously. While occasional fighting continued up and down the Savannah thereafter, the backbone of the Indian revolution had been broken by what has come down to history as "The March of the Three Hundred" and the colony clustered along the Atlantic began to live normally once more after a year of anxiety, suspense and horror. Refugees in Charleston began to return home to their plantations. The exploit of

Colonel Moore and his brave band of colonials rang down through the years as a tale to inspire coming generations at Charleston and along the Savannah frontier.

Forty years later Governor James Glen of South Carolina summed up the achievement of the Three Hundred by saying, "It is probably owing to that March that we have this opportunity, so long after, of commemorating that Era: for had the Cherokees and Creeks joined at that time, which nothing prevented but the resolute Behaviour of our Militia; it might have proved fatal, it must have been, at least very dangerous to the Province."

The Yamassees sneaked back across the Savannah, defeated and forlorn, and took their women and their children and their few remaining possessions southward toward St. Augustine. They begged a home among their one-time enemies and became a subject race, prideless and disconsolate. Their revolt had taken a heavy toll among their warriors. They were a lost tribe forevermore, mingling with the remnants of other tribes, refugees like themselves, who submitted themselves to slavery among the Spaniards. In time they disappeared completely as a tribal entity. The Creeks, likewise, retreated westward.

The English had learned their lesson from this near tragedy. Immediately they strengthened their frontier by building at Savannah Town a fort which rose, like a proud sentinel, amid the crude shacks of the trading post, a symbol that England was here to stay. It was named Fort Moore in honor of the deliverer who, himself, was promoted several grades to lieutenant general. He reopened trade with the Cherokees and his scouts were constantly wary for trouble from the Creeks.

Colonial authorities at Charleston came to see the wisdom of old Tom Nairne. At last he was vindicated in his persistent plea for strengthening the Savannah River front. For the French and the Spanish still squatted there to the south of them, at Mobile and St. Augustine, squatted and plotted. The English in 1721 built a fort in the middle of what is familiarly known to history as "the debatable land," that area between the Savannah River and St. Augustine, embraced now in middle and southern Georgia and northern Florida. It was called Fort King George and it stood at the mouth of the Altamaha River. The Spanish, reasserting, as they had constantly to do, their claim to this country, raised a frantic howl about this outpost. Charleston paid little heed to their protests, but such things were taken more seriously in the chancelleries of Europe, at least taken seriously enough to set diplomats to writing those long-winded notes couched in fine language which served to keep the status quo between wars. The fort finally burned down and saved embarrassment all around. England relented to the point of not trying to build it again and withdrew her garrison.

This, however, was only a temporary gesture to the Spanish king. England, checked in one direction, always moved in another.

So, on February 12, 1733, the Indian observer on Yamacraw Bluff, eighteen miles above the mouth of the Savannah, looked down upon a new invasion from the sea. It was only a miniature and rather pitiful affair, all things considered, a fleet composed of a sloop and five oversized canoes. Forlorn, too, were the faces of those who sat, huddled against the raw February wind. The newcomers landed at the foot of Yamacraw Bluff and clambered with little cheer up to the site picked out a few days before by James Edward Oglethorpe for the city of Savannah and the new English colony to be called Georgia for the English king.

PART 3

Utopia for a Day

CHAPTER ONE

OGLETHORPE STARTED WITH A BOATLOAD OF
IMPECUNIOUS HOPEFULS

The hundred-odd men, women and children who slept on Yamacraw Bluff above the Savannah River that first night in hastily
pitched tents embodied a variety of impulses set in motion in
England which radiated through all Europe. This colony in its
inception was the fruit of wild and beautiful dreams of Utopia.
Like all English utopias, however, it had a tough core of plain
imperialism. It was salted with practicality of the strictly British
sort. In contact with the reality of existence in the wilderness
it quickly lost its utopian complexion, as had other dreams that
men in the quiet cloisters of Europe had dreamed as they looked,
from afar, upon a new world where a paradise still might be
created. They saw then the visions that other men today, looking back, conjure up when they contemplate how America
started and what it might have been, and yet know, in their
heart of hearts, could never be.

It is not likely that any utopian dreams sweetened the

74

sleep of the men and women who threw themselves down on the hard soil of Georgia that first night, weary from two months in a small and smelly ship that wallowed in a strange sea. There must have been some that night who waked with a start, the sound of the rushing seas suddenly gone from their ears, to look out with vague fears and find the sea there no longer, even though there was still the rolling sensation of landsickness, to see instead the blank and unfriendly night and the forbidding forest and the cold stars of an alien land. And then tomorrow brought them up against the stern necessity of clearing ground and building homes and planting and providing.

The man Oglethorpe who started all this along the river here combined within himself the dreams and the practical needs of empire, and so made the two concepts one for a long time.

He was both an attractive and a forbidding figure, a strange mixture of conservatism and near radicalism. Along with many splendid qualities, he had a strain of self-righteousness, tinged with hypocrisy. For he could insist that Negro slaves be banned from Georgia while at the same time he was a director of the Royal African Company, which was a slave-trading organization and contributed slave money to his fortune. He became deputy governor of the slave company the year of the founding of Georgia. He also insisted upon the prohibition of rum from the colony, though he, himself, was fond of his wine and beer. He did permit the sale and consumption of wine and beer, and himself superintended the brewing of beer for the colonists. Both slavery and rum were proscribed in the articles creating the new colony.

He had practical reasons for forbidding both. He regarded it unsafe to have another race in the midst of an infant colony. South Carolina not long before had suffered the anxieties of a slave revolt, and the founders of the new colony were acutely conscious of such a danger. Also Oglethorpe knew that many slaves had fled from Carolina to hide away among the Spaniards, which, of itself, represented a loss of valuable property—he, himself, knew how valuable—as well as creating a class of informers among the Spanish enemies. For defense purposes, too, Oglethorpe and the founders of the colony thought it unwise to permit slaves, for it would be a temptation to the farmer to forsake his plantation for the city, and leave its operation to the blacks. This would deprive the outlying settlements of their natural defenders, the white owners. There was, furthermore, a compelling economic reason which went right to the fundamental object of the colony, that was, to establish a strong foundation in a sound yeoman class, sturdy and independent. Dependence upon Negro slaves would destroy this purpose, for it would make it hard for the poor white laborer, the principal unit in the colony, to exist. Oglethorpe saw far ahead and forecast, in this view, the ultimate deteriorating effect of the slave economy with its discouragement of the small, independent farmer, and all the evils that followed many years after he died.

Later there developed within him a passionate antipathy to slavery on humanitarian grounds, though this did not seem to be present in his prohibition of slavery when the colony was founded. Many years later, long after he had gone home to England to stay, he wrote: "Slavery is against the gospel, as well as fundamental law of England. We refused, as trustees, to make a law permitting such a horrid crime."

As for strong liquor, he knew of its degrading effect upon the Indians and his desire was to keep it from them in the new colony as far as possible. Also he had hygienic reasons affecting the settlers themselves. He thought Georgia was too warm a climate for hard liquor, a view that has never been held since.

Oglethorpe was a soldier, in essence. As a young man he had fought on the Continent under Prince Eugene of Savoy, that great military genius. His instincts were naturally conservative, for he came from a landed Tory family, the son of a father who had suffered for his loyalty to the Stuarts. As a civil leader he at first was highly successful, in the early and mean days

of creating a home in the wilderness, when the handful of settlers so needed a strong hand to guide them and an indomitable
will to push them. In those days, we learn from early letters,
he was known among them by the title "father." Later the forbidding thin lips and the hard face of duty stirred up hate in
softer and less responsible souls, when the troubled days of necessary sacrifice came upon the colony. He was always so right,
and insisted so upon it.

Basic in his character, however, was a stern strain of
humanitarianism, the sort that is so sure what people need,
yet instinctively beneficent in impulse, a conscientious recognition of the plight of the less favored of mankind. And it was
this instinct, at the start, that inspired the creation of a colony
which, in his mind and in the minds and hearts of many others,
not only in England but all over Europe, was to be something
new and glorious in the annals of mankind.

It was the harsh tragedy of a friend that set him off in the
pursuit of his elusive dream. Robert Castell, a scholar and an
amateur architect, one of those talented persons who cannot
quite adjust themselves to the strict demands of capitalism, was
thrown in jail for debt under the English law, as were so many
in those pound-of-flesh days when England was reaching out
like a grasping money-changer. He was cruelly treated by an
unconscionable jailer, and died of smallpox in a foul prison
infested with that dread disease. Oglethorpe investigated the
circumstances. He came away full of righteous fury. He was in
Parliament at the time and he forced a parliamentary inquiry
which he, himself, was delegated to conduct. It turned the light
upon a horrible condition in supposedly enlightened England.
It was discovered that thousands and thousands of Englishmen
were languishing in jail for failure to pay their debts, many of
them victims of temporary bad luck. The report of his committee
created a sensation and all England was stirred. It led to reforms in many directions.

Debtors were turned out of jail in droves. But still there was no way for them to make a living in England, and another problem was created. This dilemma led Oglethorpe to his great project, which fitted in appropriately with the purposes of the masters of England, which also were partially Oglethorpe's purposes, for he was a man also with a keen perception of England's imperial opportunities and her destiny. These people, Oglethorpe saw, might be transported to America where they could find new opportunity and, at the same time, England would be served thereby, her imperial interests advanced.

Others, it now came to light, had been having such dreams and the idea blossomed quickly into realization. It got religious backing, always very potent. There had lived in England a preacher, Dr. Thomas Bray, who was the directing genius behind two influential societies which had organized libraries in England and America and promoted education and Christianity among Negro slaves in America. Rather imposing names they bore, Society for the Propagation of the Gospel in Foreign Parts and Society for the Propagation of Christian Knowledge, commonly known as SPG and SPCK. Becoming infirm and knowing that he had not much longer to live, Dr. Bray organized a foundation to carry on after his death, Associates of Dr. Bray he called it with perhaps pardonable modesty. He died in 1730. Oglethorpe had a good friend among the Associates of Dr. Bray, John Lord Viscount Percival, who later became the first Earl of Egmont, and to him he went for help in carrying forward his plan for an American colony. Oglethorpe told his titled friend there was £15,000 in a charity that could be used to start the colonial enterprise. At the behest of the earl, the Associates petitioned the king for land in America for the colony. A grant was made of the land lying between the Savannah and Altamaha Rivers embracing the coastal islands, a group of twenty-one trustees was organized, including Oglethorpe and the Earl of Egmont, and the project was assured.

Never was such a venture so widely supported, so widely

advertised, and so pregnant with the enthusiasm and hopes of so many people, proving that people are, basically, so much more idealistic, so much more optimistic of a better world than their rulers ever will let them be. Men and women who could never see America, who knew they could not participate, were excited to a fever of charity.

The proposed colony had two elements of success. It was good, hardheaded business for the empire. It was at the same time an outlet for the humanitarian impulse always present in every age and really easily aroused.

The lords of British empire espoused it eagerly. It would provide that bulwark for the Carolina colony on the south for which the need now was so clearly shown by the ghastly experience of the Yamassee War. The mercantilists saw in a thriving and prosperous colony a market for goods manufactured at home, and they saw, too, how such a colony might produce raw materials and luxuries which England now had to buy outside her own colonies, in America and elsewhere, silk, wine, indigo, rice, and spices, and the like, in short, a very fortunate interempire trade all around. The American colony also would absorb the unemployed who haunted the thick streets of London like wraiths of bad conscience and thus ease what was fast heading into a domestic crisis.

For the idealistic, the philanthropic, the religious, the political philosophers it had the obvious appeal of a new experiment, an experiment in government, in social organization, in the education and proselyting of races then in darkness, such as the Negro slaves in neighboring Carolina, and the Indians in the mysterious recesses of the surrounding forests. All England took up the crusade. From the pulpit ministers of the gospel preached sermons about Georgia that can be found in libraries today, and a heaven on earth rises still like an ancient mirage from the stilted phrases. Their flocks contributed in cash and in religious books. Over three thousand such books were collected, far more than enough to suffice for a long time to comfort the souls of those early pilgrims about the mouth of the Savannah, even if they had had any time to read. Pamphlets were written.

Magazines and the primitive newspapers of the day provoked discussion of the new utopia in the taverns and in the homes. Fashionable folk talked about Georgia over their tea. Poets were inspired to celebrate the new Elysian Fields. Contributions poured in to the Trustees, from the plain people, from the wealthy and titled. Lord Jekyll gave £500 and, in thanks, got a Georgia island named for him later. The Bank of England even relented for a trickle of £250 from its well-stuffed coffers. The House of Commons lavishly voted £10,000. Businessmen furnished seeds for all sorts of agricultural experiments, and tools. Always the new colony was described as a veritable paradise, though with various virtues, according to the personal inclinations of the writer and his knowledge or lack of knowledge of geography. The imagination was freed for flights into the empyrean.

The masses of Europe watched as for the rising sun after a long night. The French and Spanish empires looked on with jealousy and fear. These English! How excited they could get over a barren land when they translated it into terms of new homes, and how dangerous their enthusiasms might become! Simple people, but dreadful in their simplicity.

The enterprise won favor on all sides in England, and for different reasons, which helps to explain the later inevitable clash between the cold calculations of the rulers of empire and the naïve dreams of those who foolishly saw a better world overnight on the shores of America.

Oglethorpe had many chores to do to make ready his expedition. It was a formidable task and a heavy load of responsibility. He was a man of order, patient of infinite detail. Financing took time, but was no really serious obstacle because of the widespread interest and the earnest co-operation of the trustees. Selection of the colonists was a tedious job. This was a careful weeding-out process. Hundreds applied. Only a comparatively few could go. Oglethorpe's humanitarianism was tempered with caution. He was not one to lose his balance in the fine frenzy of a dream. His purpose was to help unfortunate Englishmen, those who had run upon hard times, especially people otherwise sound, solid and respectable who had been caught in the dilemma of debt and unfairly thrown into jail under the severe English law.

But he had no intention of taking to the wilderness, where life would be rough and trying, any derelicts who would hang about his neck and endanger the success of this venture upon which he was staking his reputation. He was giving his time and services without charge, in fact, he contributed from time to time from his own ample means to the Georgia colony. Finally, after many, many interviews, after much close investigation, he picked his boatload to go to the new colony. Those among them who had outstanding debts had to arrange for terms of settlement with their creditors. As the men were selected they were put immediately to military training, for soldiers were needed for Oglethorpe's and the empire's plans, and any afternoon they could be seen drilling before Buckingham Palace. Sergeants of the Royal Guard instructed them in the manual of arms.

The day came at last when all was ready for the ship to put out into the unfriendly ocean. The thirty-five families went aboard the *Ann*, a vessel of two hundred tons packed like a bulging valise, anchored at Deptford, the port of embarkation. There must have been some among them, now that the great adventure was upon them, who were tortured suddenly with doubts and misgivings. They could find some comfort in the resolute demeanor of their leader and in the calm assurance of the Trustees, men of standing and achievement. These came aboard for a final inspection and were led about the vessel by Oglethorpe. He explained what care he had taken in fitting and equipping the tiny ship. He pointed out the provisions for the journey and the first days on shore, showed them the neatly stacked arms, muskets, bayonets, swords and ammunition, explained about the tools and agricultural implements and the stock of seeds for planting, and then, to assuage the hazards of the sea, there were the ten huge casks of beer, and, for any among the Trustees who were fearful of souls in the wilderness, there was the library of religious books.

Oglethorpe may have regretted the space necessary for these, but he was a man willing to compromise to achieve his ends. He was proud, too, of the human cargo, the prospective colonists. There were carpenters, bricklayers, mechanics, and farmers among them, men who should be helpful in coping with a wild and wooded land and making homes and farms out of it. Going along, too, to minister to their souls was a clergyman of the Church of England, the Reverend Henry Hebert; and to instruct them in the culture of silk, which the Trustees planned as a major industry, an expert from Piedmont by the name of Nicholas Amatis.

The *Ann* sailed November 16, 1732. It stopped at Madeira to take on a bountiful supply of the wine for which that island is famous, and, just short of two months from the day they saw Deptford drop under the English horizon, the now veteran seafarers got their first welcome glimpse of the New World, at Charleston, on January 13, 1733. There they were allowed to go ashore for ten hours, to stretch their legs and see the sights, and have a look at a settled colony of English folk in America, an old established colony it was now, with a character all its own, and, we may imagine, ready with a show of airs for the newcomers from England.

Oglethorpe was a man of dispatch. He ordered the ship to take the colonists to Port Royal Island, while he set out overland with William Bull, one of the leading men of Carolina, to pick a site along the Savannah River for a settlement. Much to his liking he found the bluff above the river, eighteen miles from its mouth, where lived nearby the Yamacraw Indians. He met and talked to the chief, Tomochichi, and a half-breed woman of whom we shall hear something later, and found the aged Indian friendly to the English settlement. Several days later he led his little brood through the inland passage from Port Royal to their future home.

The next day, characteristically, Oglethorpe gathered the colonists about him on the bluff and delivered them a speech. He had been known in Parliament as a dull speaker, much given to clichés and the obvious and moralizings, and while this address did not depart from the pattern, it perhaps was more dramatic because of the circumstances and the scene of its delivery—the bluff with the tents of boughs where they had cooked their breakfast, the forest behind them, and the slow red river below them on its way to the sea. He was unusually solemn this morning. He tried to impress upon them their duties as the founders of a new colony, and a colony with the high aims of this one. He told them that the seed they sowed here would, morally as well as literally, bring forth its increase, either for good or for evil, in coming generations. Nor did he omit one of his favorite topics of moralizing—rum. Though many of those before him had been addicted to this vice in England— and it seems to have been a contributing influence to the plight of some of them—he put abstinence now on a charitable basis, that is, for the sake of their Indian neighbors. He explained what liquor did to Indians. It was his hope, he told his little band, "that through your good example, the settlement of Georgia may prove a blessing, and not a curse, to the native inhabitants."

It must have been a most impressive occasion. It is, certainly, in the recalling.

Then he set them to work.

His letter to the trustees back in England written ten days later is revealing. He wrote:

> I fixed upon a healthy situation about ten miles from the sea. The river here forms a half-moon, along the South

side of which the banks are about forty feet high, and on the top a flat, which they call a bluff. The plain high ground extends into the country five or six miles, and along the river-side about a mile. Ships that draw twelve foot of water can ride within ten yards of the bank.

Upon the river-side in the center of this plain I have laid out the town. Opposite to it is an island of very rich pasturage, which I think should be kept for the Trustees' cattle. The river is pretty wide, the water fresh, and from the key of the town you can see its whole course to the sea, with the island of Tybee, which forms the mouth of the river; and the other way you see the river about six miles into the country. The landskip is very agreeable, the stream being wide, and bordered with high woods on both sides. The whole people arrived here on the first of February. (February 12th by the present calendar.) At night their tents were got up. Till the seventh we were taken up in unloading, and making a crane, which I then could not get finished, so took off the hands, and set some on the fortification, and began to fell the woods. I marked out the town and the common; half of the former is already cleared, and the first house was begun yesterday in the afternoon. Not being able to get negroes, I have taken of the independent Company (from South Carolina) to work for us, for which I make them an allowance. . . . I am so taken up in looking after a hundred necessary things, that I write now short, but shall give you a more particular account hereafter. A little Indian nation, the only one within fifty miles, is not only at amity, but desirous to be subjects of his majesty, King George, to have lands given them among us, and to breed their children at our schools. Their chief, and his beloved man, who is the second man in the nation, desire to be instructed in the Christian religion.

That was a nice proprietary English touch—"to have lands given them among us"; and the prompt notice—for the reading of the devout among the Trustees—that the Indians desired to be instructed in the Christian religion showed that Oglethorpe was a clever fellow.

The colony was communal in basis, one of the many such experiments in America, of which the Savannah River had its share. The Indians here in Georgia and elsewhere lived successfully, in their primitive state, under a communal form of social and political organization, but no civilized people in the New World ever found a formula that was satisfactory for long.

Oglethorpe laid out the city by a careful design which is preserved today in that neat, orderly pattern which seems, somehow, so appropriate in its setting. Bull Street, which he named for the friend from Charleston who had helped him select the site, led away at right angles from the river. Along this the simple houses, twenty-four feet by sixteen, made of rough, sawed timber, were built and, at intervals, there were the squares around which traffic must move today, set apart for market places in the original plan.

Each family had a building lot in town for a home, a garden plot on the edge of the city, together a total of five acres, and forty-five acres more beyond the city for general farming. Fifty acres was the limit for the average run of indigent colonists who were to begin life anew in Georgia, though provision also was made for persons of means who should desire to come to the colony, and to such larger tracts were assigned beyond the city, with a limit of five hundred acres. Subsequently some English people of substance took advantage of this provision for larger holdings, so that the colony was not long in acquiring the class distinctions that contributed to the troubles that befell later.

A quitrent of two shillings an acre was laid on all land, the payment not to begin, however, until ten years later. The property was held in tail male, that is, it could pass only to the eldest son. If there were no male offspring, the land reverted to the Trust, for the colony was essentially military in purpose, despite all the dreams of its planners, and the object was to have a male defender on every holding.

Instead of the Negro slaves that were used in Carolina for hard and heavy work in the fields, the Georgia colony had a system of white indentured servants. They were bound into service at periods varying from seven to fourteen years. An opportunity was given them to become settlers when they had completed their service. If they would agree to remain four years more, they were assigned twenty-five acres. This would be increased to fifty acres if they decided to become permanent inhabitants of the colony. Their former employers were required to furnish them with farming implements and other things necessary for an independent start in life.

Oglethorpe got his colony laid out, the people settled under the restricting form of society with its prohibitions against slavery, liquor and accumulations of property that were slowly to irk the colonists into revolt, and then set briskly about the larger business of empire building, which, we gather, was much more to his taste than the social and political reforms of the philosophers that he had carried out to the letter as required. He had set up the utopia. A practical man, he seemed to take it for granted that that was sufficient. We can feel it was with somewhat of relief that he turned, rather abruptly, from the routine of the Savannah colony to look after the more pressing demands of empire. We must remember, too, that Oglethorpe was essentially a soldier, and that he was in the prime of life, full of energy and vigor, and eager to try himself against the Spaniards. He was forty-three when he landed his colonials at the foot of the bluff along the Savannah River.

In three directions he now projected the empire program of military defense, alliances with the Indians, and development of trade.

One of his first acts was to plant five cannon on Yamacraw Bluff and to establish a fort, Fort Argyle it was called, along the Ogeechee River southwest of Savannah at the point where the

Indians from the south usually crossed the river in their forays northward toward Carolina. In the next few months he ventured, on several occasions, far to the south on exploratory trips, going even to San Juan Island at the mouth of the San Juan River, or St. Johns River, as the English called it, not far from St. Augustine, the Spanish capital. On the coastal islands he planted a string of defenses to guard the inland passage that the Spaniards used in their northward invasions—Fort St. George on San Juan Island, and, north toward Savannah, Fort William at the south end of Cumberland Island, and, on St. Simon's Island, a defense at the southern tip which he named St. Andrews Fort and, in the center of the island, the town of Frederica, and a fort to protect it. On the Altamaha River he laid out the town of Darien where a band of Scots were settled and, in time, developed a thriving and flourishing colony.

Frederica was the pride of Oglethorpe's heart, rather than Savannah, and he took the meticulous care of a soldier in laying out this strictly military town in the midst of the lordly live oaks, clean and precise against the green profuse disorder of the great trees. It sat on a bluff, on the western side of the island along the inland channel, looking out upon the wide expanse of a mouth of the Altamaha River. Here he built himself a simple cottage, the only home that he ever had in the colony. It sat, pleasantly, in the midst of a garden and an orchard, typically English, with the massive live oaks all around to shelter it from the warm southern sun. The sea breezes sweetened the air with the fragrance of wild flowers. He commuted to Savannah by boat when his business demanded, which was, perhaps, not so often as necessary, for Oglethorpe neglected Savannah, and here we may find at least a partial reason why the colony did not prosper so well as it might have.

Savannah still stands. But Frederica disappeared in a few years. All we can discover today of Oglethorpe's proud military capital and its defenses is a fragment of the fort that clings to the edge of the island. This ancient ruin is sequestered, like a refuge of history, from the modern spick-and-white seaside resort. The waters of the river lap at its moldy walls. It gives forth the dank smell of abandoned ruins.

The building of Frederica and the laying out of most of the coastal defenses were accomplished after Oglethorpe had made a return trip to England, four months after his arrival in Georgia.

On this first trip back to England he took with him his Indian friend, Tomochichi, the chief's wife, a nephew, and several more of the Yamacraw tribe. The founder of the Georgia colony and his Indian charges caused quite a sensation. Oglethorpe was received in London almost like a conquering hero. Odes were dashed off in his honor by the poets of fashion. The Indians were received by the king and queen and were made much of wherever they went. Their festivities were interrupted by the death of one of their number, for whom there were several days of mourning, and this Indian was buried in St. John's Church at Westminster, far from his native land. Eventually they went back home to Georgia with Oglethorpe, very much impressed—as they were supposed to be—by the power of England; for there was the purpose of empire in their pilgrimage to England. They could tell about it back home to the other Indians, and so the word would spread in time beyond Savannah among the tribes of the wilderness.

Tomochichi, who was now a very old man, was an outcast from the Creeks. Years before he had left the confederacy, no one ever found out why, and a little band had followed him to the new home along the Savannah. They had taken the name of Yamacraws. They were helpful to Oglethorpe in every way. Through them he arranged a conference of a number of nearby Creek chiefs who came to Savannah and bowed before England in solemn ceremonies and agreed to trade with the English, instead of the Spanish.

Too much credit cannot be bestowed upon Tomochichi as a factor in Oglethorpe's success. He was, in mind and soul, a great man, one of those rare spirits, selfless, wise and tolerant, who seem, so often, to happen into history at the right moment to serve a purpose, if there is any purpose in history. In his youth he had been a warrior of renown, so that he was a product of the vicissitudes of a hard life among a primitive people, and not just a good and kind old man.

A beautiful friendship grew up between the aged red man and the white leader half his age, somewhat akin to the relation between father and adopted son. It is a tribute to Oglethorpe that he saw at once the virtue that lay in this Indian chief, the value of his friendship and counsel. The two became constant companions. Oglethorpe relied upon him for advice. Tomochichi, old as he was, yet was hardy, and he went along on the numerous expeditions that the English soldier made to look out the islands on the coast and prepare himself for what he saw was the inevitable, and perhaps decisive, clash with the Spaniards.

He was not along with Oglethorpe, however, on the longest expedition that the general undertook. This was up the Savannah and then overland, along the trail blazed by Dr. Henry Woodward over sixty years before, to attend a great assembly of the Creeks at Coweta Town, their capital on the Chattahoochee River. It was while Oglethorpe was far off in the Creek country that Tomochichi fell ill and died. The general got word of the chief's illness and sent back message after message to his aged and ailing friend; but he could not get back to Savannah before the Indian's death. Tomochiche's body was held, however, for a state funeral in which Oglethorpe served as a pallbearer. He was buried in Percival Square in Savannah, where he rests today under an imposing monument.

Oglethorpe's activity was constant, but it was organized, and it began to show results. Beyond Savannah settlements sprang up. Living on the outposts on the coastal islands became orderly. Roads were hacked through the forests and the malaria-infested swamps—from New Inverness, a Scotch settlement on the Altamaha, to Savannah; from Savannah to Augusta, along the Savannah River, and from Frederica through the tangled woods and heavy underbrush to St. Simon's Fort at the south end of St. Simon's Island.

Every few weeks another boat would put into the mouth of the Savannah and so the population slowly grew. It is customary to think of Georgia as an English colony. Yet it was not. It was truly a melting pot.

Population statistics show that Georgia, in its first few years, was more Germanic than British. For to the Savannah came many persecuted Middle Europeans. The Salzburgers found along the Savannah a refuge finally from religious persecution which had driven them from the mountains of Austria. They had migrated first to France and then to England, where they heard about the new Georgia colony where they could live and worship God as they pleased. They were a sturdy and thrifty people, God-fearing. Their colony was virtually a theocracy, so thoroughly was it ruled by their pastors. Oglethorpe personally led them in their search for a new home. They settled first along a little stream that winds into the Savannah a few miles above the city. They called it Ebenezer. This spot, however, proved isolated and unhealthful, and Oglethorpe helped them find another along the Savannah where they built a town which they called New Ebenezer. Only the fragmentary foundations of their church still stand today to tell where they lived. They developed a prosperous settlement that stood squarely on its own feet, and they, alone, were successful in the culture of silk, which was intended to be one of the chief contributions of the Georgia colony to empire trade. Oglethorpe had no trouble whatever with them.

He was less happy in his experience with another group which also came to Georgia to escape religious persecution. The Moravians, also from Austria, were supposed to settle to the south of Savannah on the Ogeechee River, but they chose, instead, to remain in Savannah. They had specified, in their agreement with the Trustees, that they would not bear arms, as it was contrary to their religion. They insisted rigidly upon this stipulation when the Spanish invasion threatened. So unpopular did they become with other colonists, who could see only that they were not bearing their share of the military burden, that the Moravians finally left and moved, en masse, to then faraway Pennsylvania. But before they went away they settled all their debts.

For his southern military border Oglethorpe wanted strength and reliance, and who could serve him better as border folk than the Scots? The highlands of Scotland were scoured for hardy specimens of that sturdy race whose fighting qualities the English knew so well. This was fairly simple. For there were Scots ready to leave their hills and try a new life elsewhere, Scots of standing and of good family who were marked men because of their recent futile attempt to put the Young Pretender on the throne of England. Oglethorpe rounded up a hundred and thirty capable citizens who were valiant fighters and brought them to Georgia, with about fifty women and children. They were settled on the banks of the Altamaha not far from its mouth. The settlement was called New Iverness, but the whole surrounding region was known as Darien, in honor of their countrymen who had lost their lives in the destruction by the Spanish of the Scotch settlement of Darien on the Isthmus of Panama.

In time, the settlement was called Darien. The Scots spread over to St. Simon's Island and developed the plantation system which, in the following years, became the basic pattern of the southern agricultural economy. The Scots, along with the Salzburgers, bitterly resisted the movement for legalization of slavery in the Georgia colony, which began within a few years but, when slavery was legalized, they accepted it and became slaveholders themselves.

The Scots were sturdy and loyal and hard-fighting allies in the very disastrous expedition southward to St. Augustine in the winter of 1739 in which Oglethorpe struck in vain, as so often happened through the years, at the capital of Spanish empire in southeastern North America. It was a series of mishaps and, after failing in a desperate attempt to take the mighty Spanish fortress by storm, Oglethorpe led his battered and depleted army back to Frederica.

The Scots, too, were mainstays in the Georgia founder's greatest military exploit, which was his thwarting of a formidable invasion by a veritable Spanish Armada. It was the final, highly organized thrust of Spanish power northward along this coast and it is comparable, in a smaller way, to the Spanish Armada that had threatened England, herself, just exactly one hundred and fifty-four years before, for it bore great significance in the struggle for the southeastern part of the continent.

CHAPTER TWO

GEORGIA HAD HER SPANISH ARMADA

In the early summer of 1742 a fleet of fifty Spanish vessels, loaded down with men and munitions for conquest, bloomed out of the harbor of Havana and spread themselves about the southern seas, like a giant bird and her brood of ugly ducklings faring forth proudly and belligerently in search of food. For this armada, Spain had devised a bold scheme. It was to sweep northward along the coast, wreck Frederica, capture Savannah and once again establish the Spanish-American Empire's northern boundary about St. Helena Sound, below Charleston. The boundary was to be as of old, as in the days now so glorious in memory, when Spanish garrisons had sat so comfortably in all this land and Spanish priests had worked so diligently to subdue reluctant savage souls and extend his Catholic Majesty's Kingdom of Heaven into the wilderness. For Spain still claimed all this region as her own. The English were only interlopers, temporary squatters without rights. There was in this expedition as its chief of staff an able Spanish soldier and writer, Antonio Arredondo, who had only a few weeks before completed a document to establish this claim.

It was dated March 20, 1742, and constituted the White Paper for this expedition. The document is appealing and persuasive as an historical, legal argument. But the English sat here, in possession, and if Oglethorpe had his way, they would continue to sit here. There were tense days, though, when he was not quite sure. For all the odds were against him, and heavily.

His state of mind is revealed in a message he dispatched to the Duke of Newcastle, dated June 7, 1742, which also, had he failed, would have served as an alibi and a shameful warning to those who sat across the ocean, unheeding of their corners of empire.

"I hope your Grace," he wrote, "will remember that I long ago acquainted you that I anticipated an invasion as soon as the affair with Cuba was ended, and prayed for succors, which are not yet arrived. The Spanish have, as I then believed, sent more troops, and expect a general revolt of the negroes. It is too late now to ask your Grace to represent this to his Majesty and ask succors. Before they arrive this matter will be over. I hope I shall behave as well as one with as few men and as little artillery can. I have great advantage from my knowledge of the country, and the soldiers and inhabitants are in good heart and used to fatigue and arms. We have often seen and drove the Spaniards, and I believe that one of us is as good as ten of them."

Oglethorpe spoke truly about the impossibility of getting help. None came. Already the Spanish armada was on its way to St. Augustine, where it put in before heading north. Nor could he get any help as near at home as Charleston. Again Charleston chose to sit and wait until she, herself, was attacked. And, to dampen the morale of his own people, Savannah at his back was seething with discontent over the restraints of her utopia, and rumors flew through the city of Spanish successes, without foundation, started by men and women of ill will. It was backbiting defeatism of a flagrant sort.

But Oglethorpe wasted no time pining for outside aid in those anxious days when the Spanish fleet was moving north. He did everything possible to batten down his little island bulwark against the Spanish hurricane. The Spanish fleet had blithely ignored English forts and garrisons on the southernmost islands until they reached Cumberland Island, just to the south of St. Simon's on which Frederica was located. Fourteen Spanish ships were detached to attack Fort William at the southern end of Cumberland Island, but were driven off by the guns of the fort and the guns of a schooner which lay outside the fort. Four of the ships were so badly damaged that they foundered on their way back to St. Augustine for repairs. The rest of the fleet, thirty-six vessels, by-passed Fort William and headed into Cumberland Sound.

Oglethorpe brought up some of his Indian allies from

Frederica to join the garrison at Fort St. Simon's. Then, for himself, he prepared a maneuver that seemed utterly foolhardy. He loaded part of his own regiment on three vessels and took this pitiful naval unit straight into the teeth of the whole Spanish fleet. Two of the vessels, including his own, dashed headlong into the Spanish armada, shooting as they went. A third vessel was diverted and took refuge in a creek. Aboard it was the commander at Frederica who climbed the mainmast to see what happened. The sight was disheartening. He watched the other two vessels disappear into the Spanish fleet, like two harried rabbits into a pack of ravening dogs. The smoke of battle closed about the scene and with heavy heart the lieutenant of Oglethorpe climbed down to report the news. He was not a man to believe in miracles and the next day when this ship returned to Fort St. Simon's he announced that their gallant leader and all with him were lost. He hurriedly dispatched a message to Charleston to this effect and begged immediate help to save Frederica from destruction. The news threw a dark shadow over all at Frederica, for what hope was left with their leader gone?

But a miracle had happened out there in the dark confusion at sea. The lookout at Fort St. Simon's could not at first believe it the next day, when he saw the two English ships heading in toward him. But they were real, and not a ghostly vision. Oglethorpe, too, was safe, as the defenders of the island learned in time, and not only safe, but full of energy. There was no time to dawdle over the miracle of escape, which had been possible because of the smoke clouds.

Under their cover the two ships had slipped away, and taken a roundabout course, eluding the Spaniards. They had beaten the Spaniards to Fort St. Simon's. But the enemy vessels were not far behind, and Oglethorpe began issuing orders to make ready the defense. He pulled in the garrison at Fort Andrews at the northern end of Cumberland Island and brought it across the narrow inlet to join the defense of St. Simon's and Frederica. He gathered together all vessels available and had them lined up before Fort St. Simon's to meet the Spanish onslaught. He commandeered a merchant ship lying in the roads, the *Success*, and made it ready to fight, alongside of his own schooner which carried fourteen guns, and eight York sloops. On each of the last, one man was left under orders to sink the vessel or run it ashore if in danger of capture. He sent a message to Darien asking all possible manpower from the Scots, and called in all troops at outlying parts of St. Simon's for a concentration.

There was no more than time enough for these arrangements. It was an anxious and busy day, that July 4, 1742, a date then of no particular significance in the history of North America, but a date almost as significant as July 4, 1776; for events shaping up that July 4, 1742, determined that the English, rather than the Spanish, should possess this southeastern portion of the American continent to have and to hold and to develop.

The Spanish hurricane broke the next day, July 5, 1742. The lookout in the watchtower saw it first, the long line of ships proudly moving in, and it seemed to those waiting here and at Frederica and elsewhere on the island for the blow to strike that the alarm gun would never stop its doleful blasting. It was the custom for the alarm gun at the fort to fire once for every ship sighted. Soon the Spanish ships were close enough, and the guns from the fort and from the ships lying in front began to speak defiantly, and the Spanish guns answered back.

For four hours the Spaniards tried to board the *Success*. They were thwarted. Finally the fleet gave up this direct, frontal assault, and those on shore watched it withdraw and take a course up the river in the direction of Frederica. Oglethorpe, who had been on his own schooner during the attack, seized the opportunity of the Spanish withdrawal to prepare for the next Spanish maneuver. He ordered the men on ships ashore. At his instructions, the battery and the provisions at the fort were destroyed. Then he directed the ships to cut loose and escape, and they hurried off to Charleston, where all arrived safely.

He gathered the troops and the sailors about him, after the guns had been spiked and the fort dismantled, and marched them inland, all but an Indian rear guard which he left behind to cover the retreat. The Spanish fleet returned to Fort St. Simon's and disgorged its forces, a motley crew of regulars, volunteers, Indians, and Negroes. The Indian rear guard made it unpleasant for them, harassing the landing, and killed a number of the enemy and captured a Spanish soldier who estimated the invading forces at 5,000. This report was exaggerated, for presumably there were only about 3,000, and not all of them, by any means, first-rate soldiers.

Now there began in this fair and lovely island one of the momentous battles of history, the Battle of Bloody Marsh it was called, for so it turned out to be, though the participants naturally could not appreciate what they were doing or not doing for history's sake. They were men living in the mad and exciting reality of minutes that seemed hours, and hours that seemed days. Again, as in so much of modern history, it was the story of a small English army—there were not many over 500—miraculously extricating itself from an almost impossible dilemma, backs to the wall, so to speak, by bravery, by luck, and by that species of English cleverness which exhibits itself in such a crisis.

Back and forth across the southern part of the island, in the woods, in the marshes, along the narrow road, the battle rolled. From the accounts there emerges a fantastic and ironic and gory drama set in a lovely scene made for an idyll—slaughter in the woodland flowers, death among noble trees, blood splashed on the tender grass.

The Scotch accounted well for themselves that day, as always. It was the Highlanders from Darien who met the first Spanish onslaught when the invaders left the fort on July 7 and began a march toward Frederica nine miles away. The Scots joined the Indian rear guard in a delaying action, to hold back the advancing foe until Oglethorpe could organize and arrange his defense. The usually peaceful woods were noisy with the insane sounds of battle. Behind them the Scots and the Indians, fighting side by side, left the dead, more of the Spaniards than their own, as they retreated slowly before the superior Spanish army, back, back, until they were only two miles from Frederica.

Here Oglethorpe gathered his forces to check the invaders before they could reach the open prairie where they might use their overwhelming numbers to advantage. He led personally a fierce charge which threw the Spaniards back. It turned into butchery. Oglethorpe, himself, took two Spanish prisoners. The Spanish commander also was captured. Nearly all of the Spanish advance force of 140 men were either killed or made prisoner. The few who survived were pursued through the woods for a mile. Oglethorpe posted a guard at this new front line and returned to Frederica to prepare his company of marines and to allay the fears of the civilian population. The advance guard prepared an ambush about a glade, ready for another Spanish advance; but they were discovered and surprised by an enemy force and put to flight. Oglethorpe met them retreating when he came up with his fresh troops.

Now came the coup of this bloody day. A detachment of Scotch Highlanders circled around through the woods, got behind the Spaniards and laid an ambush about another open glade about two miles in the Spanish rear. Presently the Spaniards returned this way, and stopped on the inviting greensward to rest and refresh themselves. There seemed, for the moment, a respite in the fighting. They began to build fires in preparation for cooking food. All at once a horse reared up, frightened by the Scots hidden nearby. In panic, the Spaniards began to race hither and thither, to get hold of their arms, which had been stacked. But they were too late. The Scots poured fire upon them from every side. The trees were alive with bursts of flames, every way the confused Spanish soldiers turned to escape. Some two hundred of them were killed or captured.

This bloody massacre must have taken the heart out of the Spaniards, and undoubtedly was the psychological stroke that doomed this once-proud invasion. But the day was not entirely won for the English. Oglethorpe hurried back to Frederica and rounded up every man he could find. He moved his army with every available recruit, not over five hundred altogether, about Fort St. Simon's for a sudden, surprise attack while the enemy still was unnerved and reeling from the ghastly ordeal in the marsh. There occurred now one of those unfortunate incidents which might have proved disastrous, had not Oglethorpe turned it to his own advantage.

A Frenchman serving in the Georgia army deserted to the enemy and told them how small and weak was Oglethorpe's force. The Spaniards had no way of knowing. They could not be sure what reinforcements still might be concealed in the recesses of the island they had not penetrated, and one of them remarked, after the bloody encounter in the glade, that "the woods were so full of Indians that the devil himself could not get through them."

So when Oglethorpe reached the vicinity of the fort he discovered that the Spaniards were ready for him. But he never lacked a stratagem for such an emergency. He released a Spanish prisoner, on whom was planted a letter for the Frenchman. This letter intimated that the Frenchman was a spy, and advised the French deserter to induce the Spaniards to move their fleet toward Frederica so that a masked battery there could blow it out of the water. The Frenchman was also asked in the letter to hold the Spaniards at Fort St. Simon's for three days longer when reinforcements for the English would arrive, some two thousand soldiers and six war vessels. The letter, of course, found its way to the Spanish commander; and while he was not so naïve as not to suspect this might be a trick, yet it gave him pause. He called a council of war, and considered all possible eventualities with his lieutenants, the likelihood of reinforcements, the rough and uncertain terrain over which it was necessary to fight, the difficulty of moving up their artillery over the narrow road and through the woods, the proved fighting ability of Oglethorpe's troops, and the merciless slaughter that had cooled off the ardor of his soldiers. Caution ruled, and the Spaniards decided to withdraw.

So the fleet sailed away, virtually giving the English the victory by default.

It was the last real threat ever made by the Spaniards to break the line of the Savannah.

Oglethorpe left Georgia forever the next year and went home to become a prosaic country gentleman and to settle back into a neglected niche among the hazy half-gods. He was fifty-three at the time. He had lived little more than half of his life, but it was in Georgia that he had left his contribution to history, all in the short space of ten years. Calmly, like an orderly Englishman, he abandoned his bachelor's role, so convenient in his days of adventure, and married a lady of fifty. He circulated in the literary society of the day, was a friend of Dr. Johnson and Boswell and Oliver Goldsmith, and survived far beyond his era, drifting about London a tall and gaunt and weazen-faced old man, babbling rather tiresomely to bore a newer generation. He could never recapture the glory of his Georgia experience. But the colony always remained dear to his memory. There is a legend that he was offered and refused the command of the British armies in America when the Revolution broke. It is known that he thought ill of the policy that provoked that conflict.

CHAPTER THREE

MARY MUSGROVE—QUEEN OF THE CREEKS

Among the Indians at Yamacraw Village who met Oglethorpe the day he landed to pick a site for his Georgia colony was a half-breed woman. She stepped out of the crowd that day as an intermediary to clutch hold of the star of a strange destiny. It rose upward brightly, turned red and sullen, and finally exploded like a skyrocket, after Oglethorpe had gone back home to England. But it served to light up a weird scene in the streets of the city he had founded along this bluff—Mary, Queen of the Creeks, leading her Indian vassals before the terrified populace. An angry drum echoed against the boxlike wooden houses.

Then, years later, at the head of her legions, she was a hard and vengeful woman, full of the wiles of the world.

That day she first met Oglethorpe, Mary Musgrove was more innocent though not a pretty figure. She is described as "in mean and low circumstances, being cloathed with a red stroud petticoat and Osnabirg shift." She was a slattern on that occasion, uncomely as a camp follower, and she was, in truth, a slattern in heart all her life. She was not, of course, prepared for the visit of the distinguished Englishman who appeared so suddenly from nowhere. But this did not deter her from grasping her chance, as it might a vainer and even less clever and ambitious woman, and she was both clever and ambitious. When Oglethorpe and William Bull came to the village she immediately made herself known and spoke to them in English. She was promptly drafted as an interpreter.

Such services were needed. For it was apparent that the

101

Yamacraws were at the outset cool toward this English intrusion. Had not the English promised, in the treaty ending the Yamassee War of 1715, that they would not move south of the Savannah, and was not the north bank of the river rather close to the line agreed upon? Mary promptly capitalized upon her opportunity. This was her hour. She persuaded the Indians that Oglethorpe's purposes were beneficent and to their interest. The English leader was naturally grateful and saw that Mary could be helpful as a go-between.

Thus there began this day an association that proved quite profitable to Oglethorpe during his ten years in Georgia. For Mary became, in effect, an official interpreter, a post she did not abuse until Oglethorpe had left Georgia's guidance to others. Meanwhile she did squeeze out of it all the personal glory and personal advantage that she could. She was frequently called upon by Oglethorpe for counsel in Indian affairs as well as to interpret, for she knew the Indian temperament, and she thus became a familiar figure in the colony.

Mary Musgrove was in her early thirties when the arrival of Oglethorpe opened to her the door of an amazing career. For several years she had lived at Yamacraw, in virtual seclusion, with her husband, John Musgrove, and helped him with the management of a trading post.

Mary was the child of an English father, a trader lost to history, and a Creek mother who was, it appears, a sister of that vaunted chieftain, Emperor Brim of the Creeks, who had turned the Indians upon the English in the Yamassee War all up and down the Savannah and in the backwoods. She was born at Coweta, the Creek capital along the Chattahoochee, and at the age of ten had been taken to Carolina. There she had gone to school and had been baptized as a Christian. For five years at an impressionable age she had lived among the English. Her eyes had been opened to white civilization, crude even as it was in Carolina, and, like Tomochichi, she must have seen that it was ordained to supplant that of her mother's breed.

She did not hesitate when the occasion was offered to cast her lot with her father's people. Such an opportunity occurred when John Musgrove, who must have been a handsome and attractive fellow, came riding among the Creeks, accompanying his father on a peace mission. The courtship was brief. The young Englishman and the magnetic half-breed, still in her teens, were married and lived for seven years among her people. He acted as a trading agent among the Creeks. No record is left to guide us as to the reasons why the two moved to Yamacraw to set up their own trading post, but we may surmise, from what we know of Mary, that it was her doing. We can easily infer that it was the dawning ambition of a maturing woman determined to move up in the world. She was, we discover, the energizing force in this marriage. For, from what we know of John Musgrove, he was an easygoing, amiable fellow of little ambition, and not a great deal of spirit.

It was Mary's acquaintance with Oglethorpe that opened the way for her to branch out again and take the next step in her career. The English leader was anxious to protect his frontiers by outposts from which the Spaniards might be watched, and he proposed that the couple open another trading post on the Altamaha River, deep inland, about 150 miles from its mouth. It did not take much persuasion to convince the ambitious Mary. The Musgroves established the trading post and called it "Mount Venture." Not long after they had settled here John Musgrove died. Mary did not pine long as a widow. A man was essential to her purposes. One cannot be too nice in the wilderness, and Mary certainly was not very choosy nor did she have to go very far. She married herself to the commander of the twenty rangers who were stationed at the Altamaha outpost, to a man named Jacob Matthews, who had come to Georgia as an indentured servant some years before.

Jacob was a worthless fellow. Characteristic of his type, he blossomed out quickly as a man of property—which belonged to his wife—and finally burgeoned into a swaggering, bragging frontier gentleman-of-ease, one who gave himself over to long bouts with the bottle. He went off on terrific sprees, he got into fights, and altogether made himself thoroughly unpopular. He had some peculiar fascination for Mary. She clung to him, and he seems to have been, despite all his weaknesses, a man of strong mind, although surely of dark and devious purposes. He deftly began to poison her mind by feeding her ambition. He insinuated that she was not being properly rewarded by Oglethorpe for her services as interpreter. It seems there had been some sort of promise of cash remuneration that was never fulfilled.

Jacob also insinuated that she might exploit her position among the Indians, that she might weave a profitable web by playing upon the conflicting cupidity of white man and red. The pair were soon well up in the world, and dreams of a still finer fortune beckoned. They now had a home in Savannah, the trading post on the Altamaha, and the plantation at Yamacraw. Jacob was in the habit of bringing Indians to the house in Savannah, where there were frequent drunken brawls. This not only disturbed the neighbors but alarmed Savannah officials, in particular William Stephens, president of Savannah and chief magistrate, for Jacob and Mary now began to demand more presents for the Indians as the price of continued friendly relations. Jacob also set up a claim to 450 acres of land near Savannah that he much coveted. The Indians were held as a threat, and Mary now was really influential with them. Thus the one-time indentured servant and his half-breed wife had become serious troublemakers.

Then, suddenly, death intervened in a series of blows against Mary to give the plagued officials of Savannah a respite. A brother was killed in Oglethorpe's expedition against St. Augustine. Next her husband fell desperately ill. Mary took him to Savannah for medical attention. But in vain. He died after a few weeks. While she was watching at his bedside word came that the trading post on the Altamaha had been destroyed by a joint force of Indians and Spaniards. And, to cap it all, the overseer of her Yamacraw plantation was also drafted for the St. Augustine expedition, and he too died in that futile campaign. Her place left untended almost went to ruin.

But Mary was a resolute woman. She determined to build up her fortunes again, and, characteristically, the first step was to get herself a new husband. He turned out to be another rogue.

Thomas Bosomworth, the third consort, was a man of parts—most of them bad—and possessed of an imagination that seemed to arouse all that was evil in Mary. He was even more seductive in urging her on to exercise her peculiar powers than had been Jacob Matthews. The two went far before they fell victims to their own audacity.

Bosomworth had come out from England to try his fortune in the Georgia colony. He came as a mere clerk to William Stephens, but this he intended only as a starter. He aimed high, but the best he could do was "secretary to the Indian Affairs" which was not the post of consequence that its imposing title might imply. Nor was it one that justified his talents, in his opinion. He poked around, then, versatile fellow that he was, among the professions to find something to his liking, a place that would make him somebody in colonial affairs. For a while he thought perhaps the profession of arms would be the solution. He went to Frederica to become a soldier, but soon found this not much to his liking.

From this brief career in what, in this wilderness, was more like a job than a profession, and not at all gentlemanly, he turned to letters, surely a refined calling. He wrote a pamphlet bitterly arraigning the Bethesda Orphanage at Savannah, established by the famous preacher George Whitefield. When somebody accused him of being the author, however, he became indignant, writing to the Trustees: "I am sorry to find, that my good intentions are perverted to be imputed to an ambition of appearing as an Author." So he dropped that. Then, for some reason, he decided he had been called to the ministry. He took this so seriously that he returned to England for holy orders and came back to the colony a full-fledged minister. But he found even the pursuit of religion in the colony an unpleasant role. So he again left for England with the word that he was now gone for good.

All this time, all through this ordeal of trial and error, Mary was his wife, and patiently she bore with him.

But the Reverend Thomas had not gone for good. He showed up again in Georgia, after only a few months' absence. He was no longer a minister, however. Now, suddenly, he seemed to discover for the first time what should have been apparent to one of his inclinations all along, namely, Mary, his wife. It occurred to him, all at once, because perhaps he was at the end of his own resources and knew not what else to try, that *she* might be the way to power and position. So he now became devoted to her—and her possibilities.

The two began a fresh career in the business with which Mary was already familiar, one which had taken her up in the world before her late bad fortune. They opened a trading post at the junction of the Ocmulgee and Oconee rivers, a rather elaborate enterprise, which they named "The Forks." Thomas, even as Jacob before him, immediately succumbed to the delusion of being a grand gentleman, with a capable wife at his side to provide the wherewithal. He bought himself half a dozen slaves, flaunting them despite the ordinance against slavery. In short, in every way, he began to show the utmost contempt for colonial officials. The trade was in deerskins at the post, but this was soon a side issue. Mary's and his main business, for which a trading post frequented by Indians was quite handy, was a clever scheme to get their hands on land through Mary's influence with the Indians.

Oglethorpe had gone home to England for good, and the restraint he had exercised over the ambitious and unprincipled Mary was now removed, which left her free to try her wings, undaunted. The plot was simple in essence. She and her husband got Malatchee, a Creek chief who was her cousin, to sign a document turning over to Mary three islands, St. Catherine's, Ossabaw, and Sapelo, and a tract lying between the Savannah and Pipemaker's Creek—all of which had been reserved to the Creeks as a hunting ground in the original treaty with Oglethorpe. In it she was recognized formally as "Queen of the Creeks."

Bosomworth now traded on his prestige as prince consort. On credit he purchased a whole herd of cattle in South Carolina and turned them loose on St. Catherine's Island. He saw himself as a lord of the manor, a modern Abraham. To pay for the cattle he induced Mary to renew her claim for the various services she had performed for the colony. Her bill was £1,024. There is some confusion about the documents the Indians signed. Later they claimed that they thought they were merely signing a list of grievances to be presented to colonial officials. But Mary knew what she was about. The Indians were simple dupes in her hands.

Malatchee, whom she was using as her front, was a Saul of his day, a tall, handsome fellow whose "behavior is such, that one would rather imagine from his complaisance, had been bred in some European Court, than among Barbarians," this according to William Stephens, who, before it was all over, had plenty of trouble with this fine Indian. He was pleasant, amiable and tractable, yielding to the last person who talked with him, and the very sort of leader who was so difficult to deal with in a crisis, for he could be pushed about easily, and neither side could ever be quite sure where he would stand. Mary maneuvered him skillfully, though she must have been disgusted more than once with her handsome cousin. Because of his indecision, his changing moods, the crisis Mary eventually produced in Savannah dragged on for nearly a month. In the end it set time against her to her downfall.

After Mary and her husband had obtained the signatures to the document awarding her the land they sought to get it formally ratified by the Trustees. Mary went about among the Indians, like a Lady Bountiful, distributing gifts to buy their allegiance. Then she looked about for a tool on the other side. She selected a man named Heron, who was the commander at Frederica. She raised up before him the threat of an Indian revolt, and she evidently painted a very dark picture. To this she added the spice of self-interest. She would give him a share in the land, she told him, if he would get her title approved by the Trustees in England. Heron, who turned out to be as easy as the Indians, signed papers recognizing Malatchee as king of all the Creeks and approving the title the Indian had granted to Mary and Thomas to the lands they wanted. These were taken to England by Abraham Bosomworth, a brother of Thomas. But the Trustees were not deceived. They refused flatly to sanction any such business.

Mary then decided upon desperate and bold measures. Spurred on by her husband, whose mouth now was literally watering for the handsome estate that seemed almost within his grasp, the two of them, with Adam Bosomworth, another brother, turned up in Savannah with Malatchee and a few Creek warriors. They threatened that, if Mary's claims were not recognized, they would let loose a whole army of Creeks upon Savannah to establish their rights with force.

Stephens seems to have got a little panicky. He was without proper defense in Savannah. Only a short time before, the troops at Frederica had been disbanded. Mary and her husband knew this, for Thomas Bosomworth happened to be at Frederica when the soldiers were released. Thus he and Mary had timed their descent upon Savannah when it was ill prepared. Stephens tried appeasement. He staged a handsome banquet for Malatchee. He distributed presents. He played for time. But he flatly refused to agree to Mary's demands for recognition of her claims.

So the determined woman gave the signal and one night the Indians came down the Savannah in a fleet of canoes, howling and shooting off their guns. They encamped on the outskirts in the Yamacraw settlement. The city was in a fever of terror, and its plight was alleviated none by the heat of summer, for it was late July when the Indian siege began. For, in effect, a siege it was.

Summer reaches down along the river with a hot, moist hand, slowing down all human motion and activity. The nights are still, quiet, and full of strange portents which seem to suffuse the very air in tropical and semitropical lands. In these nights of anxiety Savannah slept restlessly, waiting with ears alert for the demoniacal yells that foretold the beginning of massacres, an event which its people had thus far been spared—and with hands ready to grasp a gun, even though now the city did have some military protection.

Stephens had commissioned Noble Jones, one of the city's leading men, to marshal an army; and that gentleman had gathered together a force of 170 militiamen and citizen volunteers. Also some of the young men had organized a Horse Guard which patrolled the streets at night. The occasional tramp of passing hoofs on the streets outside offered solace to the weary-eyed householder in the deep of night.

Stephens, meanwhile, continued his pacifying gifts of food and drink in order to wean the Indians away from their malevolent matriarch. He laid out a big dinner. Under the benign influence of good food, strong drink, and deference to Stephens's every whim, Malatchee warmed up to the English and denounced Thomas Bosomworth as a liar. Encouraged, Stephens invited the whole Indian assembly into the city for a big feast. Captain Jones, however, was taking no chances. He disarmed them before they paraded through the streets. At the head of the procession was Thomas Bosomworth, dignified by his churchly robes. With him came his spouse, his brother Adam, and their convenient image of authority, King Malatchee.

They gathered at Stephens's house and there the pipe of peace was passed around while drinks were poured.

Stephens pressed Malatchee as to why the Indians had descended upon Savannah. Malatchee could not say officially without consulting Thomas, who had withdrawn from the gathering along with Adam, but he said the story had gone around among his people that Mary was to be put in irons and shipped off to England. Stephens denied any such intention, but was very emphatic that, if Mary was guilty of anything detrimental to the colony's interests, he would not hesitate to tie her up and send her back home without asking anybody's leave. Mary was in the crowd. She heard this.

Immediately she began an angry tirade, shouting that she was both empress and queen of the Upper and Lower Creeks, taking in all available titles and a lot of territory, and that she owed no allegiance to the English king. Stephens had disrupted harmony again. But the chief magistrate was a patient gentleman. He let her rave. Afterward he invited the Indians to another big feast that night. Mary was against it. So was Malatchee. He ordered the Indians to stay away from this celebration, but only six of them obeyed his orders. The lure was too tempting. Stephens knew the Indian nature.

Again, with food in their bellies and drink coursing through their brains, the Indians went away happy and friendly, and it seemed that the crisis had passed. But this was just one of the deceptive periods of calm through which Stephens and Savannah were to live for many days.

For late the next afternoon Adam Bosomworth led a parade of Indians down the streets. They had a drum and it rolled menacingly. The citizens came running to witness this effrontery. Adam was arrested and thrown into jail. Feeling mounted high in the crowd that had gathered so quickly. Some wanted to start shooting and stop this nonsense once and for all. But officials finally calmed them down, and the mob broke up and dispersed. Several of the Indian leaders were spirited away by members of the council to Stephens's home for more talk and liquor. Peace seemingly was restored again, that is, until Mary came storming up. She had learned about this latest gesture.

"You talk of your white town, your general and his treaties," she screamed in a frenzy. "A fig for your general. You have not a foot of land in the colony."

In which, of course, she was in a sense correct.

She stamped her foot, and said this very ground belonged to her.

Stephens had her arrested. She was detained temporarily. But her husband went to the chief magistrate, putting on—as he did so often—the contrite front he had acquired in his brief career in the ministry. He begged that if Mary and his brother Adam were released he would see that they would both meet with the council the next morning. And he pledged that there should be no drinking that night.

Savannah was on edge all that night. The Horse Guard was on patrol until dawn.

The promise of no drinking during the night turned out to be a vain hope. The Indians all got drunk. Even Thomas, himself, got drunk. When the council gathered early next morning for the conference no one appeared. Thomas sent a message that the Indians were all drunk. Word was sent back for him to come anyhow. Mary and Adam did show up, but not Thomas. He was still drunk. A meeting was arranged for the afternoon.

At this some of the Indians appeared, but not Mary, nor Thomas, nor Adam, nor Malatchee. The king sent word that he had a headache. Later, however, he did come, and was in a most repentant mood—perhaps the effects of a hang-over. The council lectured him at length, telling him that Mary and Thomas were only using him for their own purposes, that these two would get a third of the presents that rightfully belonged to the Indians. Malatchee seemed to be convinced that he was being hoodwinked and observed naïvely that he had not understood before "that he was being Ranked with an Old Woman," as the records put it.

His repentance lasted for several days, and Savannah settled down to a peaceful interlude. He and his chiefs went to church on Sunday with members of the council. They strolled about the streets with them in a beautiful display of brotherly love. This respite seemed a propitious time for what was hoped would be the clinching ceremony, the distribution of gifts. The Indians were all invited.

But no—Malatchee had again been twisted around the finger of Mary. Again, she was to him the wronged woman. He came with a long document, drafted by Mary, which purported to be a declaration from the other kings of the Creeks recognizing her as their ruler. The council now talked back, and most frankly. They told Malatchee that Mary would never have been anything had it not been for Oglethorpe, who helped her and gave her an opportunity. This was the wrong tack with the Indian, for, after all, Mary was a cousin and had Creek blood in her veins. He resented such talk. He got very angry. He foamed at the mouth, so the records of the day say. But the council members went ahead with their distribution of gifts, making a great show. This was too much for Malatchee's avarice. He decided it would be the part of discretion to calm down. He proposed that they "spend the Evening with the Beloved Men in Mirth," with a quick change of mood so characteristic. The council accordingly foregathered at a tavern that evening. They all fraternized very sociably, with games and drinks, until Mary, as usual, broke in to disturb the peace. She invaded the tavern, a noisy army of one, and raved and ranted all over the place. The councilmen brusquely told her to go home and go to bed and not to make a fool of herself. She wouldn't budge. They threatened to arrest her. This brought Malatchee to her side again, her in-and-out champion. He defied them to seize her. He put on his foaming-mouth performance again. But Mary was arrested and carted off to the guardhouse.

During the argument, the Creek king had declared that he would free Mary if they took her. He sneaked away in the night to the Indian encampment and summoned his warriors to arms. Luckily, Captain Noble Jones was ready. He hurriedly marched his soldiers to the camp where the Indians were preparing to carry out the command of their king. He ordered them to throw down their arms. They obeyed. Thomas burst then upon this warlike scene along the bluff. He pranced up and down, hurling hot bolts of profanity toward the stars. He swore he would "spend the last drop of his blood" before he would let Mary lose her birthright. He denounced Oglethorpe, now at home in England, saying "By God, General Oglethorpe has ruined her and deceived every man in the colony."

Savannah slept little that night. The Horse Guards and the militia were joined by the citizens in patrolling the streets in preparation for trouble. But nothing happened. Captain Jones's alertness had ended this sorry affair. For the next day, unexpectedly and happily, the plot collapsed.

Thomas sobered up overnight and appeared before the council the next morning in his best sackcloth-and-ashes manner. He had been wrong. Mary had been wrong. Hereafter he would conduct himself as a clergyman. He blamed Mary for most of the trouble, and would see to it that hereafter she behaved herself. This time there was the ring of sincerity in his desperate plea. The next day he proved it when he appeared publicly before the chiefs in front of the courthouse, where gifts were again being distributed, and apologized. Malatchee likewise was repentant, and suggested the usual prescription for that mood, which was, as it is always recited in the record of those days, to "spend the Evening with the Beloved Men in Mirth," adding this time, "to convince them that all was forgot, and to make amends for what passed last night." So there was another bout at the tavern, and, not only that, but the Horse Guards had another party the following night, at their own expense, for some of the chiefs. The last occasion was a great success.

The next morning the Indians left the city and went back to their homes.

Just at this denouement, Abraham Bosomworth returned from his futile mission to London to get Mary's title cleared. He was most amazed to find out what had gone on during his absence. He was of a higher caliber than his brothers, and undoubtedly would have swung his influence against the descent upon Savannah which might very well have ended so tragically for the colony. The city saw the siege lifted with relief. For if an explosion had occurred, it would have resulted in bloodshed and perhaps the destruction of Savannah plus an Indian war that might have blazed into the fury of the Yamassee War and held back the development of the colony for years. Perhaps Stephens had been wiser than it seemed in his food-and-drink policy of bribery and appeasement. It did take a long time. The ordeal lasted nearly a month. It was July 24, 1749, when Thomas and Mary arrived in the city with their demands. The Indians departed and left Savannah in peace on August 19.

But Mary was not through, nor was her husband, nor the wayward Malatchee. She was not repentant when she was driven from Savannah, despite the pious mouthings of that reverend man, her husband, nor was her cousin, King Malatchee. Like a scourge he sent his Indians marauding through the white settlements along the Ogeechee, to the south. After he had left the vicinity of Savannah on his way home, they began killing cattle and stealing corn and potatoes. Later he formed an alliance with the French, and boldly flung the fleur-de-lis from a flagpole in his village, as another sign of his scorn of the English.

Only three days after the Bosomworths left Savannah Thomas composed a letter to the Council with a plea for funds. He used his best abject style to recite his plight. He was under arrest, he wrote, for £400 due some Carolina traders for the horses and cattle he had bought for his St. Catherine's Island estate. He was being called on for payments on his debt. Would not the Trustees give Mary her share of the presents being distributed to the Indians? Again he told how abased he was for all that had happened, and begged mercy. But the Council thought Mary had been paid enough, and told him so.

Mary, of course, did not stop with this temporary setback. She was still resourceful. Again she decided to use the Indians. Undaunted, she started back across the trail that had led her and her vassals into Savannah. She set out on a long journey far back inland into the Creek country, and was so persuasive that she got seven "kings" of the Creeks to sign a document acknowledging her title and her land claims. Her success was such that Stephens saw he must do something to counteract her continued influence with the Indians. He brought some Creek chieftains to Savannah, wined and dined them, and got their backing against Mary, and, what was more practical and effective, he sent an emissary among the Creeks. For the land he exchanged beads, paint, cloth, guns, ammunition and hatchets. Stephens now had a document to pit against those which Mary could acquire so easily.

The half-breed queen saw that she was not likely to get anywhere with the colonial authorities. They knew her too well and had their fill of her machinations. She decided on an appeal to England.

For four years she and her husband battered away at the Board of Trade with all sorts of spurious documents. But the Board of Trade was not easily convinced. It delayed and delayed. She must go to England herself. She and her husband sold some of their Savannah properties to raise money for passage and expenses and in 1754 went to England. Meanwhile, in 1752, the Trustees had finally abandoned their Georgia project as too troublesome an enterprise, and the colony reverted to the king and became a crown colony. Mary was referred back to the royal regime now established in Georgia, with a royal governor. In 1759, ten years from the time of her mad Savannah invasion, her claims were recognized. She was paid £2,050 in cash, the returns from the sale of Sapelo and Ossabaw islands by the colony, in settlement for all her claims for services to Oglethorpe, and she was given, as a present, the island of St. Catherine's.

Here she retired. Here the couple, now getting along in years, built themselves a splendid new home. Here she passed her last years. Here, in time, she died. Her third husband survived her and, ironically, married soon afterward her chambermaid, an indentured servant, just as she had married Jacob Matthews, her indentured servant, after the death of her first love, John Musgrove.

CHAPTER FOUR

THE END OF UTOPIA

Even before Oglethorpe went home to England to stay, the original noble aims of the colony began to disintegrate right before his eyes. The people were loud in lamentations over the restrictions imposed upon them. They wanted slaves, so they could be gentlemen, like their South Carolina neighbors, and not be compelled to work in the fields themselves, under the hot sun. They wanted rum. They wanted to be able to own more land. They wanted to be as other people were, which is the rock upon which most utopias eventually split. They did not want to be regulated for their best interests, nor did they agree with philosophers who had defined their "best interests" from the cloister.

The elaborate agricultural program designed to sustain the colony languished as a wan memorial to the impractical ideas hatched by dreamers in England. The exotic plants set out in a garden along the banks of the Savannah, a veritable bower of Paradise it was to be, withered away and died. Only a dream was the vista of olive trees and vineyards. Silk culture was almost entirely neglected. The rows of mulberry trees stretching away in fruitful and orderly avenues to the horizon to provide food for millions of silkworms were a reality only in ambitious engravings made in England. Some indigo was planted, and rice was produced to some extent in the lowlands.

The colonists began to desert the city. Some went across the Savannah to South Carolina. Some went farther. Savannah almost disappeared as a city at one time toward the end of Oglethorpe's tenure, dwindling to a population of about five hundred from a peak of about five thousand reached in the first six years of the colony. It is interesting to note that of this peak five thousand only about half were what might be called charity cases, some fifteen hundred of these being unfortunate debtors from English jails. The other thousand of this refugee category were persecuted Protestants from Germany and Austria and other parts of the Continent. It is also interesting and significant that two-thirds of the original settlers for whom the Trustees had provided a home at the Trust's expense left the colony before Oglethorpe, proving something or other about such benefactions.

Prohibition was a failure, only reacting in lawlessness. Rum was bootlegged into the colony. Grogshops operated openly on Savannah street corners. Juries would not convict their fellow citizens. Liquor cases were transferred to trial before judges, without a jury. But the judges were equally lenient, for they indulged in drink themselves. Finally, in 1742, the Trustees relented and permitted the importation of rum, but required that it could be purchased only with an exchange of products of the colony, so that trade would benefit. The agitation for abandonment of prohibition was led by a group of prominent citizens of Savannah who were interested in the liquor business.

Oglethorpe was sound and farseeing in his opposition to slavery and continued, to the end, to resist its extension to his colony; but this utopian dream vanished, too, after he had gone back to England. Those who could afford slaves found a way around the law. The scheme was to lease them from Carolina on a hundred-year lease, with payment of the full market price. In 1748 the Trustees yielded on slavery, worn down by the agitation and the discontent. They prescribed certain conditions. In an effort to maintain the spirit of the white indenture system it was required that there must be one white indentured servant for every four slaves owned by a planter. Other restrictions were imposed common to the slavery system as it existed . elsewhere, such as no labor on Sunday, registration of the slaves in the colonial records, no intermarriage with whites, instruction in the Christian religion.

Likewise the land laws were modified to abolish the limit on the size of holdings and do away with tail male, that is, the requirement that only sons could inherit, so that, thereafter, land could continue to be held in a family where there were only daughters.

The Trustees were growing weary of their Georgia venture, worn out with the constant and continuous complaints. In 1753 the Trust was liquidated and Georgia became a royal colony under direct control of the king, who designated a royal governor to take charge of the recalcitrants on the spot. Over a million dollars had been spent on Oglethorpe's experiment. The king did not intend to let this expense go on. Georgia henceforth must begin to pay her own way. This, in time, she did. Again the colony began to prosper, now that the people were satisfied, now that the utopian reforms they had come to abhor were lifted and they could be as other people. Many new colonists were attracted to Georgia by the liberal conditions offered and they were provided for most handsomely, in the way of land, by the Trustees, who, in a final profuse gesture in the two years before they relinquished their trust, made grants right and left, some to friends in England, and in large acreage. In the year 1752 alone, such grants added up to 75,000 acres.

For the first time, with the beginning of royal government under a royal governor, the colony had an organization of local government. It was not notably democratic, but at least it provided the forms through which the colonists could express themselves, even if they were somewhat circumscribed. There was a council, in effect an upper branch, and an assembly. Any act of the assembly could be vetoed by the governor or the king. There were property qualifications both for voting and for membership in the council and the assembly, quite common of course in those times and for long afterward. Yet both of these bodies proved active in the colony's behalf. Savannah, for the first time, got a decent wharf along her river front, much bettering the movement of shipping and trade.

Previously the only semblance of local government had been a series of courts, to which the people could go with their grievances, but not with benefit of counsel. For lawyers were not admitted to the colony. Georgia, it was decreed, should be "free from that pest and scourge of mankind called lawyers."

Oglethorpe, in his time, was actually the supreme ruler of the colony while on the ground. The powers of the Trustees had been channeled through him, but with widest discretion left open to him.

With the advent of royal government the colony settled into the routine—not often calm and peaceful and undisturbed—of the other British colonies in America. As usual the clever, the acquisitive, and the strong gradually extended their influence into local government often making it serve as the instrument of their selfish ambitions.

Lawyers eventually were permitted in the colony. Before long there was a flourishing bar in the city. One of the first acts of the assembly was to frame and adopt a code for slavery as a substitute for the earlier "regulations" of the Trustees. And it soon became apparent that slavery was really to be slavery, and not a mild imitation.

This slave code of 1755, which was re-enacted and revised from time to time, but not much on the side of humanity, said that "all Negroes, Indians, (free Indians in amity with this government and Negroes, Mulattos or Mestizos who are not free excepted) mulattos or mestizos who are now or shall hereafter be in this province and all their issue and offspring Born or to be Born shall be and they are hereby declared to be and remain hereafter absolute slaves and shall follow the condition of the mother and shall be deemed in law to be chattels personal in the hands of their owners and possessors . . ."

Enslaved were their bodies, their childlike minds, and their simple souls. They were kept in the blindness and darkness of ignorance. They could not learn to read or write and a fine of £15 was fixed for anyone who tried to teach them. They were consigned to labor in the fields and about the house and in the kitchens from before daylight until after dark. It seems that, in neighboring Carolina, some masters were working their slaves too hard and too long, in the opinion of the elected representatives of the Georgia colony. So the Georgia statute decreed that no slave should labor more than sixteen hours a day! But the fine for working Negro slaves beyond sixteen hours was only £3, as compared with £15 for teaching them to read and write.

The lives of slaves in Georgia, as elsewhere, were hedged about with all sorts of restrictions, some of them written in chill fear of such slave insurrections as had occurred from time to time in South Carolina, one contemporary with the Oglethorpe regime in 1738. Slaves could not leave the plantation without a ticket signed by their master. If found without a ticket they were to be whipped, so said the law, with a maximum of twenty lashes across their bare, black backs. To prevent any congregating of slaves it was forbidden for more than seven to travel together in a body on the highroads, unless accompanied by a white person. They could carry no firearms except by a license from their masters, and this only for hunting or killing game, cattle, or "mischievous birds of prey." They could not carry guns between sunset Sunday and sunrise Monday. Justices of the peace were clothed with broad powers to disperse any assemblages of slaves and to search for arms, ammunition or stolen goods. They could not keep canoes, breed horses or cattle, or trade for their own benefit. They could not hire a room, a house or a plantation.

An elaborate patrol system was organized to keep slaves under constant surveillance. Every plantation, in regularly prescribed order, must furnish members of the patrol for a period. The colony was divided into districts which corresponded to militia districts, and these were subdivided for purposes of patrolling. The patrols were armed, and they were required to visit each plantation within their district at least once a month to check up.

The law also prescribed that the slaves should be taught the Christian religion!

The fear of the patrols came down the years, a haunting echo, even into the early days of the twentieth century; for I remember a refrain, sung by an old Negro cook, of which the only words that remain to me are:

Run, run, the pater-ol will git you.

So the Georgians got their slaves. They became as other folks, even as their Carolina neighbors. And in time, with the opportunity to expand commercially, to dream big dreams of wealth and rich living, they got the opportunity to pile up debts; for this is one of the privileges of civilization. And so it came about that laws were passed to punish debtors in this colony originally founded for those who fled from harsh debt laws in England. People were thrown into jail in Georgia for their debts, and reformers came along to try to soften these laws, even as had happened in England. The circle of "civilization" was thus completed.

Now, in the next few decades, the Savannah River valley and the adjoining coast to the south began to take on the comfortable contours of planter life. About the mouth of the river, during the fifties and sixties of the eighteenth century, a planter aristocracy began to flourish. Rice was its sustenance. Negro slaves waded in the marshes in the plantations along the lower reaches of the river busy with the growing of rice. It was a short life and a hard one. Fever seethed through the lowlands and malaria permeated the bones of the black men and women.

Slavery was coated over with kindness for the most part, which was the ready excuse that flew to the lips with criticisms. There were some among the planters who had summer camps for their families in the pine barrens above Savannah, and it was not unusual for them to send their slaves, when debilitated with fever, to these healthful spots for a time in the hot months. Such kindnesses soothed consciences sensitive to the plight of a slave race.

The marshes were crisscrossed with shallow waterways, arms of the river, spreading out in an elaborate network. These were the primitive avenues of commerce over which moved the flatboats heavy with rice, bound for deep-water harbors at Savannah, Beaufort, and Charleston for shipment to England. Most of these flatboats also carried sails, and they sped along right merrily when there was a breeze. Against the horizon of marsh and marsh grass, against the weird giants of live oak ancient with their straggling wisps of gray beard, there appeared the symbol of this early planter regime—the black man with his long pole, leaning at his toil, or standing, one hand at the rudder, beside his sail when the breeze was up, his eyes straining for the channel. Behind him, somewhere in the distance, was the house set amidst the magnolia trees and the flowers, where other of his kind, trained to the ways of civilization, came running, pell-mell, when the visitor called, to take care of the horse and carriage and to bow the gentlemen and ladies to the hospitality of friendship within. It was all carried on a broad black back.

The slave was, in those early days, mostly an ignorant being, whether man or woman. He was not long from the African jungle where the monkeys screeched in the trees and the huge snakes coiled up their trunks. His life in America if somewhat less primitive was nonetheless deadly laborious routine. He could not be depended upon to exercise much judgment, so he was taught his tasks by rote, as it were. Cultivation, accordingly, was of the most primitive sort. Clumsy hoes were almost the sole implement for cultivating rice on most plantations in the first few years. The planters would not trust their slaves with plows.

The king among blacks on the plantations about the mouth of the Savannah was the boatman. The most apt won this coveted post. This master of the boats was known as the "patroon." He must know all the tricks of boating. He must be familiar with the channels, which constantly shifted, and with the shallows and the currents. Often, on large plantations, he had field hands under him as helpers.

Up the river, to a harder and more lonely life, went the pioneer with his family. His existence was bleak and barren, though not without its excitements and compensations. He lived in a bare frame house, usually of one room, fashioned after the manner of the Indians who still lived in this country. He had a patch to grow his food, a few cows and pigs, a horse. The river valley, from Savannah to Augusta, and beyond, was a land of small farms in the early days, inhabited by just the type of sturdy, independent yeoman, for the most part, of which Ogle-thorpe had dreamed. They could not afford slaves, or at most one, two, or three in the more prosperous families.

In time many of these settlers branched out into fairly large-scale farming which was more than a bare living. They raised cattle and hogs, which had the run of the woods. They raised corn, wheat, peas and indigo, and, as they cleared the forest, they established a small lumber industry. The river valley was lush and green with its forest borders. The ax and the sawmill had not then flattened it out to the dreary waste we see today.

Georgia rapidly became the new El Dorado, the end of a rainbow trail, for the other colonies. The region was made safer for settlers, especially the lower reaches of the Savannah and the coastal lands to the south, by the outcome of the French and Indian Wars, which ended in 1763. Spain had wormed her way

into that war, unwarily, in the latter stages, just in time to
have to pay part of the costs, and the cost to her was the loss of
Florida, which was ceded to England in lieu of the captured
Havana. So England now held sway clear down to the Florida
keys. England had tried in vain to induce the Georgia colony to
supply troops for this war. Except for a few raids along the coast,
the war was far away from Georgia or Carolina, in the north
and west, and the Georgians pleaded in excuse that they could
not afford to weaken their forces, because of the constant threat
from the Indians on their borders.

Once the ban on slavery was lifted, Carolinians began to
move across the river into Georgia. Over a thousand slaves were
brought into the Georgia colony the first two years. A colony of
Puritans who had migrated from Massachusetts and settled in
Carolina in the early days of that colony moved into Georgia in
1752. They occupied a tract of 32,000 acres between the Savannah and Altamaha Rivers below Savannah. This settlement
they called Midway, as it was halfway between the two streams.
They brought 1,500 slaves with them. A thrifty, intelligent,
hard-working people, they established a neat and prosperous
community. Like a lighthouse of their religious inclinations rose
the trim Congregational church, a delicate man-made spire
among the live oaks, a pin point of New England conscience
amidst the prodigality of luxurious southern nature. From the
loins of Midway sprang some of the leading spirits of the colony
in the years to come. Their principal crops were rice and indigo.

They first traded overland to Savannah, along the road that
Oglethorpe had hewn through the wilderness which he found
along that coast. Later they built a port of their own, Sunbury,
which for several years was one of the leading ports along the
entire Atlantic coast. Its harbor was alive with vessels that took
away its produce and brought finished goods from England
and elsewhere.

A small colony of Germans was established at Bethany near
Savannah. A community of Quakers, seeking the quiet retreats of

the wilderness, found a refuge on Little River, about thirty miles from its junction with the Savannah just below Augusta, and called their settlement Wrightsborough after Governor James Wright, the most distinguished of the colonial governors of Georgia. Wrightsborough was situated in pleasant, rolling and fertile country.

In time there was a great invasion of this settlement by Virginians. They came down through the back country and spread all through this section, reaching inland from the Savannah. The region came to be called Wilkes County, a considerable area later subdivided into other counties, so that Wilkes eventually was pushed back from the river. This tide of immigration began to flow when a great stretch of territory, hitherto reserved to the Indians, was opened through a treaty with the Cherokees and Creeks in 1773, just before the Revolution. The white man now was beginning to push the Indians slowly backward toward the hills. This first cession, called the New Purchase, extended almost as far north as the junction of the Keowee and Tugaloo Rivers, tributaries of the Savannah. It was the first of a series of nearly a score of such cessions by treaty which finally drove the Indians, in fifty years, clear out of this country and to the west. Some "treaties" were preceded by the shedding of blood. This one was peaceful, negotiated about the council table and under the old formula, that is, Indian debts. The price of the gimcracks of civilization to which the white trader had accustomed the red man always was too much for his slender resources, and debts piled up. When they mounted too high, the white man demanded payment in the one coin of which the Indian possessed plenty, land! So the debts were extinguished in exchange for land.

Along the river, above Savannah, the little villages began to bloom. Like the flowers they appeared with succeeding springs. A family would decide to venture the wilderness. They would tumble their few household belongings into a wagon, gather together what livestock they owned, a cow or two perhaps, a few pigs, and off they would go. A cache of corn was included to feed the cattle and, if there was a pinch, to feed themselves. Some such families had a Negro slave or two. They would find a suitable location, where there was a spring and where the forest land looked promising. First they would clear way the ground for a home and build a crude log cabin with a dirt floor. Then they would clear a larger tract for planting their crops. Before the food crops came in they would fish and hunt for their meals. Another family would come along and settle near to become neighbors. Another family would join them. Eventually there would be a group of settlers and a village would grow up. In time the families would extend their holdings and cultivate larger fields. The merchant would come and he also would act as a factor for the farmers, assisting with the financing and moving of produce. Then there would spring up a rude church; the preacher would come among them to tend their souls; a doctor to look after their bodily ailments, and, presto—civilization with all its trappings.

For many years living generally was primitive and niggardly along the river above the Savannah, though here and there prosperous enough for some energetic pioneers who were especially thrifty or had the knack of making a good living. Augusta gradually grew into a city as the center for the trade that moved up and down the river and across the trails that radiated away from it.

Another town appeared at the junction of the Savannah and Broad Rivers. It was named Dartmouth. It grew up naturally about a fort built there in the early days, Fort James—this was erected in 1775—to protect the stream of settlement moving into the rich Broad River valley from Virginia. Other small towns grew above Augusta along the river owing to the movement of produce from the inland and more fertile back country to convenient loading points. Population thickened away from the river, rather than along it. Only a few towns sat immediately on the riverbanks.

PART 4

The Beginning of Revolution

CHAPTER ONE

IN TONDEE'S TAVERN THEY HATCHED IT

Tondee's Tavern, in the heart of Savannah, was the cradle of the Revolution in Georgia. In the beginning it was, figuratively, the capital of Georgia, but not for long. Government in Georgia was constantly on the run, once the colony was caught up full in the sweep of war, and frequently was carried in the hats of a few bold men.

It was not a likely place to plot a revolution, having nothing dark or secretive in its atmosphere. It was a comfortable and congenial refuge, warm and cozy in winter with a big fire always murmuring in the "long room," cool and quiet in the summer away from the heat that drenched Savannah's streets. It was a place for the family and the children. Peter Tondee, the proprietor, saw to that. Here, of an evening, the families would gather. The elders would sit about with their ale. The young folks would play quoits. Some of the young blades formed a club— "All Saints Quoits Club," they named it—which assembled here

127

weekly. Peter would set out a flowing bowl for their refreshment. The tavern sat on what is now the corner of Broughton and Whitaker Streets and was a community center. Here came the sea captains fresh from the oceans, with news of the world, to find a most receptive audience in old and young. There were tales of the English homeland, of wars in Europe and on the high seas, of storms and shipwrecks, and the "latest" court gossip.

Tondee's Tavern began its career on the threshold of exciting and troublous times. It was built in 1766 or 1767.

The Tondee family had come from Switzerland and settled on a lot granted in the city of Savannah. His father and mother were both dead when Peter, who was sixteen, and his brother Charles, who was ten, bobbed up in Savannah history. The two boys were apprenticed to a magistrate of the colony, Henry Parker, for such jobs as boys of that age can perform. Apparently they were good and steady workers, for when Bethesda Orphanage was planned, and the two boys were selected to live there, their sponsor complained right bitterly at losing them. The orphanage had not been finished when the Tondee brothers were enrolled and they lived for a while with another family in the city. Peter helped to build the orphanage which, it may be recalled, was the project of the noted preacher, George Whitefield.

From the annals of the times we get occasional glances at the young man, Peter Tondee, as he rose to a position of prominence among his fellow citizens and acquired substance and a family. We find in 1750 that he was one of three young men who associated himself in what was first called St. George's Club, later Union Society, an association that provided financial help for the orphanage during its emergencies. It was composed of a mixed trio—Tondee, a Catholic, Sheftall, a Jew, and Richard Milledge, an Episcopalian.

In time Peter began to acquire land—a tract on the edge of the city, a lot in the little town of Hardwicke. Then he took to himself a family, a wife and children, by marrying a widow, an Acadian woman. A number of Acadians came to Georgia

when they were dispersed by the English from their Nova
Scotia homeland, though very few stayed long. Later we find
that Tondee got more land, a tract of five hundred acres of
timber land below Savannah. From this he cut the timber out
of which he built his tavern. He had been busy all the while
at his trade as carpenter. Among other assignments he had
erected a building for the courts of the province, and in 1767
he was honored by appointment as culler and inspector of lumber for the port.

Keeping a tavern must have been, however, his destined
calling, for his business flourished and his tavern was frequented
by the leading figures of the community and the surrounding
countryside. It was only natural, then, that it should become a
meeting place when the spirit of revolution began to spread
among the citizens of the colony. Peter Tondee's revolutionary
fervor, it must be said, seems to have had the usual amount
of inspiration in self-interest. He was required to pay a tax of
£40 sterling to the British government on a slave he owned,
and taxation without representation had its own little tyranny
for him. But revolt, too, had its personal risks.

He discovered this when the Sons of Liberty began to use
his long room to plot their plots, for official eyes began to look
suspiciously toward his tavern. It is presumed that the revolutionaries met under the guise of the All Saints Quoits Club or as if
for a session of the Union Society to conceal their purpose.

The first meeting was on July 27, 1774. It was summoned
on news from Boston, delayed naturally, that the British had
closed the port of America's leading city. There was much talk
and many speeches. The long room was heavy with the voice
of the masterful George Walton, who was very impassioned
in demanding a stand against such practices by the mother
country.

The group decided to do nothing yet, but to call another
meeting which would be more representative of the whole
colony. That was set for August 10. Then Governor James

Wright got word of the plotting and forbade the meeting. It was held, of course, but in great secrecy. Peter Tondee was assigned to stand at the door and check every man who came to make sure of his loyalty. At this meeting they voted to send supplies to Boston and drew up a resolution of grievances which, as far as those present were concerned, lined up Georgia with the other colonies.

There were many meetings from time to time, as events pushed the colonists closer to the breaking point. It was a time of indecision and, in Georgia, a time truly that tried men's souls.

This comparative newcomer among the English colonies did not flame up overnight into an unquenchable revolt. Quite to the contrary. Georgia had been most kindly treated by England and in James Wright the province had for many years a wise, tolerant and exceptionably able governor. The colony, furthermore, was isolated from the center of dissension and revolt to the north. Nor did the grievances about which other colonies complained bear upon it so heavily. The navigation laws, which restricted and confined the operation of trade, colonial merchants and ships, were not such a burden upon Georgia as upon some of the other colonies. For very few ships were owned by Georgians. Also the pinch of taxes levied from England was less severe, because of the colony's lack of large-scale business and industry.

Governor Wright was influential in holding back any precipitate rush to revolution. He was particularly effective with the older generation, which had strong ties with England.

The American Revolution was, in truth, a civil war in this far southern English colony. Families were divided, father against son, brother against brother. For example, Noble Jones, a leading citizen of Savannah, he who had taken command when Mary Musgrove's Indian legions had descended upon the frightened city, remained loyal to the crown, but his son, Noble Wymberly Jones, joined in the revolutionary movement. James Habersham, another leading citizen, who had been so active to get slavery legalized, stood by England, while his two sons, James and Joseph, took up the colonial cause. James Spalding tried to be a neutral and removed his family to East Florida to sit out the storm there, although this entailed a great sacrifice of his material interests. He was a young Scot who had come to Georgia, built himself a prosperous trading business with the Indians, and established himself as a lord of the manor in the rich community that flourished on Sapelo Island, as on the other "Golden Isles" along the Georgia coast. He returned after the war to find his estate confiscated and in ruins. The story of divided families was repeated over and over.

More and more tense grew the recurrent meetings in Tondee's Tavern as open war drew nearer. Perhaps as much responsible for the final break as anything else was the influence of the Puritan settlement at Midway, with its early Massachusetts traditions. Its natural sympathies lay with Boston, and sprang from an inherited distaste to the mother country that stemmed back to the reasons for the original settlement in New England a century and a half before.

Midway emissaries to the Tondee Tavern sessions were persistent in demands for an open break with the mother country. There was Lyman Hall, who later signed the Declaration of Independence, and Benjamin Andrews and Nathan Brownson. All three were members of the Congregational church at Midway, and all three afterward became governors of Georgia.

Theirs was, however, an uphill struggle with many setbacks before Georgia finally wrenched herself loose. Patriots got their first disappointment when their colleagues at the Tondee Tavern sessions refused to appoint delegates to the First Continental Congress at Philadelphia. Later they failed in an effort to have Georgia join the nonimportation association approved by the First Continental Congress. Discouraged by these rebuffs, the Midway malcontents sought an outlet elsewhere for their zeal. They went to South Carolina, which was warm for revolution, with a plea that they be permitted to work with that colony. But South Carolina was disdainful of its shy and faltering neighbor. Its leaders flatly turned down the request for an alliance from the Midway minority. They went even further. They broke off commercial relations with Georgia, declaring that Georgians were "unworthy of the rights of freemen", and were "inimical to the liberties of their country." At one point South Carolina almost reached the point of an invasion of the hesitant adjoining province.

A majority of Georgians who assembled at Tondee's Tavern in the colony's First Provincial Congress in January, 1775, still were unwilling to go the whole way. They still were hopeful of some show of leniency from England. The congress addressed a plea to the throne to repeal the acts imposing taxes on the colonies by a Parliament in which the colonies were not represented. The king, they thought, surely would heed. The king, of course, did not, since he could not repeal an act of Parliament.

It was "the shot heard round the world," fired far away from Georgia, at Lexington, that finally stiffened the backbones of Georgians desirous of joining in common action with the other colonies. The news of that incident in Massachusetts arrived, belatedly of course, on May 10. It set off a great and exultant celebration throughout the city as the news was carried from mouth to mouth. The patriotic fervor had its release in a raid upon the colonial powder magazine, the property of the king's government, led by four of the more belligerent of the group that had set about plotting, to no avail hitherto, in Tondee's Tavern—Noble Jones, Edward Telfair, Joseph Habersham and John Milledge. The seized the powder and sent part of it, with a shipment of rice and some money, to Boston. An old legend has it that this powder was used in the Battle of Bunker Hill. Governor Wright ordered the arrest of the raiders and offered a reward of £150. But no arrests followed, due to the state of public sympathy for the rioters.

CHAPTER TWO

Now the spirit of revolt was kindled. Georgians had perpetrated an act of defiance, and there is nothing like a concrete act to rally the wavering. Another opportunity for a show of defiance came a few weeks later with the king's birthday, June 4. The usual celebration took place. But when it came time to fire the customary salute to the king from the cannon set up along the bluff along the Savannah, it was discovered that the guns had been toppled into the river by some mischievous spirits.

The very next day a liberty pole, the symbol of revolution, was erected in front of Tondee's Tavern, and Georgia had joined the parade. Two weeks later, on June 21, at a meeting in Tondee's Tavern, a Council of Safety was organized and instructed to correspond with the other colonies. The assembled revolutionaries decamped in a body to the liberty pole in front of Tondee's Tavern, hoisted the liberty flag to the top of the pole, and then, having done a good day's work, returned to the tavern to a cheering dinner that Peter Tondee had laid out. Thirteen toasts were drunk in an excess of patriotism and good fellowship, and some Savannah wives learned that night with the arrival of tipsy husbands that liquor is a natural accompaniment of revolution.

The next step was taken with boldness and vigor. Over a hundred delegates, this time from all parts of the colony, gathered again in the tavern on July 4—just a year before the Declaration of Independence—in the Second Provincial Congress. In a session lasting until July 17, they transacted all manner of business that set them squarely off on the road to revolution. Still they were shy of shattering the awful and traditional majesty that shone about the throne. Rather than upon "his sacred majesty," they sought to lay the blame for their troubles on men like themselves—on the ministers, members of Parliament, the army. They issued another and final appeal to the king as to some higher divinity. Then they poured out their indignation in another series of resolutions, bristling with vehement language—"despotic ministry," "corrupt Parliament" (King George had done some of the corrupting), and "army of mercenaries." In a direct appeal to their own people, the colonial leaders at Tondee's Tavern told how the blood of their fellow citizens had been spilled in and around Boston, and how bravely Americans had stood up against British regulars, and concluded in a ringing sentence:

"A civil war in America is begun."

The Provincial Congress voted to join the nonimportation association and, among other things, Georgians discovered that hereafter they must forgo their tea, since the "genial herb" was included on the proscribed list, along with mourning cloth, and other things made in England. The Congress also re-elected three delegates who had been chosen at the First Provincial Congress as representatives to the Continental Congress, but who had declined to go to Philadelphia on the ground that the First (Georgia) Provincial Congress was not truly representative. Archibald Bulloch, Noble Jones, and John Houstoun were again returned with two more, Lyman Hall, the ardent Midway revolutionary, and Dr. John Joachim Zubly, a minister. Bulloch, as well, became the executive of the Provincial Congress, being elected its president.

Dr. Zubly turned out to be a wavering spirit, manifesting the ordeal of conscience through which so many in Georgia went, when confronted by the actual decision to separate from the mother country. One day at Philadelphia, during a session of the Continental Congress, he said frankly that he did not want independence from England.

"A Republican government," he declared, "is little better than government of devils."

He was of the Established Church and a man of wealth.

The conscience-stricken cleric was denounced by Samuel Chase of Maryland, who accused him of carrying on a correspondence with Governor Wright revealing the plans of the Continental Congress and warning the governor of the impending separation from Great Britain. He left Philadelphia hastily when he became suspect and the center of controversy. Subsequently, when royal government was resumed in Georgia after the capture of Savannah by the British and loyalists, he returned to his church and remained in Savannah until 1781.

But there was no longer any wavering now for the men who had directed the course of the Second Georgia Provincial Congress. They advised Governor Wright openly of just what they had done. There was no longer any secrecy. In vain he tried to convene the regular Georgia Colonial Assembly to check the tide of revolt and keep the colony in the empire. But most of the members of the Assembly were also members of the Provincial Congress. Rapidly they acted to establish their own government. They took over the courts and the militia and seized the customhouse. In alarm Governor Wright appealed to England for troops, but the home government did not want to stir up armed resistance, still hoping that the Georgians might see the error of their ways and be saved to the empire. The governor asked for his recall, but was instructed to remain "to stem the tide." Finally, early in 1776, the governor was arrested as a precaution, when two British warships sailed into the river and anchored off Tybee Island. He escaped and took refuge on the ships. Georgians generally were relieved when he got away, for they did not want to persecute the man who had been a good and able administrator of affairs.

The appearance of the two war vessels excited the city, and the leaders immediately began to prepare Savannah for an attack. Fortifications were erected along the waterfront. In early March the British, unable to get supplies, decided to appropriate for themselves a fleet of rice vessels. They turned the noses of their two ships up the river toward the wharves where most of the rice boats were tied up. Before the Georgia authorities could act, the British had seized the rice-laden boats. Savannah leaders instituted peaceful negotiations for recovery of the boats. They got nowhere. Outraged, they enlisted the help of South Carolina and, assisted by men from the neighboring province, they boarded some of the ships and set fire to them. The British then slipped away to sea with only a few of the prizes. Eight left behind were taken over by the Georgians and dismantled.

This was the first brush with the enemy, but war had not started yet.

This show of British force was so disturbing, however, that the Provincial Congress, meeting in its third session, left Savannah and moved up the river to Augusta. The legislators became maneuverable, and it was just as well, for in the next few years they had to hie here and there with the changing fortunes of war. At Augusta they now organized the new state government, formally electing Bulloch the first president of Georgia and commander in chief of its military forces. They drafted a temporary constitution, reorganized the Council of Safety with the requirement that the president must consult with it, organized a judicial system, and decreed that all existing laws not in conflict with the new state of affairs should continue. They also filled two vacancies in the delegation to the Continental Congress. In the places of Dr. Zubly and Noble Jones, who wanted to retire for a time to his plantation to be with his aging father, the Congress chose Button Gwinnett and George Walton.

When the scare at Savannah blew over, government officials and legislators returned to that city. Again Tondee's

Tavern was the scene of a memorable event. There, in the long room, the Declaration of Independence was read to the Council of Safety by Bulloch. The day was August 10, 1776. A copy of the document had just been received.

Afterward, Bulloch went outside and read the declaration in the public square before a great throng which had gathered, excited and jubilant, at the news of what had happened in Philadelphia on July 4. He read the signatures at the end. The names of three of their own citizens were there—Button Gwinnett, Lyman Hall, and George Walton, The other two delegates had not been present when the declaration was signed.

The people could not hear it often enough. Again Bulloch read it, this time before the liberty pole in front of Tondee's Tavern, and through the city and up and down the bluffs of the Savannah reverberated the noise of the cannon in a salute of thirteen guns. The word was passed around swiftly that the declaration was to be read still another time. People hastened to the battery along the banks of the river, where Bulloch read the challenging words again. When he had finished the battery guns broke forth in salute.

Savannah stopped its work and gave itself up to a holiday. Everywhere, in the streets, in the taverns, the declaration was discussed, its words quoted, its meaning conned. We have no record, but Tondee's Tavern and others in the city must have done a flourishing business that day. During the day the news was carried to the outlying settlements and the celebration went on, settlement by settlement, as the word was spread. It was the most exciting night in Savannah and its environs since Mary Musgrove had led her Creeks upon the city. As on that other occasion, Savannah slept little this night. The streets were crowded with exultant crowds making merry over this new thing that had happened in their world. Little did they know that night what it was going to mean in the hard and bitter days to come. They cheered and clapped their hands when a great procession streamed by, a mock solemn funeral cortege, with the effigy of King George III in the coffin. There was a formal burial ceremony. He was no longer sacred.

There was one person missing in all this hilarity, one who deserved to see this day and night. His wife had to superintend the rushing business at the tavern, and she must have been sad as she looked after the gentlemen whom Peter Tondee had known and served in those critical days when all that now was coming to its climax was being plotted in the long room about the tables that he had fashioned himself with his own hands. Peter had died nearly a year before, on October 22, 1775.

CHAPTER THREE

IT WAS A FAMOUS FEUD

Georgia now found herself caught tight in the vise of war, and an unhappy situation it was for many of her citizens who did not want it, who still clung to the ancient loyalties; and trouble enough it was for those who had forced the decision and who now had to take responsibility. The burden was magnified by factional feuds and divisions of counsel. Georgia was ill prepared, and had not the English been so busily engaged far to the north, trying to stamp out the revolutionary fire at its source, seeking to corner a Continental general by the name of George Washington, who was proving so elusive, the southern colony might have been in real danger. For she had at her disposal, ready for offense or defense, only a battalion of 236 men under command of Colonial Lachlan McIntosh, a force of cavalry—

sixty men—along the Florida border, and a few scattered troops on the frontiers for protection against the Indians.

Button Gwinnett came home presently from Philadelphia with his saddlebags full of resolutions adopted by the Congress, containing instructions for the raising of an army in Georgia. He rode the eight hundred miles on horseback, stopping in Virginia and Carolina to visit friends. He rode, unwittingly, into a situation created by the clash of personal ambition that was to lead eventually to his doom. For he was sore at heart with jealousy and thwarted ambition and carried a chip on his shoulder.

Gwinnett had been responsible for putting through the Continental Congress the resolutions providing for Georgia's military establishment. With that confidence which grows in the secret places of the souls of most men, he pictured himself in the role of a military commander, though he had had no experience. He wanted to command the brigade that was to be raised in Georgia. Instead, the Continental Congress had selected Colonel Lachlan McIntosh, who had an effective friend in George Walton, a man clever at pulling the strings politically. So Colonel McIntosh became General McIntosh.

This was the beginning of a feud famous in Georgia history.

Lachlan McIntosh was a familiar figure about Tondee's Tavern in the days of deliberation before the final break with England. He had taken part in the debates and was a member of the successive Provincial Congresses. The tavern was to him, we can imagine, more than just a public house; for he and Peter Tondee had known each other as boys at Bethesda Orphanage and there the two, one a scion of the distinguished McIntosh clan, the other the son of a Swiss immigrant, training to be a carpenter, had lived and played and worked together, symbols of the almost classless society in those days in Georgia.

The McIntoshes had come to Georgia as refugees, but the determination and high purpose that ran in their Scotch blood

had exhibited themselves in their new wilderness home and
they had become leading people in the colony, a numerous
clan respected and honored not only in their community about
Darien, but through the whole of Georgia. They owned large
plantations on the mainland, about the mouth of the Altamaha,
and had spread into the neighboring islands.

The Georgia coast now was a highly cultivated, civilized,
and prosperous community. Negro slavery, abhorrent to the
earlier Scots, had become an accepted fact with the newer
generation, and the black man was making this land to bloom.
Spacious rambling houses sat at the end of long white roads
lined by giant live oaks among peaceful fields, green with growing things, that stretched away on all sides.

The approach of revolution found Lachlan McIntosh settled
comfortably in this fruitful land of plenty won from the wilderness. He had a home of his own in the vicinity of the
Altamaha and a family growing up about him. He had become
a surveyor, after a few years in Charleston in the mercantile
business, and had been able to acquire highly desirable lands
for himself. He was an established figure and nicely accommodated to grow old gracefully among his kinsfolk and his friends.

But all this, of course, could not hold a member of the
Borlam McIntosh clan when the tocsin of revolt sounded,
revolt against the traditional foe, England, a revolt, too, to give
him, and others like him, clear title to their heritage in a new
land. Military adventure was, likewise, an inborn trait. He and
his brother William, as youngsters, had fought the Spaniards
at Bloody Marsh. Later the two of them had plotted another
adventure, which was foiled only by the intercession of General
Oglethorpe. The banner of revolt was raised again in the
Scottish highlands, and they heard about it through rumors that
Oglethorpe, who was going back home to England, was to lead
the English against this new uprising which was on behalf of
the Young Pretender, Charles Edward Stuart. Once again the
Scots were busy in that fruitless crusade to recapture the throne

of England for the Stuarts. The two young men decided to stow away on the vessel that would take Oglethorpe back to England, make their way to Scotland, and enlist under the Stuart banner of their forefathers and of their father. They hid in a boat tied alongside the ship in which Oglethorpe was to return. The general learned about their conspiracy. He had them brought to him and told them how fruitless was this new uprising of the Scots, reminded them how good a friend he had been to their father, and told them as an English officer he could arrest them, but that if they would give up this reckless adventure he would let them go unmolested. They were persuaded. That was the last time they saw the man under whom they had loyally fought at Bloody Marsh.

Lachlan McIntosh was well acquainted in the Georgia colony and was recognized as a man of ability and distinction. It was natural, therefore, that if he enlisted in the revolutionary movement against England he would be accorded a place among the leaders in his community. That was his due. He had important connections and contacts, not only in Georgia but in South Carolina. As a young man he had become a protégé of Henry Laurens of South Carolina, who later was president of the Continental Congress at Philadelphia and a leading spirit in the Revolution. Laurens had found a place for the young Scotsman in his mercantile business in Charleston, had taken him into his home almost as a son. There Lachlan McIntosh had every opportunity to improve himself in the midst of a cultured family. In those days he acquired the ease and grace and polish of Charleston society. Eventually he had his fill of this sort of life and went back to the Altamaha to marry and make a place for himself among his own people.

William was now the head of the clan. His daughter, Margery, had married the wealthy Scotsman, James Spalding. The McIntoshes were connected on all sides with the lords of the plantation and trading aristocracy that had developed in St. Simon's Island and Sapelo in the years before the Revolution.

William's wife had been Katherine McKay, the only daughter of Donald McKay. He had come over with the original Scotch refugees and had bought all of St. Simon's Island after Oglethorpe had gone home to England and the island had lost its status as a purely military outpost of the empire. Lachlan McIntosh became chief magistrate of Frederica, now a quiet town and no longer a fortress. Lachlan's younger brother, George, had the ancestral Borlam McIntosh lands on the Altamaha, which he had developed into a profitable plantation, raising rice in the lowlands as well as beef cattle and corn.

George McIntosh was active in the plotting that went on at Tondee's Tavern. He was honored by election to the Council of Safety. But a cloud had come up about him when he was suspected of not being entirely loyal to the colonial cause, because of trading operations with the enemy with which he was connected indirectly.

The younger brother, in this way among others, became involved in the family feud with Button Gwinnett.

Gwinnett, the ambitious and mercurial gentleman who was such a bright and fiery figure in the early days of the Revolution in Georgia, had the shining ardor acquired often by those who come late to the altar of revolution, but he was without a long background in the land and among the people from which it springs.

He arrived in Savannah presumably about 1765. He had been in the exporting business in England, at Bristol, and had become imbued with the romance of America and its opportunities through those business contacts which possess their own allure—the names of places on bills of lading, the stories of ship captains and sailors who rode the boats that carried his goods. He had an especially thriving trade with the West Indies in the Caribbean, and the islands of that southern sea sparkled in the imagination of all Englishmen.

Why he selected Savannah we do not know. There he

opened a general store. His wares were advertised in the *Georgia Gazette*. But this business did not hold him long. Perhaps it was too prosaic, this life of a shopkeeper. After a few months of it he bought St. Catherine's Island from Abraham Bosomworth and Mary Musgrove and blossomed forth as a planter and a man of large affairs, larger presumably than he could handle, for he was never very successful, was continually in debt, became entangled in the courts with his creditors. He was, in short, constantly harassed to live up to the expansive role he had picked out for himself.

It was only ten miles from his landing on St. Catherine's across the inland passage to Sunbury, and he was constantly in and out of that then bustling seaport, enlarging his acquaintance, impressing himself upon the community by his personality. He undoubtedly was a magnetic fellow with considerable charm, also ambitious and, from all we can observe, somewhat of an opportunist, not a handicap in politics. He had no roots in America. But he learned fast, and he was eager to be up in the world. Here was opportunity in the creation of a new political order, such opportunity as could never come to an exporter in Bristol, where he was only an atom in a vast empire. There is no incident in the rather sparse record of Button Gwinnett in England to indicate that he ever raised his voice in political protest, or was even interested.

Lyman Hall, that zealous spirit of revolt at Midway, seems to have been the influence chiefly responsible for Gwinnett's conversion to the revolutionary cause. Perhaps the Midway patriot saw in the attractive Englishman a useful vessel, and Gwinnett was ready for the chance to advance himself in a community red hot for revolution. He suffered from no indecision. He sat with the First Provincial Congress at Tondee's Tavern and was elected, as we have seen, one of three delegates to the First Continental Congress, who never got to Philadelphia, and re-elected the next year, when they did get to Philadelphia.

Presumably he met Lachlan McIntosh, his future rival, at Tondee's Tavern, in those early councils. There is no record of their meeting, such things always being provokingly missing from the annals. But it is not difficult to imagine a basic conflict in character. McIntosh had the reserve characteristic of his people, nor apparently did he have that warmth which attracts easy and quick friendships. We do not know about the relations of the two before their ambitions clashed, but we may imagine that Gwinnett had not greatly concerned himself about McIntosh until the latter suddenly was awarded the military post that Gwinnett coveted.

Though McIntosh had won the military post, Gwinnett still had his foothold in civic affairs and one day found himself catapulted to a position from which he might hamstring his rival and realize his ambition to conduct military operations. President Bulloch died and a successor must be chosen. Gwinnett was elected by the council as acting president, until a regular election could be held.

It was incidental to his election by the council that the feud between the McIntoshes and Gwinnett got a public expression, and this through George McIntosh. The younger brother of Lachlan was not present the day the election was held, his wife having died that day. But he turned up at the meeting on March 4, 1777, and refused to sign Gwinnett's commission. In the presence of the whole council he rose and said that Gwinnett would be the last person in the world he would choose for the office. Gwinnett, nettled, retorted angrily:

"By God, then, this will be the last day you and I will ever sit together in council."

This was public notice that war was on between the prominent Scotch family and the interloping Englishman.

Now in the seat of power, Button Gwinnett immediately sought to realize his ambitions as a military commander. The project to which he turned was the familiar and plaguing one that had fired the minds of Georgians for many years—the old dream of capturing St. Augustine. Spain had disappeared into the mists. But England now held Florida as a heritage from the Spaniards, and, as in other wars in which coastal settlers had been involved, St. Augustine still sat at their backs, threatening. Only the year before, in 1776, the Georgia colonials had undertaken another futile expedition toward St. Augustine. Everything had gone wrong. The terrific heat of summer—it was August—had taken its toll. Men died at the rate of fifteen a day on Sapelo Island. The army, scattered along the coast, never did encounter the British foe. Lachlan McIntosh had participated in that expedition.

But Button Gwinnett refused to be deterred or discouraged by this setback. St. Augustine loomed as a star he could pluck for his crown. He had a good excuse in the active marauding expeditions of the English in southern Georgia and along the coast. In February, 1777, just before he was elevated to the presidency, the British had captured Fort McIntosh on the Satilla River and had almost won Fort Howe on the Altamaha.

Now was his big chance. This was to be his show. He assumed complete command as president and insisted that civilian authorities were charged with responsibility for military operations. A military council was created embracing militia and colonial military officials over which he presided. He insisted that this council should direct operations and that military commanders in the field must report to it.

But General McIntosh refused to accept this division of authority. He ignored the council. Finally Gwinnett, himself, took the field. The council meanwhile bickered over the division of authority and recalled both the president and General McIntosh to Savannah and turned the expedition over to Colonel Samuel Elbert. It was the old story, in the end, of other such ventures. Colonel Elbert was to proceed down the coast, as

Oglethorpe once had done, to meet the Georgia militia under Colonel John Baker in a junction of forces at Sawpit Bluff on the St. Johns River. They never met. Each had to fight British armies separately, and Elbert was badly defeated. The expedition straggled home, and Gwinnett's ambitious dream withered. He had assumed responsibility, and the blame fell upon him.

His fall from power was not long delayed. When the new Assembly met May 1 to elect a successor to Bulloch, it passed over the acting president and chose John Adam Treutlen, though Gwinnett made quite an active campaign and had some support in the Assembly. The people needed a scapegoat and the Assembly had one ready to hand in the man whose military ambitions had overreached themselves.

Two weeks later, May 15, Gwinnett, now a private citizen again, and General McIntosh appeared before the Assembly, at its summons, for a post-mortem on the Florida debacle. Meanwhile there had been developments also in another affair involving the McIntoshes and Gwinnett which had intensified the increasingly bitter personal feud. This was the case of alleged treason involving George McIntosh.

Let us go back to that. It all began only a few days after the spat in the council between Gwinnett and George McIntosh over Gwinnett's election. Gwinnett received a very disturbing communication from John Hancock, president of the Continental Congress at Philadelphia, accusing George McIntosh of treasonable conduct.

"This gentleman, it seems," Hancock wrote of George McIntosh, "is a member of the Congress in Georgia and under that character is secretly supporting by every act in his power, the designs of the British King and Parliament against us."

Hancock enclosed an intercepted letter from Patrick Tonyn, British governor of East Florida, which set forth that George McIntosh was helping a Mr. Preston to procure rice for the British forces in Florida. Supply of the British in Florida from the Georgia coast surreptitiously was one of the problems that was causing Georgia officials much concern at the time.

In his letter, the British governor described George McIntosh as one "who is compelled to a tacit acquiescence with the distempered times, and is one of the Rebel Congress of Georgia, intentionally to mollify and temporize, and to be of all service in his power." George McIntosh's principles, the governor said, "are a loyal attachment to the King and Constitution."

"He would, my lord, be in a dangerous situation was this known," Tonyn concluded.

These were serious charges. Hancock's letter was dated January 8, but it was over two months in reaching Georgia. The Assembly had already adjourned when it came into Gwinnett's hands, and he was unable to get together enough of the council for a quorum, so he took responsibility, himself, and ordered a militia colonel to take two men and arrest George McIntosh, as Hancock had instructed in his letter. The accused man was brought to Savannah and turned over to the provost marshal, who took rather extraordinary and extreme measures and put McIntosh in irons.

This provoked a bitter outcry from McIntosh's friends. They proposed bail of £50,000, but Gwinnett refused. In time the president got his council together; after hearing Hancock's letter read, however, the council ordered the irons removed. George McIntosh's brother-in-law, John Houstoun, one of Savannah's leading businessmen and citizens and delegate to the Continental Congress in Philadelphia, protested that McIntosh's health was such that he would die if confined in the common jail at Savannah. A few days later Gwinnett went to Sunbury to supervise preparations for the Florida expedition, in pursuit of the military command he had assumed. The council, in his absence, voted to release the prisoner on £2,000 bond. Four members of the council signed his bond, so that the treason charges apparently were not regarded as seriously among some people as by Hancock and Gwinnett.

It was when the affair had reached this stage, and against the background of the personal bitterness between the McIntoshes and Gwinnett, which the issue had engendered, that Button Gwinnett and General Lachlan McIntosh stood before the council in mid-May to give an account of the abortive and disastrous Florida expedition and the divided command.

Gwinnett's talents as a politician served him well on this occasion. He spoke so persuasively in his own behalf that the Assembly adopted a resolution approving the conduct of himself and his council "so far as these matters were laid before them."

The usually composed McIntosh went into a rage. He lost his temper completely. He called his rival "a scoundrel and a lying rascal." This unparliamentary outburst was ignored by the speaker and the Assembly, though it was clearly a breach of the rules of procedure.

But Gwinnett must act. This was one of those "affairs of honor." He could not let it pass and hold up his head among his fellows. He consulted friends and they agreed there was nothing for it but to challenge his detractor to a duel. As his second, Gwinnett selected George Wells, a member of the Assembly from Richmond County in which Augusta was situated. That night Wells presented to General McIntosh a letter from Gwinnett saying that, since he had been called a scoundrel in a public convention, he desired to meet McIntosh the next morning before sunrise in satisfaction of his honor. The general accepted, with an ironic quip. He would be very glad to accommodate the gentleman, even though it was earlier than his customary hour of rising. As his second, he chose Major James Habersham. The seconds got together and made the necessary arrangements. McIntosh would provide the pistols. As the site for the duel they picked a meadow in the property formerly belonging to the royal governor, who had now fled, and so known as "the Sir James Wright meadow." This was on the outskirts of Savannah on the road to Thunderbolt.

Despite his pert rejoinder to the challenge about the unusual hour of rising, General McIntosh was first on the scene the next morning. He and Major Habersham arrived fifteen minutes before Gwinnett and his second. The two gentlemen who had come to salve their respective honors greeted each other with frigid politeness. The general presented his pistols. They were examined, as was usual, to see that they contained only one charge. These preliminaries went on in low tones of voice appropriate to the solemnity of this private occasion in the gloom of early morning. The four men then discovered, somewhat to their surprise and chagrin, that the affair was turning into a public occasion. Several persons had gathered on a nearby hillside to watch the two heroes shoot it out. It was agreed to move to a place farther away, where the field of honor could not be observed by the curious. Another place accordingly was selected.

Gwinnett was asked at what distance the two should stand.

"Whatever distance the general pleases," he replied.

The general was pleased that the shooting should take place at three paces, about nine feet. This was measured off by the seconds, and Major Habersham, after taking a look, suggested another pace, another three feet. This was agreeable. The seconds recommended that the two men should stand back to back, pace off the distance, turn and fire. But McIntosh didn't like any such arrangement.

"By no means," he interposed. "Let us see what we are about."

So it was decided that the two men should take their places, face to face, four paces apart, and fire at a signal. They took their places. The signal was given. The two shots rang out simultaneously in the early morning.

Gwinnett crumpled and fell. The general's bullet had struck him above the knee and broken the bone.

"My thigh is broken," he cried out.

His own shot had lodged in the muscular part of General McIntosh's leg. The general still stood. He did not know the extent of the injury he had inflicted and called out to ask if his antagonist wanted another shot. Gwinnett replied that he did, if someone would lift him up. The seconds interceded at this point, insisting that the honor of each gentleman had been satisfied. The general was led over to his fallen foe and the two shook hands. The participants were helped from the field and taken to their respective homes.

Neither wound apparently was serious. But Gwinnett had a doctor who was not skillful. The weather was hot and gangrene set in. Three days later, on a Monday morning, he died.

The duel quickly became a cause célèbre, attesting to Gwinnett's popularity among the rank and file, magnetic interloper though he was. Resentment spread among his followers in the Popular Party and a petition with 505 signatures was presented to Governor Treutlen demanding that General McIntosh be removed from the state. Public feeling was so high that William McIntosh, head of the clan, resigned his position as commander of the light cavalry in Georgia.

Before he was fully recovered, General McIntosh sought to clear himself of the ignominy heaped upon him from all sides by champions of the dead leader, who was now rapidly being elevated to a martyr. A letter that General McIntosh wrote to Colonel John Lawrence, George Washington's military secretary, three days after Gwinnett's death, has recently come to light. In that, McIntosh said that the death of his one-time rival "was evidently owing to the unskillfulness of his doctor." He pointed out that Mrs. Gwinnett, the widow, "publicly declared me innocent and blameless and often requested of my health.

"Mrs. Gwinnett I am informed has entered a prosecution against the doctor who seems to be generally blamed for the death of her husband."

The letter obviously was written to help pave the way for a project initiated by the general's friends, which was to have him transferred to General Washington's army. For such a transfer was arranged after his recovery through the influence of his friend, George Walton, who interceded with the Continental Congress and with General Washington. McIntosh joined the main American army in time to go into the winter camp at Valley Forge and suffer the privations in the snowbound wilderness of Pennsylvania. That was certainly penance of a sort.

Button Gwinnett flashed brilliantly across the horizon of colonial Georgia to light up dramatically the mixed motives and passions of the era. He lives forever in history by that pinched, but very neat, signature on the Declaration of Independence which now is his only claim to fame, and that among a select group; namely, those who have a penchant for the collection of rare signatures. His autograph has become a collector's item. Only thirty-six known signatures of his name are extant, and, every so often, a paragraph appears in the newspapers to announce the sale of one of his autographs for a fabulous sum.

"Button Gwinnett"—there is still a charm in the strange name.

His ghost still seemed to pursue the McIntoshes. Governor Treutlen was caught up in the vortex of popular resentment that swirled now about George McIntosh. The governor ordered his arrest and removal to Philadelphia for trial on treason charges before the Continental Congress.

The McIntoshes rallied for resistance. General Lachlan McIntosh interceded and ordered his friend Habersham, now a colonel, to arrest the recruiting officer who had been detailed by the governor to take the prisoner to Philadelphia for trial. The general's orders were carried out summarily in defiance of the state authority. Governor Treutlen countered by designating a militia colonel to seize George McIntosh and take him to Philadelphia. This order, however, came too late. The younger

McIntosh already had escaped and fled to the McIntosh strong-holds in the swamps along the Georgia coast. There, on his own estate, he sat with his back to a tree and wrote letters that tell of his plight. His house had been burned, his barns and other buildings destroyed, and his Negro slaves had been confiscated and sold. It was in the midst of summer, in July, that he sat dismally among the ruins and composed his lamentations.

"They have taken possession of my estate," he wrote, "destroyed my crops, by turning their horses on to them, killed and driven off my stock, of every kind, broken open my house, barn and cellar, plundered and carried off everything of value they could find, wantonly committing every act of waste and destruction."

That was written July 3. Two days later, he wrote again:

"I am just informed one of my most trusty Negroes, on my indigo place, has been cruelly whipped, until he died in the rope, because he would not tell my hiding place."

He added, "Excuse this handwriting, for it is done on my knee, and under a tree in the woods."

This was typical of the merciless personal and factional warfare of the Revolution in Georgia. Incidents of that sort are repeated again and again in the annals of the times.

Eventually, George McIntosh was lured from his hiding place and went to Philadelphia. A committee of three was appointed to investigate the charges against him. Before the committee could make its report it was discharged by the Congress. Another committee was appointed subsequently and ultimately reported that there was insufficient evidence to hold McIntosh. He was released and went back home to the ruins of his plantation to start again.

The three other McIntosh brothers served throughout the Revolution. The youngest, John, distinguished himself at Fort Morris, the outer defense for Sunbury, and gave Georgians a heroic incident and a slogan that rang wherever they talked of the war that raged along their shores and up and down the

Savannah River. When the British sent Colonel John McIntosh a demand to surrender the fort he sent back the message:

"Come and take it."

These words were engraved on a sword which the Georgia Assembly presented to the fiery youngster of the McIntosh clan to commemorate his brave feat.

Lachlan McIntosh's military experience was the most varied and checkered of the family. He exhibited an unfortunate quirk of temperament which may have been sharpened by his feud with Button Gwinnett. After a period of service with Washington's army he was assigned to the Virginia and Pennsylvania frontier. There he was in constant difficulties with his subordinate officers and with the inhabitants.

Colonel Daniel Brodhead finally wrote in protest to General Washington that the Georgian was almost universally hated by "everybody in the department, civil and military." He was transferred back to Georgia in 1779 to serve under General Lincoln, at that time in command of the Southern Department, only to find that the antagonism still persisted. The Executive Council gave it voice. The council drafted a letter to Congress in which it said that "the people at large in the state had such a repugnance to him that the militia would not turn out under his command." The vengeance of Button Gwinnett still pursued him.

Congress, however, paid no attention to the protest and General McIntosh served with the combined American army and French fleet in the siege of Savannah in 1779, a siege which failed to regain that city from the hands of the British. Later General McIntosh was stationed at Charleston and was captured by the English when that city fell to them. This, however, did not end his service. He was exchanged, returned to the army and was stationed in Virginia when the war ended. Eventually he was restored to favor, for, two years after he went back to Savannah to live with his family, he was elected to the Continental Congress and was also designated to be a member of the

commission that settled the dispute over boundaries between
Georgia and South Carolina. He died February 20, 1806.

But this was a long time after the war that rolled up and
down the coast and back and forth through the Savannah River
valley, in only some of which McIntosh had a part, and we return now to the war in general that left its imprint upon the
entire valley and its people. Georgians discovered that they had
merely been playing at war in the futile expeditions southward
of the early days of the Revolution, though these southward
thrusts would have been good tactics had they succeeded.
For the English came from the south, as well as from the north,
in the pincer movement that developed in late 1778 to catch
Georgia in a squeeze. It poured the British wrath in a wall of
fire that blazed along the coast and far up the Savannah into
the backwoods and left a wasted and impoverished wilderness
where only the hardy could survive.

CHAPTER FOUR

WAR ROLLS UP THE SAVANNAH VALLEY

It was the Battle of Saratoga, hundreds of miles to the north,
that turned the British to the south. This staggering defeat of
English arms caused a reorientation of British strategy, which,
as now envisaged, was to conquer the south, eliminate it from
the war, isolate that section from its northern neighbors, and
then gradually to move northward. This strategy looked most

attractive on the maps British generals and ministers studied, and it was, indeed, most fruitful of result for quite a while.

The grand plan called for invasion from the south by an army operating out of East Florida under Lieutenant Colonel Mark Prevost. This army was to be joined by a fleet coming down from New York under command of Colonel Archibald Campbell. Prevost did not fare so well. His army was turned back in its first attempt, before he could reach Savannah. But in his retreat southward he wreaked destruction along the coast by burning and pillaging. A victim of this British vengeance was that symbol of revolution at Midway, the little Congregational church. It was burned to the ground.

More successful, however, was the mission of Colonel Campbell, who arrived off Savannah in December with an army of two thousand aboard his vessels. He landed them near the mouth of the river and prepared to infest Savannah. The city was defended by General Robert Howe with an army of six hundred men. Though outnumbered, he should have been able to hold the city, as it had excellent defenses in the maze of swamps surrounding it with only a few approaches available, and these were capable of being blocked off by the proper disposition and handling of his forces. But the American general left one entrance open and the British were told about this by an old Negro with the strange name of Quamino Dolly.

Of the Negro's motives, who he was, why he betrayed the American forces, we do not know. We only know his name. He was perhaps a slave with a grievance of some sort. But he acted as guide for the British army and led them through the one unguarded passage in the swamps and to the rear of the American army. The garrison was caught and completely surprised. The English chased the American soldiers clear through the city in a shameless rout. It was an easy victory. Over half the American army was killed, drowned or captured. The British lost six dead, with nine wounded.

General Howe fled across the river into South Carolina. He

washed his hands of Georgia and ordered the garrisons at Sunbury along the coast, and at Augusta, up the Savannah River, to join him in South Carolina. They refused. Gloom spread through Georgia and a resentful clamor went up for the luckless general's head. He was acquitted by a court-martial, but relieved of his command of the Southern Department. He was succeeded by General Benjamin Lincoln in one of those shifts in command in this beleaguered department which occurred so often in the next four desperate years.

One patriot leader who spoke out against General Howe in a biting letter, Christopher Gadsden of South Carolina, got back a challenge to a duel for his temerity. In that combat, Gadsden had his ear clipped by a shot from General Howe's pistol. This seemed so comic to the clever Major André, then the toast of all the Tory ladies in Philadelphia, that he dashed off a satirical poem to celebrate the event in his best drawing-room manner, one verse of which ran:

> He missed his mark but not his aim,
> The shot was well directed;
> It saved them both from hurt and shame,
> What more could be expected?

It was two years later that the handsome English officer met his own doom for his part in the attempted plot with Benedict Arnold, the disgruntled hero of Saratoga, to betray West Point to the British.

The fall of Savannah was the beginning of dark and evil days for the revolutionary cause in the south. For Colonel Mark Prevost was on the way again, moving up the coast from Florida, this time by sea, leading an army of two thousand men. On this second invasion he captured Sunbury, so successfully defended on the previous foray from the south by Colonel John McIntosh, and entered Savannah to join Colonel Campbell. This gave the English a combined operating force of four thousand men, quite a formidable army for those times. Colonel Prevost was given control of Savannah with his army, while Colonel Campbell turned his command up the Savannah River in a triumphant sweep.

Bethesda, the flourishing little town established by the Salzburgers, was the first objective. Most of the inhabitants were sympathetic to the American cause, but their pastor, Christopher F. Treibner, deserted them and the British took over the town. In spite of the pastor's loyalty to the English, the invaders converted the church, known as Jerusalem Church, into a hospital and a stable. The Salzburgers were scattered from their homes and Bethesda disappeared as a town as the war wore on. They returned eventually to the primitive wilderness that this religious sect had found with General Oglethorpe half a century earlier, when they were first settled here close to the river.

Colonel Campbell continued his advance up the river. He met some resistance from comparatively small American forces under the command of three patriots who were to distinguish themselves, among others, in the devastating guerrilla warfare that raged along the Savannah River in the next four years. These men were William and Benjamin Few and John Twiggs. But resistance was futile in the end, and by the end of January the English army marched into Augusta and took over that city.

Colonel Campbell then dispatched bands of raiders upriver from Augusta into Wilkes County, the now fairly populous and prosperous agricultural center settled by immigrants who, as we have seen, had come down the backwoods trail, from North Carolina, Virginia, and from colonies even farther north.

At the approach of the British some of the more timid inhabitants of Wilkes County scattered across the river into South Carolina. Some resolute souls, with small holdings, who had little to lose, remained behind to create a refuge for the Revolution in Georgia. There, from time to time, its fugitive leaders, including its political officials, and its harried little armies, battered but indomitable, would retire for a breathing spell, but always to go back to the fight. Here, out of hardship and suffering, was re-kindled the revolutionary ardor that finally won the day and drove the British from the river valley.

Along the Savannah the Revolution assumed aspects of class warfare. This derived from the still pioneer nature of the river valley, outside of Augusta, and from the character of the people who had settled there. There was, among them, a fundamental strain of discontent. They had come here, most of them, from more civilized communities to the north, and had left those more highly civilized centers because they were irked by, and restless under the restraints of, a settled and sedate existence —its rigid government with restrictions on the individual, or its established church, which looked critically at religious dissenters, or its social organization, which pivoted about a few leading families that dominated by virtue of wealth or blood. They were looking for more liberty, some of them for more license, for there were among them the reckless fringe avid for adventure and not too careful about the conventions. England, for long, had represented established authority, and they were easily enlisted in the fight to overthrow this symbol of authority. Their appetites for revolution were whetted because they saw it was their betters, socially and financially, who were inclined to stand by the status quo of established English authority. There were some of these loyalists even in this frontier community, and there were more of them across the river in upper South Carolina. Upcountry South Carolina, in contrast generally to up-country Georgia along the river, was basically loyal to England.

This was because of the kind of people who had settled there and their backgrounds. Many of the early settlers in upper South Carolina were Germans who had pushed into the back country and set up the towns of Orangeburg, named for William of Orange, and Saxe-Gotha. A few years before the Revolution, in 1764, these Germans were joined by others. This emigration was assisted officially by the English government, so that there was a friendly and sympathetic attitude toward England.

These people had none of the feeling for individual liberty that was instinctive with colonists of English derivation. There was, among them, no tradition akin to that inherent among Englishmen stemming from the struggle, through the centuries, for the right to have a voice in their own affairs, to be represented in parliamentary bodies that assessed taxes, no battles over freedom of worship, of assembly, of press and speech. Here in upper South Carolina these Germanic refugees had more freedom than they ever had enjoyed in their homeland, so they could have no grievance on this score.

They had little commerce, and the issue over freedom of navigation for ships that concerned the coastal settlements had, of course, no meaning for them. They used no tea, so that the controversy over the tax on tea likewise meant nothing to them. Furthermore, they felt no impelling desire to join coastal South Carolina in the attempt to get representation in the British Parliament in London as they, themselves, were not permitted by the South Carolinians to have representation in the colonial assembly at Charleston. They had tried to get such representation but, when they had proposed to go down to the lower parishes to vote, they had been denounced as rioters and the Charleston militia had been turned out ready to march upon them.

In addition to the Germans in the forks of the Saluda and Broad Rivers, there were also Scotch-Irish Presbyterians who had come down the back trails from the northern colonies and settled. They, too, were denied representation in the colonial assembly, and had few representatives in the Provincial Congress. They had few contacts with the coastal settlements and had not been long enough in this region for any assimilation into the colony or to have any real identity with it. The colonial government was too far removed and too weak to protect them and, as a consequence, they had been compelled to set up their own government of "regulators" to protect them from roving bands of robbers who infested this area. It was a long time before they could get the colonial government to set up courts, and when this finally was done the courts turned out to be debating societies devoted to political harangues to stir up opposition to an English king, who seemed a very long way off, rather than to keep order and punish criminals. Arguments about tea and ships were pure abstractions to them, for they had no use for either. Altogether, the quarrel with England that so agitated the lowland folks seemed to be only a struggle for political power.

So this upriver region in South Carolina was a compatible and comfortable refuge for the timid and hesitant and well-to-do on the other side of the river in Georgia.

But those who had not got along in the world, the underprivileged, who had nothing to lose, or those wild and untrammeled beings who loved fighting for fighting's sake, and adventure for adventure's sake, or who just rebelled naturally at any sort of authority—these welcomed revolution, and it was they who stayed behind to fight the British armies, to spend their lives hiding in the wilderness they knew so well, and emerging to fight again.

All this contributed to the cruelties and barbarities that characterized the war along the Savannah, the bloody vengeance, the cold-blooded murder, which made the river valley and the back country literally a shambles, especially in the last two years of the Revolution. Nowhere in America perhaps did the Revolution reach such a low and inhuman level.

There were here, even in these early days, some of the hopeless and shiftless class known as "poor whites." They lived on the edges of pioneer civilization, as they did later in this section at the outer gates of the cotton kingdom, uncouth, illiterate, virtual savages. Often they were inbred and amoral. Some had drifted in from the north, from Virginia and North Carolina, where William Byrd, the Virginian, had first discovered them in his travels into the interior from Tidewater Virginia, and described them for us, portraying for literature the "poor white" of fact, including those who were addicted to chewing clay, and known as "clay eaters." Some had come up the river from Savannah, the less favored outcasts from Oglethorpe's utopia. They lived in filth and squalor, in hovels in the pine barrens which stretched away from the river above Savannah toward Augusta, an infertile and inhospitable land, and in the forests farther up the river. They grew a few scraggly crops and hunted in the woods and fished in the streams. They reproduced their own destitute and listless progeny, generation after generation. They were, for the most part, a mean and low order of human being, but among them there were always a few bright spirits with a strain of crude humor and wilderness philosophy to spice up the breed and lighten their barren lot, and occasionally they were sketched by the wandering traveler or novelist. They were ingrown, suspicious, and jealous, and from this embittered folk came some of the brutalities of the Revolution along the Savannah. Life was cheap among them, and they murdered with a certain cool and unfeeling nonchalance. They were not a brave people, but a sneaky and crafty crew.

Though the Revolution in Georgia had many aspects of a class war, as has been said, it was not by any means altogether that. There were many deviations from class patterns. For about Savannah and Charleston and along the Georgia coast the Revolution attracted leading spirits in the community, as we have seen. Some took the step from inherited conviction, like the Puritans of Midway, and certain outstanding families who had lived so long in South Carolina that they had established an aristocracy of their own, by right of self-bestowal rather than by blood and lineage. Others revolted because of an innate and shrewd instinct at gambling with fortune, people who saw that this was the means to power and self-aggrandizement, the way for a chance to improve their positions, an opportunity not in any sense to be deplored. Still others espoused the new order because of mercantile, English restrictions on their trade and business, but this was not so considerable a factor in Georgia as elsewhere.

Yet the upper classes, as they may be so designated for lack of a better, hard and fast definition, were severed and split, some within families, as we have seen. Generally the less favored were the more united. These, as a matter of course, formed the basic ground for the implanting of revolutionary doctrine. They became its fighters in the ranks. Some of them, it must be admitted, deserted, often from hardship and weariness, and others changed sides, while some recanted and returned to the loyalist fold. Others rose above the ranks, becoming leaders with opportunity.

Sir James Wright, Georgia's British governor, saw the Revolution in terms of a class war from his uncertain and uneasy and quivering seat of authority at Savannah. The city was shaken by the turbulent masses as the plain people were fired by the propaganda of self-appointed champions.

"The communities in the parishes were a passel of the lowest people, chiefly carpenters, shoe-makers and blacksmiths," he wrote. "It is really terrible that such people should be suffered to overthrow the civil government and most arbitrarily sport with other men's lives, liberties and property."

This was distinctly the class viewpoint of an empire satrap nettled by the changing order.

One of the well-favored ladies of Savannah, Elizabeth Lichtenstein Johnson, put it more snobbishly when she wrote in a letter to a friend that everywhere, at the approach of revolution, "the scum rose to the top."

This "scum" foamed out of the woods along the Savannah to harry the red-coated armies of British authority.

Sir James had the confidence of his class that the rabble could be put down by a little show of panoplied force from regulars of the British army. When Savannah was captured he returned to that city and resumed his role as royal governor, issuing orders for confiscation of the property of those who had taken the field against the crown and Parliament, holding out promises to those who would return to the fold. He got together a legislative assembly of sorts to give the semblance of re-established government; but his sphere of control was narrow and confined, going little beyond the city of Savannah. He directed a puppet show in the midst of chaos.

CHAPTER FIVE

KITH FOUGHT KIN FOR BLOOD

Guerrilla warfare, bloody and without quarter from 1779 on, raged along the Savannah above Augusta. The British gathered armies of Tories in upper South Carolina to strike at the ragged and ill-equipped Americans who set up headquarters in Wilkes County and sent out bands that roved the country, crossing and recrossing the Savannah, sniping at isolated British outposts. This conflict engendered all the hatred of a family feud, for that is exactly the character it assumed.

One American detachment laid siege to Fort Carr on the upper river, which had been seized by the British. This siege was almost at the point of success, when the Americans investing the fort got word that a Tory army of eight hundred men under command of Colonel Boyd was heading toward the Savannah from Ninety Six, South Carolina. The siege was lifted and the Americans retreated toward the Savannah, sounding the alarm through the countryside.

They crossed the river near Fort Charlotte, which was on the Carolina side just below the junction of the Broad and Savannah Rivers. Wilkes County and the frontier responded to the call under the direction of General Elijah Clarke, a rugged, tough,

and able leader, and John Twiggs and John Dooly. Colonel Andrew Pickens hurried from across the river in South Carolina
with a complement of South Carolina troops to join the Georgians in a stand against the British.

Colonel Boyd, the British commander, selected a crossing
for his redcoats which was guarded by a blockhouse, manned by
an American lieutenant and eight privates. This "fort" mounted
two swivel guns that swept the river. He asked for a quiet passage. The Americans refused. So he moved his army five miles
upstream and, under considerable difficulty, finally got his men
and equipment to the Georgia side of the river. Rafts were constructed hastily to transport the men and baggage, and the
horses swam the stream. This crossing was contested by a small
force of Americans on the Georgia side who poured a stream of
fire into the oncoming British army. But the colonials operated
under handicaps, because of the tall canes in the marshes along
their side of the river. Colonel Boyd, however, lost about a
hundred men in the crossing, either killed or drowned.

Captain Anderson, commanding the American force that
had attempted to prevent the British passage of the river, was
now joined by other American forces which had been assem-
bling, and they set out in pursuit of the Tory army as it headed
down the river on the Georgia side. Colonel Boyd halted his
loyalists eventually at a farm on the north side of Kettle Creek
where that stream enters the Savannah. The horses were turned
out to forage among the weeds of the swamp, and the men busied
themselves about food. They had been on short rations for several days. They rounded up some cattle and slaughtered them,
and gathered corn and began to parch it.

In such disorder they were surprised by the American army.
They were quickly rallied, however, and had the advantage of
position, for the Americans had to cross the swamp to get at
them. The American advance was stubbornly contested and dead
bodies were strewn through the muck of the swamp. Colonel
Boyd was mortally wounded. A horse was shot out from under

General Elijah Clarke. But the Americans would not be denied. After several hours they completely routed the Tory forces. Colonel Boyd died the next morning, and his troops, discouraged by the loss of their leader, scattered through the forests. Only about 200 of them were collected afterward by Colonel Moore and led in retreat back to Augusta. Some of the Tory fugitives sought refuge among the Creek Indians, some among the Cherokees, while others took flight southward clear across Georgia and ultimately reached Florida. Some returned to their homes in South Carolina and sought mercy from the patriots in their communities, promising to be loyal thereafter to the colonies. During this contest along the Savannah, as elsewhere in the country then, there were many men who changed sides with the vacillating fortunes of war.

Kettle Creek—February 14, 1779—was a great victory, and it caused rejoicing throughout the upper river valley. It alarmed the British so that Colonel Campbell gave up Augusta and moved his army southward again. But the sudden revival of the patriot cause along the river was short-lived.

This was so, despite elaborate preparations in another quarter that seemed most promising. General Benjamin Lincoln, commander of the Southern Department, had taken up quarters at Purysburg along the river between Savannah and Augusta on the South Carolina side, where there had once been a settlement of Swiss and Germans. They, however, had been compelled to move away because of malaria. General Lincoln was gathering an army which, with the various units arranged here and there, would amass for him a force of 8,000 men. With this he planned to sweep the British from the valley and then recover Savannah. Hopes were high for his success, for the British armies in Georgia, along the river and in the port, numbered only 4,000 men.

But the British outmaneuvered the colonials. Colonel Mark Prevost acted quickly to stop this planned concentration of American forces under General Lincoln. He surprised one of the larger units headed toward Purysburg, an army of 2,300 under

General John Ashe. This force was encamped along Brier Creek, where that stream joins the Savannah. Its right wing was deployed along Brier Creek, while its left lay along the edge of the swamps bordering the Savannah. Seldom has an army been so swiftly annihilated. The British struck the center of the American lines, which crumpled in five minutes and broke away in disorder. The men fled helter-skelter through the encompassing forests. Quickly Prevost turned his attack on the right wing lying along Brier Creek, and that too was scattered almost as quickly. Only the left wing drawn up along the edge of the river swamps put up resistance. This wing, under command of Colonel Samuel Elbert, fought back furiously, refusing to give ground, so that Prevost was forced to bring up his reserves. Nearly every soldier in Elbert's command was either killed, wounded, or captured in the bloody battle in the swamps. Elbert's stand was futile, for he stood alone. The rest of the Americans thrashed through the swamps wildly, trying to escape the British fury, and those who could swim jumped into the river to get away. Some reached the Carolina side safely. But many others were drowned.

General William Moultrie, who was serving under General Lincoln, neatly summed up this catastrophe:

"We never could ascertain the number that were lost in this unfortunate affair, as many of them did not stop anywhere until they got to their own homes in North Carolina."

It was, he said, "nothing less than a total rout."

In Moultrie's opinion this disastrous defeat prolonged the war for a year, for if Ashe's army could have joined General Lincoln the total forces available would have been sufficient to drive the British out of Georgia. This reverse had another result. It cooled the ardor of numerous volunteers who were on their way to join General Lincoln. Many of them now turned about and returned to their homes.

Deep gloom settled upon the Savannah River valley. Georgia appeared lost to the colonial cause. The British strategy of cutting off the south seemed to be working out most successfully.

It would take a master stroke to shake their grip and free the state. Such was not long in being planned.

It was General Lincoln's idea. A French fleet under Count d'Estaing, which was operating with great success against the British in the Caribbean, offered the opportunity. The French admiral had brought his fleet to America with the object of bottling up the British fleet in the Delaware River, but the British had escaped and the count had turned south with his vessels to cripple the British in the Caribbean area. General Lincoln conceived a combined sea and land assault to recover Savannah. Count d'Estaing, exultant over his easy victories in the southern sea, was induced to come to Savannah to play his part in what appeared to be another chance to add to his triumphs.

He arrived with his fleet off Savannah before General Lincoln had moved up his army. Cleverly, when the French admiral demanded surrender of the port, the British delayed their reply long enough to get reinforcements from South Carolina. Even with those, however, the British defenders were heavily outnumbered by the combined French and American forces. These eventually enveloped the city, by land and by sea, when General Lincoln brought up his troops. The American and French numerical advantage was almost three to one—6,500 against 2,500. For three weeks the allies sat about the city in a ring of siege without result. Then they joined in a co-ordinated assault which turned out, however, sadly unsuccessful. Not only were the allied losses heavy—1,000 American and French dead and wounded, as compared with 150 British casualities, but the psychological blow of defeat was costly. D'Estaing withdrew his fleet and General Lincoln hurried his badly beaten army back into South Carolina. Georgia was now given up for lost, and General Lincoln's purpose was to hold South Carolina, if possible.

This also proved a luckless enterprise, for in six months the British captured Charleston and took General Lincoln a prisoner of war. The storming of Savannah had cost the American cause the loss of General Casimir Pulaski, the gallant Pole, who was killed in the assault. It also left behind a treasured legend in the death of Sergeant William Jasper, who had distinguished himself by exceptional bravery during the fighting about Savannah, where he fell mortally wounded.

Now the valley of the Savannah was, in truth, sown with dragon's teeth. With the disappearance of organized armies, which could always keep some semblance of order in the areas they controlled, the valley returned literally to brute nature and human lawlessness, with barbaric warfare between Tory and patriot neighbors. Bands of bandits and thieves roved the desolate and devastated countryside, killing hapless inhabitants still left on the farms, stealing anything and everything. These bands posed as either Tories or patriots, depending upon the convenience of the particular situation in which they found themselves. Starvation and privation bred disease and a scourge of smallpox spread through the land, laying low for a time one of the still valiant spirits, Elijah Clarke. The homeless government of the state took refuge in the depths of Wilkes County, and Wilkes County *was* Georgia for all practical purposes. With the fall of Charleston the British moved back into Augusta again, once more giving them control of the upper valley. This they were able to do through the easy betrayal of that city by its American commander, Andrew Williamson, whose abrupt change of sides was nothing unusual in those days. For it did seem now, indeed, that the American cause was a lost cause, and what Tom Paine not so long before had called "sunshine patriots" were alert to get on what looked liked the sunny side.

Augusta came into the hands of the now notorious Colonel Thomas Brown, one of those figures who still bear a stigma in the tradition of revolutionary Georgia. The gruesome tales of the guerrilla warfare along the Savannah undoubtedly were exaggerated to some degree by the hatreds nurtured in this conflict of brother against brother and family against family. The brutalities attributed to the turncoats are almost beyond belief.

Brown was the villain in many of them. When war first broke out he was outspoken for the English and against talk of independence. He was well known in Augusta, for it was there in late June, 1775, that he had the experience that transformed him into so cruel and implacable a foe of the colonials. What happened and how he was regarded in his time may perhaps best be seen by quoting from an article in the *Georgia Gazette,* as follows:

This day a respectable body of the Sons of Liberty marched from this place [Augusta] to New Richmond, in South Carolina, in order to pay a visit to Thomas Brown and William Thompson, esqs., for their having publicly and otherwise expressed themselves enemies to the measures adopted for the support of American liberty, and signing an association to that effect, besides their using their utmost endeavors to inflame the minds of the people, and to persuade them to associate and be of their opinion. But upon their arrival they found the said Thompson, like a traitor, had run away; and the said Thomas Brown, being requested in civil terms to come to Augusta to try to clear himself of such accusations, daringly repeated that he was not, nor would he be answerable to them, or to any of them, for his conduct; whereupon they politely escorted him into Augusta, where they presented him with a genteel and fashionable suit of tar and feathers, and afterwards had him exhibited in a cart from the head of Augusta to Mr. Weatherford's, where out of humanity they had him taken care of for that night; and on the next morning he, the said Thomas Brown, having publicly declared upon his honor, and consented voluntarily to swear that he repented for his past conduct, and that he would, for the future, at the hazard of life and fortune, protect and support the rights and liberties of America, and saying that the said Thompson had misled him, and that therefore he would use his utmost endeavors to have his name taken from the association he had signed aforesaid; and further, that he would do all in his power to discountenance the proceedings of a set of men in the Ninety-Sixth District of South Carolina, called Fletcher's Party; and upon which, the said Brown was then discharged, and complimented with a horse and chair to ride home. But the said Thomas Brown, that time having publicly forfeited his honor and violated his oath voluntarily taken as aforesaid, is therefore not to be considered for the future in the light of a gentleman, and they, the said Thomas Brown and William Thompson are hereby published as persons inimical to the rights and liberties of America; and it is hoped all good men will treat them accordingly.

N.P. The said Thomas Brown is now a little remarkable; he wears his hair very short, and a handkerchief tied around his head, in order that his intelligence by the cold weather may not be affected.

Throughout that newspaper account exudes the grisly passion of the day. It is not hard to understand why the young man was embittered by such treatment for his opinions. He went over wholeheartedly to the royalists. He decamped to Florida and there got a commission as colonel of the Florida Rangers, an outfit composed of loyalists who had fled from the Carolinas and Georgia. Thereafter he became a plague to the Americans. In local legend he was one of the minor Benedict Arnolds of the Revolution in the south. Now, in command at Augusta, he took his revenge for the shame he had endured there a few years before. He rounded up patriots, had their property confiscated, and others executed. Like a scourge his troops were turned loose upon the whole surrounding countryside, and so alarming were their depredations that Elijah Clarke gathered together some four hundred women and children from Wilkes County and hurried them away for refuge in the mountains of eastern Tennessee.

There was a general exodus, too, of fighting men from Wilkes County, a strategical retreat to bide their time for a better day. They traveled about in small bands, harrying the Tories where they could. Clarke came back home in a few months, and gradually others returned. With a reassembled force he prepared for an invasion of the area held by the British. His first objective was Augusta. He attacked that city and it seemed to be in his grasp when reinforcements for the British garrison arrived suddenly and unexpectedly from South Carolina. The fighting had been desperate and bloody, fiendishly hand to hand. Brown, besieged in what was known as "the White House," was wounded in both legs and was carried about by two of his men to direct the fighting. Some of the Americans, thinking Augusta was safely in their hands, left the city on expeditions about the countryside, some to look up old friends, others to take away plunder. At this strategic moment, with the American forces in confusion and disarray, the British reinforcements arrived from Ninety Six and retook the city. Clarke disconsolately saw the victory vanish before his eyes.

Left behind were a number of American dead and wounded and twenty-eight prisoners. Brown had thirteen of the wounded hanged from rafters at the "White House," choosing this place of execution, so the story goes, in order that he might witness the death of the men from the bed where he lay wounded. Their bodies were handed over to Indian allies, who scalped them, mangled them, and pitched them into the Savannah River.

That abortive attempt to capture Augusta was in the autumn of 1781. Several months later, in the next year, Augusta finally fell to the Americans. Clarke and his Georgians were joined by an American army that was dispatched to Georgia under command of Light-Horse Harry Lee and Andrew Pickens. General Lee directed the successful strategy that eventually pinned the British defenders under Colonel Brown in Fort Cornwallis. To beat this last loyalist stronghold into surrender, Lee had a tower built on which he mounted guns to pour fire effectively into the fort.

Brown and another Tory scourge of the Revolution along the Savannah, Colonel Grierson, whose name likewise was a byword, were taken prisoner. Both were confined in the fort. Grierson was murdered by someone who dashed up to the fort on a horse, slipped into the room where he was being held, shot him, and then escaped. Though the murderer obviously was known, he was never identified officially. Tradition credits this act of vengeance to one Samuel Alexander, whose aged father had been treated cruelly by Grierson.

General Pickens, who reported this "very disagreeable and melancholy affair" to General Nathanael Greene, now commander of the Southern Department, took no chance with his other captives. Colonel Brown and the other prisoners were spirited away across the river, because, as Pickens reported to Greene, "the people were so much exasperated about some individuals." Later Brown was escorted under careful guard by the road along the Savannah River. He traveled through a veritable gantlet of insults. These reached a bitter climax when a grieving and desperate mother, a Mrs. McKay, was admitted to the presence of the Tory commander at Silver Bluff. Her seventeen-year-old boy, Rannel, had been hanged by Colonel Brown's men some time before, along with five other American prisoners. She poured her venom upon the Tory now, recalling with angry tears how, when she had learned that her son had been captured, she had followed Brown's army from camping place to camping place and entreated for his life. One reason that Brown had been guarded so carefully after he was taken prisoner was that a younger brother of McKay had sworn to kill him.

But the loyalist leader escaped any such fate. Three years after the end of the Revolution, in 1786, he wrote from Nassau a long letter in defense of his military conduct in Georgia and South Carolina, this in reply to a critic. Later he went to London to live and was convicted there in 1812 of what is termed by a local South Carolina historian as "a grand forgery upon the government," and, the historian concludes, "ended his days in disgrace and ignominy."

To offset the vileness and iniquity of Tory villains, the people raised up their own local heroes, and here, too, perchance, there was some pardonable exaggeration. Fancy intertwines so with fact that we shall never know the real truth. But the real truth of details matters little when the fate of nations is at stake. Raw and violent colors were used broadly in painting both villains and heroes, and the shedding of blood was the measure of prowess, held cruel and inhuman on one side, but glorious and patriotic on the other.

Every school child in Georgia learns the story of rawboned Nancy Hart, the local Boadicea and Judith of Bethulia combined, a cross-eyed hoyden, tall, angular, strong-limbed and muscular, her face pockmarked with smallpox, who could shoot and swear like a man and is, in all respects, the typical Spartan wife and mother of the time and place. She is perhaps not altogether a caricature, for those were hard times when only the rugged could survive. Not for Nancy Hart the safe refuge away in the mountains when the enemy was on the loose. She refused to join the women and children of the Broad River settlement who left the community of Fishdown Ford in Elbert County under the protective guardianship of Elijah Clarke. No, she would not run away and leave the primitive home that she and her husband, a captain of the local guerrillas, had established in the wilderness. She remained behind to become the heroine of the fireside for years to come.

Nancy had her date with history one morning with the sudden arrival of a squad of Tories at the front door of her rude cabin. Only her children were with her. The captain had left the house, though she knew he was still in the neighborhood. The enemy wanted breakfast. Cheerfully Nancy invited them into the cabin, and there on the walls, in the antlers of a number of deer, her guests saw the trophies of the hunting prowess of her and her husband. She had a reputation as a good cook, and her Tory visitors perhaps had heard this. She could prepare pumpkins in seven ways, so the legend goes, one for every day in the week. She now set out some pumpkin pie, a mess of venison, hoecake, and fresh honeycomb. To signify her comradery, she picked up a jug of corn liquor that one of the Tories had as part of his equipment, threw back her head and took a healthy swig, and wiped off her mouth with her sleeve in a jovial gesture, all prefaced by her outburst:

"I'll take a swig with you, if it kills every cow in the land."

Her geniality was disarming. The Tories had stacked their guns in a corner of the room as they prepared to enjoy a hearty breakfast. When they were all seated, she stepped quietly over to a corner, snatched down an old fowling piece from the wall and, pointing it at her guests, delivered her ultimatum: she would blow out the brains of the first man who made a move to get up or to taste her food.

She had, meanwhile, sent off one of her children to hunt up her husband and bring back help for her private little war in the wilderness. Back of her, at her command, her oldest daughter, Sukey, took her place, ready with another gun, loaded for business, to hand her mother if the going got tough. She was a menacing figure, truly, but one of the Tories did not take her seriously. He rose and started toward her. With a vengeful oath she pulled the trigger. The cabin shook with the explosion. He fell dead at her feet, shot through the chest at close range. Just then, in the nick of time, her husband arrived with help and the Tories were made prisoner.

So Nancy Hart shot her way into history that morning.

Another figure of local fame as a terrifier of Tories was Robert Sallette. He roved around doing ill deeds against the enemy. The story connected with him that comes down to us is about a wealthy Tory who had offered a hundred dollars for the head of this American avenger. Sallette, hearing of the reward, picked a pumpkin, put it into a sack, called upon the Tory, and announced that the sack contained the head of Sallette, and claimed the reward. He demanded the money before he would open his bag. When the Tory handed him the money, Sallette jerked off his hat and pointing to his head, cried out:

"Here is Sallette's head."

Frightened, the Tory started to run. Sallette raised his gun and brought him down.

Bloody tales of bloody days.

CHAPTER SIX

LAST OF ALL CAME "MAD ANTHONY" WAYNE

Into this blighted land there came, last of all, to rescue the Savannah valley from the enemy, the dashing "Mad Anthony" Wayne, the hero of Stony Point, and a veteran campaigner with George Washington. He didn't like the assignment much when it was given him by General Washington, and he liked it even less when he arrived on the scene. After some experience in the swamps around Bethesda, the point which the Georgians had reached in their progress toward Savannah, only twenty-five miles from that city, he made the observation:

"I find this country a desert."

He did not exaggerate much.

General Wayne came fresh from Yorktown, where, much to his chagrin, he had been unable to participate in his usual vigorous manner because of a wound in his thigh. It had been inflicted by an American sentry who had shot the famous military figure when he pranced up on his horse in his usual theatrical way and failed to identify himself properly. After his wound had healed, he had asked Washington for a furlough for a few weeks, but the general told him that he already had enjoyed more leaves than any of his other commanders. He was ordered to join General Nathanael Greene, who had been detached from Washington's army only a few days before to go south and clean the British out of that region.

This was familiar territory, of course, for General Greene. It had been he who had chased Cornwallis northward and into the trap that Washington had laid at Yorktown in conjunction with the French fleet under de Grasse. But in the deep south, Yorktown was only a battle far away. The British still clung to Charleston and Savannah, hanging on to the edge of the continent in the southeast, and that section still was in a state of war.

Riding alone, Anthony Wayne traveled southward, about two days behind Greene's army. He did not hurry. In Virginia he stopped here and there to visit at the plantations of friends and occasionally he stayed overnight at taverns which, as he got farther south, became more and more primitive. The civilized Pennsylvanian, who liked his creature comforts, got into a more and more morose frame of mind with the cramped quarters in the tiny inns where everybody slept in the common room, family, guests and all, and the ham and eggs at breakfast were poorly cooked and unpalatable. He was glad when he finally joined the army in South Carolina.

He pleaded with Greene to assign him some of his Pennsylvania troops for the campaign in Georgia, but Greene was adamant against it. He needed experienced soldiers with him for the conquest of Charleston. Georgia was not so important. Wayne was given five hundred assorted veterans and in due time crossed the Savannah from South Carolina into Georgia. He found relatives in Georgia who were proud of so great a kinsman. But this adulation was not much relief for the situation he found in Georgia about which he complained in letters to General Greene and friends back home in Pennsylvania. Only a handful of troops was available. The Georgia militia could furnish only five hundred raw infantry. The state government was in confusion, practically no government at all. Food and supplies were lacking. He sent into South Carolina for rice and beef for his soldiers and for the nearly starved civilian population. To get additional recruits he had placards smuggled into Savannah and posted at prominent places offering two hundred acres of land, a cow and two hogs to any British or Hessian troops who would desert and join him. He got less than a hundred soldiers by that device.

But, worst of all for the Wayne temperament, was the state of idleness to which he was consigned. Greene had ordered him to remain at Bethesda and not to move closer to Savannah for the time being. His assignment was to keep a barrier between Savannah and the few British detachments and Tories still at loose in the upcountry, so that Savannah could not be relieved. The Bethesda encampment became intolerable. Many of his men went down with fever bred by the swamps. Finally, in desperation, he did disobey orders to the extent of moving to higher ground at Sharon, only five miles from Savannah. As was his nature, he became gloomy and irritable with the enforced idleness and, having no fair ladies near to distract him, he took to drinking. That did not improve his temper or his health.

From time to time, however, there were occasional distractions of a military sort. Only a few days after he had settled himself at Bethesda, the British made a foray out of Savannah, but he skillfully deployed his troops in such a manner that his little army looked much larger than it was and the British returned without giving battle. There were other adventures. Once, by a ruse, he captured a number of Indians and some sorely needed supplies. Learning that a sizable pack train in charge of twenty-six Indians and six white traders was headed toward Savannah to be paid off with gifts of various sorts for their services, he sent some South Carolina dragoons to meet the caravan on its way home from Savannah to the Altamaha River to the south. The uniforms of the dragoons were red, and Wayne's theory was that the Indians would think they were British troops. The trick worked. The Indians were lured into an ambush by the troops they mistook for friendly British, made prisoner, and their ninety-three pack animals and the goods and supplies were confiscated for use of the American army.

The trick was tried again with the Choctaws. But it did not work this time. The Indians discovered the deception after a number of them had assembled, one by one, in the American camp on the promise of presents. All of them escaped.

On one occasion General Wayne and his little army barely escaped extermination in a surprise night attack by some three hundred Creeks led by Guristersijo, who had been dispatched on this mission by Alexander McGillivray, the great half-breed Creek leader in Alabama who so detested the Americans.

General Wayne and his command, so many of whom were sick, had relaxed their vigilance somewhat. They were completely unaware of Indian spies who hovered unnoticed in the tall grass about the camp, watching for an opportunity. These lookouts noted that the camp was poorly guarded, and one night, when they discovered that the Americans had only one sentry at their rear and only a handful of guards in their front toward Savannah, Guristersijo prepared his coup. Advancing quietly in the dead of night from the rear, the Creeks killed the lone sentry there and, with wild war whoops, swarmed toward the camp. Their fiendish outcries were their undoing. For the main camp was farther than they had estimated and the Americans were aroused in time. Wayne was one of the first out of his tent and he burst forth ready for business, his pistol in one hand, his sword in the other. Quick witted as always under stress, he sized up the situation in a flash and began to shout orders. He rallied his command from its initial confusion and finally the attack was repelled. The general almost lost his life. He had mounted his horse to better direct the counterattack and Guristersijo, lying on the ground, sent a bullet into the animal. The horse fell under the American commander. But he got himself clear without injury.

Wayne found out afterward that the Indian chieftain, his midnight assailant, was a familiar figure connected with his own venture in statecraft as a member of the Pennsylvania Assembly ten years before. At that time Wayne had warned the legislature that the British were lining up allies for themselves among the Indians and suggested that the Pennsylvania colony, for its own defense, should do likewise. He foresaw the probability of an eventual conflict with the English, though that was four years before war broke out. His advice was to deal with a rising young Indian leader in Pennsylvania of that time in making the alliance, Emisto-Siguo he was called then, Guristersijo, as he came to be known later. The Indian had left Pennsylvania and gone to the south, where the talents for leadership that the then legislator in Pennsylvania had sensed were recognized also by Alexander McGillivray, and the half-breed had used the young Indian in his own plans.

The surprise night attack, which could have been so disastrous, but which had turned out otherwise, was the last battle of the Revolution for the tempestuous and temperamental American general. It had occurred on the night of June 23, 1782. Nineteen days later, on July 12, the Americans marched down the streets of Savannah with General James Jackson at their head. This intrepid and tireless Georgia fighter, who had been so faithful through all the vicissitudes of the war along the Savannah, was assigned by Wayne the honor of taking over the city formally when the British finally evacuated on orders of Sir Guy Carleton, who had succeeded General Clinton as commander in chief of the British forces in America.

General Wayne found a charm in the physical aspect of Savannah, which he now saw for the first time, chiefly because its broad streets and its friendly atmosphere reminded him of Philadelphia. When he inspected the city formally he found it pockmarked here and there by the seven years of war. Damage from British cannon balls, at the time of the city's capture, still had not been repaired. Churches and public buildings showed signs of their wartime use as hospitals. Many of the fine private homes had been looted. When Wayne arrived in the city there was a scourge of smallpox. The many Negro slaves who had been left behind by the British preferred to remain idle, rather than work, and this was among the administrative problems that confronted him.

Despite his delight with the city, the general was anxious to complete his Georgia assignment, and, if possible, to get back to Philadelphia. But there were necessary delays. The ships bearing the British troops from Savannah still hovered about the harbor and he could not leave until they had cleared out for home. For it was still feared that if the American army withdrew the British might return. Formal peace had not yet been signed and was not, as a matter of fact, for many months. Colonel Thomas Brown, who had been exchanged and again had a British command, also was still a threat. Though he had announced his intention to retire to St. Augustine, he suddenly turned up near Savannah with a motley army of Tories and Indians. But, when General Wayne left Savannah with an army to confront him, he withdrew. Finally, on August 6, the American troops were permitted to leave the city. But, meanwhile, two events occurred which changed the general's personal plans and identified him, for a much longer period than he had expected, with the state where he had ended his Revolutionary War career.

One was an act of the Georgia legislature. For his services in lifting the British yoke finally from the state, the legislature voted him two estates along the Savannah—Richmond, twelve miles above the city and overlooking the river, and additional acreage along the river which went under the name of Kew, and also a plantation and large cowpens in southern Georgia.

The other event was one familiar through Wayne's life—a pretty girl, Mary Maxwell by name, of a prominent Georgia family. She was much younger than the general and was attracted to him as one of her years is to a reigning hero. But she had also another purpose. This was to get her nineteen-year-old brother removed from the rolls as a proscribed Tory by Georgia law, which was very broad in its terms. Wayne made promises about her brother, though he did little about it and never accomplished anything.

But, on a furlough which he took for himself after his Savannah military tour of duty, he saw much of Mary Maxwell, another of the many women to whom he paid court through the years while his wife, Polly, remained on the family estate at Waynesborough, Pennsylvania, in neglect except for an occasional cold and formal letter. He was, in truth, a ladies' man.

During this time, too, he went out often to inspect his estates along the river. They were run down and dilapidated and would take much money and much work to rehabilitate to their former productivity as rice plantations. Typical of the Wayne ego and self-centeredness, he was envious because Georgia had granted a much handsomer estate, the famous Mulberry Grove, also along the Savannah, to his superior, General Nathanael Greene, and Greene had not even served in Georgia as he had. But the disgruntled Wayne found consolation in the fact that he would have as neighbors two people of whom he was very fond, the general and his much younger and very vivacious wife, Catherine Greene, who was known in the service as "Cathy." The two plantations were near each other.

But, before he took up life in Georgia, there was an interlude back in his home haunts in Pennsylvania and, as far as his friends there knew, Pennsylvania rather than Georgia was to be his home. He was, as a matter of fact, back and forth for several years.

Pennsylvania prepared a grand welcome for the returning hero. But nature played him a nasty trick. He was taken ill on the boat from Savannah and was still abed when the boat docked at Philadelphia and had to be lifted off, not at all his gallant self, so that his return was not all that he had envisaged it. He soon recovered, however, and began again the merry life of fashion with his cronies, male and female, the latter including an old flame, Mary Vining, who was a lively figure at the frequent parties. Cathy Greene was there, too, on a visit, so he was again flatteringly surrounded by charming women. Polly remained as usual at Waynesborough, though his daughter, Margaretta, was with him in Philadelphia and joined the round of festivities. Official honors came, one after another, to satisfy his ego. He was presented with a special medal in commemoration of Stony Point by Congress; he was elected to the Board of Censors of the state, a sort of Supreme Court that reviewed acts of the legislature every seven years; he was also elected to the state Assembly, where he joined the conservative faction. His one pet project, repeal of the law that barred theatrical productions in Pennsylvania, failed, and so after a couple of years he turned to the south again. His trouble, as always, was finance. Finally, however, he got some money together through loans, piling up debts again, bought himself some slaves, and prepared for the life of a planter.

On the business side of this venture he was a miserable failure, but his plantations formed a background for social life to which he devoted much of his time. And this at least was a success. He was often at the Greenes' and because the general, a sober Quaker, took his farm work seriously and had little time or aptitude for society, Wayne became a constant attendant upon Cathy, squiring her around. This provoked gossip. Somebody finally went to the master of Mulberry Grove about the friendship of his wife and the dashing neighbor. Greene found no reason to be disturbed. The explanations of his wife and his friend satisfied him. Cathy, however, had perhaps a woman's triumph in the fact that she had weaned the gay cavalier away from Mary Maxwell, who soon dropped into the background, out of sight and out of mind, to join the discarded women along the path of the peripatetic lover. But Cathy Greene, too, dropped out of the life of Wayne when her husband died after an attack of sunstroke. She returned to the north and social life at Mulberry Grove was interrupted for several years though, as we shall see, it bloomed eventually again. On General Greene's death his compatriot in arms and neighbor in Georgia spoke feelingly and highly of his character as a soldier and a man.

General Greene's death came in a fashion, somehow completely out of character, by which the careers of military men are so frequently ended. He and Mrs. Greene had gone to Savannah for the day, and on the way home had stopped at the neighboring plantation owned by William Gibbons. The general and his neighbor went out in the hot sun—it was June—to inspect the latter's plantation. The general wore no hat. He began to complain of pains in his head and he and Mrs. Greene left and went home. Wayne had been invited to Mulberry Grove for dinner that night, and he met the general and Cathy when they arrived, having reached the house before they did. The general was ill and uncomfortable and was put to bed. He never got up again. He was ill for months and died in November. The year was 1786. Wayne was with him when he died.

Over Wayne's social life on his plantation and on neighboring plantations and in the town there hung constantly the cloud of his mounting debts and his failure as an agriculturist. He had mortgaged his two plantations in Georgia and his own place at Waynesborough and was under constant pressure for payment. He let other bills run and, in his desperation, so demeaned himself as to ask the Georgia Assembly for another grant for his war services in Georgia. He claimed that he should be awarded the difference between the value of his holdings and Mulberry Grove on the ground that he had done more for Georgia than had General Greene. The Assembly turned him down. But there was another way out. If he were an officeholder in Georgia, which would establish him as a citizen there, then he would be protected against attempts to collect from him in Georgia on obligations in Pennsylvania, as Georgia had protective statutes for its citizens as regarded their debts to outsiders. His citizenship status was most vague. He claimed citizenship in both states at one time or another to suit his particular needs of the moment. Before he could investigate carefully his prospects of winning public office in Georgia, he had to return to Pennsylvania. Immediately his creditors there popped the law on him. He knew, however, that it would take time for the legal processes to reach the ultimate limit of sending him to jail for his debts under Pennsylvania law.

Soon after he returned to Pennsylvania he wrote to James Jackson in Georgia asking for election to the Georgia Assembly. He was rejected. Then he inquired into the chance of running for Congress from Pennsylvania, which also would give him immunity wherever he happened to reside, and he very frankly confided to a friend, Sharp DeLany, that this was purely a subterfuge to protect him from his creditors. He found, however, that election to Congress from Pennsylvania was equally impossible, whereupon he went back to Georgia. There he did run for the state Assembly, only to meet defeat. Then he sought election to the United States Senate, but another was chosen by the Assembly for that post.

He was persistent. After a canvass of the situation, he decided to try for one of the two Georgia seats in the House of Representatives in Washington, the one for lower Georgia that was occupied at the time by James Jackson. For wholesale fraud and chicanery, that election was the match of any ever staged since by our most notoriously corrupt political machines, even though there were far fewer voters to deal with in a new and sparsely settled election district. The fraud was participated in personally not only by Wayne himself, who supervised the distribution of rum to a troop of Georgia militia and rounded them up to vote for him, but by two outstanding citizens and officials— one the chief justice of Georgia, Henry Osborne; the other, the mayor of Savannah, Thomas Gibbons, who was Wayne's campaign manager and who baldly directed the stuffing of ballot boxes and other illegal tricks. There was also some questionable activity by zealous partisans of Jackson, who was busy in Congress at Philadelphia at the time and did not return to the state for the election, but it was minor compared to that of the reckless and callous Wayne lieutenants. Wayne quickly got the election certified and went to Philadelphia and took his seat in the House. Jackson returned to Georgia and was elected subsequently to the Georgia Assembly.

It was a year before Jackson found out fully the extent of the fraud perpetrated by the Wayne forces in the Congressional election. He thereupon brought a contest for the seat, and the fraud was shown to be so flagrant when the election was investigated that the House voted unanimously to unseat Wayne, who, of course, was not permitted to vote in his own contest. But Jackson was not seated, either. The seat was left vacant.

Even before this action by the House the election had its repercussions in Georgia. Jackson brought impeachment proceedings against Chief Justice Osborne in the Assembly, and he was tried and impeached by the Senate, the verdict barring him from holding any public office for thirty years. In addition he was fined $600. As for the other principal in the fraud, Jackson challenged Mayor Gibbons to a duel. Neither hit the other after three shots. Honor was thus satisfied, and Gibbons lived to become a central figure in one of the most famous lawsuits in our history before the Supreme Court, as will be related later in its proper place. Jackson afterward was elected to the United States Senate.

Wayne, meanwhile, had finally extricated himself from his web of debt. Gibbons, who was his lawyer as well as his political manager, was discovered to be acting also on behalf of his creditors and moved in for a judgment for the long-standing debts on Wayne's plantations. In the settlement, Wayne disposed of all his Georgia holdings, except the cowpens, and in exchange was able to lift the mortgage on his own estate at Waynesborough in Pennsylvania. That ended his strange and stormy career in Georgia.

He went home to Pennsylvania to land eventually on his

feet as commander in chief of the American army by appointment of President Washington. He achieved new fame for restoring order in the Northwest Territory and retrieved by a
great victory the all but fatal defeat suffered earlier by Arthur St.
Clair. He died in bed (as had his friend, General Greene) in a
lonely blockhouse on Presque Isle in Lake Erie, of a complication
of ailments, in his fifty-second year. When his body was removed
from a grave there several years later, at his daughter's wish, and
reburied in St. David's churchyard at Radnor, Pennsylvania, there
stood in the crowd at the ceremonies sponsored by the Society
of the Cincinnati a veiled figure. It was Mary Vining, the faithful.
She had retired to seclusion when she heard of his death and
emerged for this final ceremony over his remains.

PART 5

Hail King Cotton!

CHAPTER ONE

THE SAVANNAH BECOMES CIVILIZED

For seven years the haggard and harassed armies of the colonists had fought stubbornly for liberty along the coast and up the Savannah River valley. But what they possessed, when it was all over, was hardly a river-goddess. She was, rather, a gaunt hand-maiden, starved and listless, ragged, hungry, and sick of soul.

This first civil war of the Savannah River valley had been most costly, and left destitution on all sides. Agriculture had been trampled down by the armies marching up and down the river. Weary soldiers returned to ruined farms. Owners of the big plantations on the coastal islands below the city came back to desecrated homes and ravished and impoverished fields. Augusta was scarred with battle wounds from fighting in her streets. Savannah, likewise, suffered—physically, mentally and spiritually. Fortunes had been wiped out in the struggle for independence. Commerce had degenerated into barter. Money was worthless. Paper currency, toward the end of the Revolu-

189

tion, was at the rate of $16,000 to $1—"not worth a Continental." The governor of the state, now finally able to rule again in the open, no longer a wanderer, dealt out a whole quire of bills for a night's lodging for his party in a Savannah tavern.

But these were sturdy folks in this Savannah River country. They did not stop to mourn and ask whether it had been worth the battle. They set about their individual jobs of reconstruction. The rice plantations began to thrive again along the lower river about the city and on the sea islands to the south. Indigo, once a small but profitable crop, was abandoned, for independence from Great Britain shut off the former colonial bounty from the mother country that had stimulated the trade in it. In the up-lands about Augusta, tobacco plantations again flourished under the vigorous management of the Virginia and North Carolina settlers. Now, with the end of the Revolution, these earlier set-tlers were joined by others from the same states who came streaming down the back trails and across the Savannah. New towns sprang up along the river and its tributaries as centers for the movement and marketing of tobacco. Here were located the inspection warehouses to grade the tobacco that came in from the surrounding countryside. Flatboats carried the tobacco down to Augusta, where there were more inspection warehouses. From the plantations about Augusta, in South Carolina and Georgia, the hogsheads of tobacco were trundled in by mules. A big shaft was run through the center of the hogshead and mules were hitched in front to roll the valuable cargo down the tobacco roads, as they were called, which followed the ridges so that no streams would have to be crossed. Other flatboats then carried this tobacco crop down the river to Savannah to be hoisted aboard oceangoing vessels for markets overseas.

The country began to come alive again.

The upriver section surged ahead. A generation after the Revolution it was twice as populous as the coastal region, having about two thirds of the eighty-odd thousand inhabitants counted for the state in the first census of 1790.

On the contrary, Negro slaves, who made up over a third of this total, were concentrated more heavily on the big rice plantations in the five counties of the coastal area. Some 13,000, nearly half of the 29,000 slaves in the state, lived and toiled in this region, which was only about half the area of the six counties upriver. Slavery was on the increase again. It looked for a time, during the depression that followed the Revolution, that slavery might be abandoned as an uneconomic venture. The Negroes were useful mostly on the rice plantations about the mouth of the river and along the Carolina and Georgia coast, and the war had cast a blight here. Many slaves, too, had been dispersed and lost during the Revolution. But the return of prosperity in the lowlands and the rapid development of agriculture as a whole in the Augusta community, particularly tobacco culture, demanded constantly fresh supplies of labor. Virginia and North Carolina found a ready market for their excess slaves in

Georgia during these years. A rushing business went on in healthy and able-bodied blacks.

They were, of course, available only for those who had the means, and not a great many agriculturists could qualify. Only a fourth of the families in the state owned slaves at this time, which was about the percentage maintained through all the years of slavery, and many of these, especially in the upcountry, could afford only a few.

The black man and his wife and progeny formed the solid foundation of the plantation system about the mouth of the Savannah and on the nearby coast and coastal islands. Negroes made up nearly three quarters of the whole population in this flat and flourishing spot of earth so favored by nature, and their toil created the riches that enabled their white masters to enjoy leisure and a certain amount of luxury, to live amply and hospitably, to entertain and be entertained.

Along the coastal islands some planters were beginning to experiment with sea-island cotton which had been imported for cultivation into Georgia and South Carolina from the Bahamas, but it was little more than a hobby at this time. It was too difficult to separate the fiber from the seed, though the long-staple sea-island cotton was more easily picked apart than the short-staple variety that a few planters in the upriver section were beginning to raise on a small scale. Negro slaves, squatting about in groups, could clean only a pound or two apiece in a whole day. This was too expensive for any but the largest planters.

During and shortly after the Revolution some of the bigger plantations—and there were a few covering several thousand acres—were broken up, and slave holdings were somewhat smaller thereafter. For example, before the war, Sir James Wright, the colonial governor, had 523 slaves working on the eleven plantations he owned in various sections, along the Savannah, the Ogeechee and the Canoochee River. There were others with relatively large holdings. The 1790 census listed James Spalding, the Sapelo Island planter, as the biggest single owner of slaves with 94. The average size of rice plantations was four hundred acres, though there were some, of course, considerably more extensive. The big plantations required abundant supplies of clothes, shoes, bedding, simple furnishings for their slaves. These the planters ordered in wholesale lots from England, still doing the bulk of their business of this sort with that country in the absence of a substantial manufacturing industry as yet in the fledgling republic.

Savannah drew upon the prosperity of the plantations to expand its business and financial interest, its banks, and its shipping. Oceangoing vessels sailed into the harbor to bring finished goods and to take away the produce of the lowlands and the upper valley. The waterfront was a lively place. Here, amidst the ocean and coastwise vessels, might be seen the rafts that had come down the river from Augusta, and points even north of Augusta, loaded with tobacco, lumber, beef, corn and wheat.

Savannah was incorporated as a city in 1789, with a mayor and a council to manage its civic affairs. The year before, Catham Academy had been chartered by the state legislature to provide schooling for young men. The theater was now added to the social life of the city. Messrs. Godwin and Kidd, who had previously brought their Charleston troupe to the city to put on plays, opened their own theater in Savannah in 1785 with performances of *Cato* and *Catherine and Petruccio*. A few years later the theater was renovated into what became known as "the New Theater." Godwin started at the same time a dancing school where "young ladies and gentlemen might receive expert tuition in the polite and necessary accomplishments of dancing." The dancing masters of the day seemingly had a bottomless reservoir of young folks in the fashionable homes that were rising on the Bay Front and on the squares leading down the center of the city along Bull Street. For a French gentleman by the name of John Frémon, who had run away from Virginia with the young wife of an elderly man, earned a living as a dancing instructor for several months.

In a house along West Bay Street, which still stands, there was born to this couple, out of wedlock, so to speak—for a divorce never had been granted—a boy who was given his father's name, but who added a "t" to it when he grew up, to Anglicize it. John Frémont later became a famous man in the history of the American West. Savannah claimed him proudly as a native son then, but later, when he ran for president as the first candidate of the new Republican Party, she scoffed that, after all, he had only been born in Savannah and had lived there only a few months as an infant in arms. Savannah really could not be responsible for him.

The city was gay and pleasure loving then, as it has always been, and never took the business of the world so seriously that it could not take time out for the theater and balls and the fast-trotting steeds that the young blades raced about the city, or for careless conversation over a drink in the taverns, or over a cup of coffee at the coffeehouses along the waterfront. Life was comfortable and amiable and cultivated after a fashion in this city along the river, with its broad, sandy streets lined with graceful palms and handsome live oaks.

One of the first acts of the city council, after it was created with the incorporation of the city, was to issue a strict ordinance prohibiting "galloping through the streets," which seems to have been quite the thing to do. During the first year of the city's government there were sixty-one summonses for fast driving, more than for all other violations of the law put together. Even doctors liked to drive a fast pace, and some of them were haled before the magistrates. The fines imposed ranged from two to forty shillings.

Savannah had a Jockey Club which sponsored frequent racing meets. From far and near the horse lovers gathered for a big event in 1793. On Sunday before the races began the council assembled and passed a special resolution against "practicing" on the Sabbath. The city fathers solemnly resolved:

"That the mayor shall be directed to call on the stewards or committees of the Jockey Club and request them to use their influence with those gentlemen who have horses to enter for the races, to prevent them from practicing on this day, as a hint from them will probably prevent the necessity of putting the law into effect."

Savannah seemed to be a law-abiding place in those days. There was not a single violation of this edict.

All this, as with whatever else went on in the city, was discussed no doubt at the coffeehouses strung at the time along the waterfront, perched like lookouts overlooking the busy river below. Here forgathered not only shipping men and importers, but other worthies of the city, for these were comfortable places for an hour of gossip. Much business was transacted in these congenial surroundings. Here news was exchanged and spread through the community. For hither repaired the captains off the ships from foreign parts, or from New York or Philadelphia or Boston. These coffeehouses, too, were depositories for letters to be sent aboard outgoing vessels for destinations along our own coast to the north or south, or abroad.

Anyone who wanted to travel from Savannah to Augusta, or to some point in that upriver country, could go by the road on either side on horseback or could ride in the stagecoaches that were just beginning infrequent trips, or could venture in a small boat bucking the stream. The valley was deep wooded country, with occasional farms, but mostly lonely and uninhabited through the pine barrens, as a good deal of it is today, until you were well up the river toward Augusta.

For miles back on either side of the river from Augusta, itself now a thriving town just beginning to crawl back from the river, there was pretty country with many farms and every so often a cozy hamlet that was beginning to perk up brightly. About forty-five miles above Augusta was a busy crossroads community. Here a wagon road from South Carolina came down to the Savannah at the point where the Broad River flowed into the Savannah. Four little towns, only recently built, sat here at this junction point: Vienna on the Carolina side and Lisbon, Petersburg and Southampton on the Georgia side. Here, in those days, and at other points a few miles above and below, were the ferries that carried across to the Georgia side the wagons, piled high with family treasures, wagons that were bringing immigrants from the north to the fertile land of Wilkes County and the then newly created Greene County, which had been carved from Wilkes County as others were to be cut from that once huge domain in the next few years.

There were considerable bustle and stir at this crossroads of the river, with all the activity and the going and coming about the new tobacco warehouses and other rude business houses ambitiously thrown up out of raw timber to capitalize the tobacco trade and what the promoters thought would be a continuous and profitable traffic in other commodities along the river. But in a few years, when tobacco succumbed to cotton and trade moved southward to Augusta, all these towns but Lisbon, still a tiny relic, disappeared from the face of the earth. They joined in oblivion the other dead towns of Georgia—Ebenezer above Savannah, Sunbury and Frederica on the coast—and became just as extinct as Fort Charlotte, which also stood in this neighborhood, the first trophy of the Americans in this section in the Revolution. Other defenses built nearby to protect the early settlers from the Indians, Fort James and Fort Prince George, among them—all these were gobbled up by the ravenous forests.

The name of Petersburg survived along the river long after the Revolution in a type of flatboat. The "Petersburg boat," so called, was devised to meet the peculiar needs of the tobacco trade in the way of river transport. It was a permanent vessel, not just a raft to be broken up at the end of the journey such as was used later to carry cotton down the river. The Petersburg boat varied in size from 35 to 85 feet in length, with a beam of 6 to 7 feet and a draft of 10 to 20 inches. A deck was built over each end, and a plank laid flat around the gunwale provided a walk for the polemen. They would move slowly from bow to stern to propel the boat upstream. On the downstream run no poling was necessary, only steering. The pilot would stand at the prow and call back directions to a steersman behind who used a pole or sweep to guide the vessel. For a right shift, he would call back "Georgia," and to swing left he would shout "South Carolina," the familiar signals heard up and down the river, through the years, in guiding all sorts of craft. Each boat usually carried a crew of seven or eight boatmen, both white and Negro. For cooking their food they set up a box in the caboose at the rear end, covered it with a thick layer of dirt, and made their fire there. The huskies who operated these boats did not deign to pad the ends of the poles; no, nothing so soft and civilized! So it was with the pride of the primitive that they stepped from their vessels at the end of the journey frequently with blood streaming from their armpits and chests. They were a hardy lot, and proud of it.

The Petersburg boats were built at various points along the river, constructed of 1½-inch long-leaf pine. They were owned and operated by a number of people living in the riverbank towns. At one time there were as many as thirty-five or forty on the river, going back and forth between the upriver towns on the Savannah and its tributaries down to Augusta. Navigating the rapids just above Augusta at Bulls Sluice required skill and experience. It was full of dangers for boat and crew. Difficult, too, was the upstream pull through the tricky waters. The Petersburg boats also were used later to transport cotton when it replaced tobacco as the staple crop in the midlands and upper river valley.

Tobacco had only a brief heyday in the lands of the middle Savannah, from shortly before the Revolution until about the turn of the century. But, during this period, it was a boon to this fertile region. It offered the means for recovery from the post-Revolutionary depression and attracted more and more settlers. The hogsheads of tobacco came rolling down the tobacco roads to Augusta, and down the Savannah and its tributaries on the boats to the river settlements and to Augusta's inspection warehouses. Altogether fourteen inspection points were designated by the state, but the bulk of the business went to the three warehouses at Augusta, known as Call's, Richmond, and Augusta.

Here expert inspectors superintended the grading of the tobacco, its weighing, its packing or repacking in hogsheads for shipment down the river, stamped the hogshead "Georgia" and marked on it the name of the warehouse, the quality of the leaf, net weight and tare. Inspectors were forbidden by law to have any interest whatever in the production or manufacture of tobacco. They were civil servants above suspicion and reproach. The inspector got a fee of two shillings a hogshead, and the coopers who coppered the hoops about the hogshead received a shilling and sixpence per hogshead.

Five miles upstream above the crossroads with its four towns, on the Carolina side, was a settlement which survived the plaguing tide of trade and economics that wiped out the others. It, too, had its ups and downs. New Bordeaux, as it was called then, Bordeaux as it is known now, was created along the river in 1764 by 212 French Huguenot émigrés who got a grant of thirty thousand acres from the British government for a grape and wine industry.

The British government had the usual strategic interest in fostering this settlement, like others, as a bulwark against the Cherokees to protect the line of the upper Savannah. It was the jealousy of the French government that helped to contribute to the failure to transplant a lucrative wine industry to the New World. Fearing competition, France sent over only the poorer quality of grapevine shoots. The Revolution and the introduction of cotton did their share, so that Bordeaux was in an uncertain and shaky state of transition at the end of the Revolution. But it survived.

One of the French settlers left a heritage along the Savannah in a school for orphan and indigent children. This survived all vicissitudes of wars and economic changes and is now operated by the state. John de La Howe, a physician, had his own ideas about the education of children. Among them was to provide them with healthy bodies and teach them to do for themselves. The instructions he left in his will about the selection of the children for his school, their care and training, were most specific, and, among others, he prescribed that their beds should be stuffed with beech leaves "gathered before frost and dried in the shade." This, he said, would furnish a more healthful bed than feathers. He may have had other idiosyncrasies. At any rate, his wife left him a few years after he had established himself along the Savannah, and moved to Charleston. Rebecca Woodin, his housekeeper, looked after the doctor thereafter, and seemingly in a very satisfactory manner. She died before he did. In his will he ordered that his grave be beside hers, deep in the forests of his estate, that a brick wall eight feet high be built around the two graves, with a wrought-iron gate. The gate, he instructed, should be locked, and the key thrown into the Savannah River. All that was done. You can see the graves today, inside the brick wall with the wrought-iron gate.

Farther back from the river on the Carolina side and to the east and north was a land of mixed races, Scotch-Irish, German, and French Huguenots, all seeking in this rolling, fertile Carolina countryside refuge from religious persecution. They were independent, sturdy and thrifty. This was yet a crude country filling up with rough and lusty but solid folks. It was still, too, a homemade land, where women—as well as most men—did their own work. It was not a "store-boughten" land, except for a few things; that is, when they could scrape up the money to buy them, or the surplus of produce to barter for them. Always first on the list of purchases, of course, were a gun and some powder, for Indian marauders still preyed upon the pioneers here. After that came coffee, medicine, iron tools for the farm work, needles and buttons, a Bible, or maybe a stray magazine

or book. But these items were rare. Neighbors got together to
help put up the two-room cabins which, for a long time, were
the accepted type of home. There was a big room on each side
and a hall down the middle, sometimes a porch. The windows
were covered with large, heavy wooden shutters to be closed
and barred at night against prowling Indians. Later, when the
Indians were no longer a menace, glazed paper was used for
windows to let in some light for the day. Floors usually were of
sand.

It was well put in one all-embracing sentence by one of
Georgia's governors, George R. Gilmer, in his book of sketches
about the first settlers of upper Georgia, thus:

"All work, little play, no fruit, poor eating, thin clothing,
open houses, hard beds, and few blankets."

Land holdings were small, for the most part, though there
were exceptions even in the early days of settlement. This back
country was opened for settlement under the head-right system.
The head of a family was allotted two hundred acres for himself
and fifty additional for each member of the family. Slaves were
included as members of the family for purposes of land grants,
which accounts for the few larger holdings of the affluent
minority. The head of the family had to pay the cost of surveying his land. A settler with a small family and no slaves could
not cultivate the whole tract. It was too much for him. Consequently, many farms still had their wood lots. The trees were
left standing until the settler could live up to his acres, so to
speak.

In contrast with the coastal region, whites outnumbered
Negro slaves in the upper river country nearly three to one.
Those who owned slaves usually had only three or four, though
there were a few who had as many as fifteen, and very rarely,
even more. Of the 192 settlers in Greene County in 1788 who
were slaveowners, 136 had five or less, and only five owned
15 or more. One planter owned 32. By 1800, however, more
slaves had been brought into this section as cotton began to

spread over this country, and one plantation boasted seventy
slaves. This was owned by Joel Early, one of the first settlers. He
was a veritable lord of the manor of his day, but quite the exception. He had a large house built of brick which was brought
over from England and up the Oconee River. His was a stylish
ménage in imitation of the English. He required his children to
dress formally for dinner every day at six, a bit of ultra-ultra in
the wilderness.

These people in the Savannah midlands were, for the most
part, God-fearing folks, living close to nature and the fundamen-
tals. If they owned no other books, most families had a Bible.
Churches sprang up early, Baptist, Methodist and Presbyterian,
to become the nuclei of social life. There was also a smaller
and still restless worldly element that liked to gamble and drink.
Some worldlings were among the more prosperous who could
afford such vices; others among the shiftless and indigent who
couldn't afford it but persisted, humanly enough, in these
pleasures.

Bishop Francis Asbury of the Methodist Church, who had
ridden through this country in the interest of salvation, left his
righteous imprint upon it and its people. He had held a church
conference at "Old Liberty Chapel" in Greene County. It was at
this chapel, according to legend, that the "mourner's bench" first
came into being. A revivalist by the name of Stilth Mead roused
his congregation to such a pitch of hysteria and got so many
"convictions for sin" that the converts flocked up the aisles in
numbers that overwhelmed him. He couldn't talk to each one in-
dividually, so he invited them to take seats in the front row.
This, because of the miserable aspect of its grim occupants,
was thereupon named "the mourner's bench," whether humor-
ously or seriously, the legend naturally does not specify.

Bishop Asbury left behind him in this region tiny cells of
Methodism. They grew slowly, year by year, and then bloomed
into that great empire of Protestantism which had so great an
influence along the Savannah River valley. His southern cam-

paign was in the midst of the American Revolution. The war was just a bothersome incident to him. He rode bravely and nonchalantly in and out of the path of armies. Augusta became one of the two capitals of this campaign to conquer the south for the Methodist Church; Natchez, Mississippi, being the other. From these centers missionaries streamed out over the outlying provinces. The first Methodist church was established in Augusta in December, 1779, in the brief breathing spell between the first and second occupations of that city by British and Tory armies.

The vigilant bishop was constant in his condemnation of the vanities of the world and the flesh, and he frothed in his soul over any artificial devices to make religions soothing or attractive—architectural flourishes and furbelows in churches, steeples, bells, or organs. He boiled over when he saw a bell over the church at Augusta. The bell was cracked. He blurted out vengefully that he hoped it soon would break asunder.

"It is the first I ever saw in a house of ours in America," he ranted. "I hope it will be the last."

The righteous in these Savannah midland communities were hard on sinners and "backsliders."

They carried over a species of zealous and jealous fury from their religion into their political institutions. Punishments decreed by their courts smacked of the Inquisition, or of the most extreme development of New England Puritanism. Murderers were branded with an "M" across the forehead and hanged publicly for all to see. Thieves were marked across their shoulders with a telltale "R." Women too loose with their tongues were ducked in the creek in the sight of all. In the most public position in various towns stocks were erected where offenders stood in the pillory for the scorn of their neighbors, after first being whipped with many lashes across their bare backs. Debtors were thrown into jail.

It was a harsh society, indrawn and introverted. The pleasure-loving minority who liked to gamble and race horses, who drank and used profanity, were condemned severely by the good church folks and, likewise, the grand juries of the day digressed in their charges of specific violations of the law with discourses upon the morals of the community. Juries accepted the folkways of the strict religious element as the standard of morals, just as happens today in most societies, but particularly in primitive society.

Horse racing was a popular sport. It spread from Savannah and Augusta to the smaller communities in the back country, to such towns as Washington in Wilkes County and Greensborough, as it was first spelled, in Greene County. Dancing began to tap its light and tempting toe, too. But never, of course, with the consent or approval of the righteous.

Bethesda Baptist Church in Greene County brought charges of "immoral and un-Christian conduct" against one of its members who was accused of "aiding and abetting in the un-Godly practice of horse racing, in that, he allowed visiting horse owners to quarter their horses on his land, and that he sold them corn and hay for said horses." The erring member insisted that he had a perfect right to rent his barn and sell his hay to whom he pleased. He minced no words in his defiant challenge. Finally he was let off with a lecture.

A grand jury reprimanded a couple of local justices for "suffering and admitting the disorderly and unwarranted conduct of profane swearing, drinking, fiddling and dancing at the time of holding their courts." This same jury also condemned public card playing and gambling and "the custom of leading and parading stud horses in the main street of Greensborough on public occasions . . . and the profane and indelicate practice of showing stud horses on the Sabbath day at places of public worship."

Isolation had its influence in the reactionary severity of the society of the times.

Easier contact with the outside world came around the turn of the century with the opening of a network of stagecoach lines which led from Washington in Greene County to Augusta, and thence across the river to various points in South Carolina. Easier and more graceful living, too, softened some of the sharp contours of pioneer society, and this came with prosperity. But prosperity came with cotton. And the benefactor who spread cotton across this country, like snow, bestowed his gift unwittingly and by accident.

CHAPTER TWO

ELI WHITNEY FASHIONED A PANDORA'S BOX

It was an alien green world, heavy with dark mystery, into which Eli Whitney came bringing his Yankee knack with tools. He had left his home in Westboro, Massachusetts, in the melancholy autumn he knew and loved. But here, about the mouth of the Savannah, Nature sported herself still in the bright garments of May.

This was a forbidding land to the New England Yankee. Catherine Greene assured him he would come to love it in time, as had she. She also was from New England. And Eli was reassured by Phineas Miller, likewise a New Englander, who had come here to manage the Greene plantation. But the young man knew instinctively that he never would like it and in truth he never did. For underneath the gentle glove of hospitality he came in time to feel the hard and grasping hand.

It was one of those happy, or unhappy accidents—as you choose to regard it—that brought Eli Whitney to linger at Mulberry Grove, and another that led him to sit down and devise the cotton gin. He had met Catherine Greene on the ship that

was taking her back to Savannah from Rhode Island, after visiting her people there, while Whitney was going south to fill a teaching post at the then almost brand-new University of Georgia, situated at Athens, well up in the back country along the Oconee River. There the strong-minded Abraham Baldwin, its president, was earnest about building up his college which had been chartered only seven years before. It was the first state university in the new nation.

From this casual meeting aboard ship there developed a warm friendship in the long days at sea between the twenty-seven-year-old Whitney and the older woman. She invited him to visit Mulberry Grove while he awaited further word from President Baldwin. He had acquiesced.

The young man had accepted the offer at the university so that he might keep himself alive while reading law. Why he wanted to be a lawyer is hard to understand at first glance, since his bent was plainly mechanical, but it becomes clearer if we dig into his background. His father, who was a farmer, was very clever with his hands, and was busy constantly at odd times in a workshop he had fitted up in his home. The boy inherited this mechanical talent and improved it with an early start in his father's shop. It seems, as a matter of fact, to have possessed him completely, so that he locked himself away for hours in the workshop alone with the tools. He would lose himself in his concentration and grew to be a moody young fellow, unsociable, living largely to himself.

Perhaps this was held up to him critically. The young country in which he was growing up was not an industrial nation, as yet, and dawdling with tools in a community where most people were concerned with something more real, with getting a living from the land or in trading in goods that somebody else had made, was very likely looked upon as a foolish waste of time and not in the energetic, thrifty Yankee tradition. He was, in short, a misfit, just as if he had been addicted to writing poetry.

In self-defense, we may assume, however unwillingly, he decided to shake off this all-consuming and apparently useless hobby, for so it seemed to others, and force himself into something normal and accepted. Being a lawyer was respectable, highly respectable. Lawyers had been the guiding spirits of the Revolution, and they had framed the new government that came from it—and New England was most ardent for the Revolution and for the new republic. Lawyers were enjoying public esteem. So the young man, though he had never been much of a student, went to Yale, although somewhat late. There, however, in order to make the expenses of his education for a gentlemanly profession, he was still forced to rely upon the less regarded talents of the mechanic. He did various odd jobs of a mechanical sort about New Haven. He had graduated only a short time before he took passage for Savannah, which was to have been only the first stop in the long trip into the unknown country, far from home, in the virgin forests of Georgia.

Perhaps, on the ocean voyage, he had opened his heart to Mrs. Greene and told her about himself or about his secret; how he yearned to do something with machines. Perhaps he confessed his unhappiness about the career he had chosen for himself or disclosed his fears of the new country to which he was going, a land so unlike his own in every way. Perhaps that is why she invited him to tarry at Mulberry Grove, to pause there while she could figure out some way to adjust this wistful young man to the world in which he must live and make a living.

He discovered an even more alien land than he had imagined when the vessel finally turned into the mouth of the Savannah and sailed slowly inland on that tawny and sluggish stream, a lonely ship in a lonely world of water and sky and marsh grass. It was as if they were suspended in an empty world above the world. The air was heavy here in the river. It lacked the invigorating freshness to which he was accustomed at this season at home. The bare expanse of water, like a stage from which the actors had departed centuries ago, was relieved eventually by the busy, friendly dock, with its proof that humankind did exist in this other world. For there they moved about, talking in soft accents like the conversation of drowsy bees in a midsummer afternoon.

When he reached Mulberry Grove, twelve miles above the city, he found a way of living he had never known. For a time it must have seemed the paradise that had been described to him—the thick foliage at the water's edge, a jungle of wild and exotic plants and flowers and shrubs that almost smothered each other in striving toward the sun, the long sandy road that led up through overhanging live oaks to the wide house with its porches across both first and second stories. Then there were the Negro slaves, grinning a welcome to their returning mistress, chasing about at her bidding, busy with the little attentions and necessary chores to make her and her guest comfortable. The mansion was the center of an independent, self-sufficient world of its own. There were many outhouses scattered about, the kitchen standing separate from the main house. He saw the chicken house and runs, the barns, the coachhouse, the little cabins where the slaves lived, and beyond, glimpses of vegetable and flower gardens.

It must have seemed like something out of the feudal ages. Born as he had been in a land of stern necessity, where frugality was the first of the virtues, he may have despised this prodigality inwardly. He may even have felt for these planters a twinge of conscience that their prosperity flowered from the evil soil of Negro slavery. Yet these Negroes here seemed happy—and that, too, he could not understand. No, the picture did not seem to fit together. Nor did he know, as he looked upon all this, that he should be the instrument for enlarging the realm of slavery, for expanding it until it bankrupted this land and brought down bloody war from the North whence he came.

It was a corruption of human society that he could see. And yet every day he repeated the round of pleasant living that softened the soul, ate away its resistance, while the nights brought candlelight in lovely rooms, and the gleam of delicate china and old silver. And there was delightful conversation in the moonlight, on the porch or in the gardens.

With the help of Phineas Miller the capable widow had improved and embellished the family's legacy from the state and warmed it with her radiant personality. It was a happy home for herself and her children—two daughters, Martha, fifteen, and Cornelia, thirteen, and a son, George, nineteen, who was at the time away in school in France with Lafayette's son. It was, as well, a hospitable port of call for her friends and neighbors up and down the river. There were nearly always guests.

Here, two years before, Mrs. Greene had entertained President Washington. He had called to pay honor to the widow of his able lieutenant of the Revolution, during a visit to the southern battlegrounds along the river. He had stopped at Augusta and Savannah to receive the tribute of the people of those two cities, and there were all sorts of colorful ceremonies and formal functions, grandly appointed for the times, which lingered for a long time in the talk of the valley.

A few days after Eli Whitney took up his abode at the widow Greene's mansion a group of planters on their way down the river stopped and, as was customary, were accorded the hospitality of the house for a few days' visit. With his thrifty Connecticut background, Whitney must have shuddered at the lavish style of entertainment, although it was entirely routine and normal, especially at the inroads upon the larder and the wine cellar, even when he discovered that this was all taken for granted.

There was a great deal of talk about cotton. For the first time the Yankee learned about this plant. The visiting gentlemen kept saying that if only some way could be found to separate the plaguey seed from the fiber, some more efficient method than the old-fashioned rollers that were *so* clumsy and slow, then they would have a new and valuable crop for this region that would turn the river valley into an Eden and make them all rich. The weather here, they said, was so favorable to the growth of cotton. Experiments already had proved that. They built bigger and bigger conversational dreams as they warmed with the widow's wine over their dinner.

Mrs. Greene injected herself into the conversation to remark that perhaps her guest from the North could help. He had fixed her watch for her. She knew he had a fine mechanical talent. Confidently she turned to Whitney, who had thus far sat quiet and unobtrusive among this company which was so foreign to him. He was shy and subdued.

Mechanics again! How he had tried to put all that behind him, out of sight and out of mind. But Mrs. Greene was sweetly insistent and he agreed to try his hand. After all, he was a guest here, and the lady had been most kind to him. He could do something for her in return. But he did not share her calm assurance that he could turn the trick. He knew too much about the problems involved. Other clever men must have tried.

He locked himself away in his room with a few bolls of cotton and some tools, and again he was lost in that world which so few could enter with him, once more a lonely fellow, moody and unsociable. The stories vary about how long it took. Some have it a matter of ten days; some, weeks. One story is that he almost gave up and that Mrs. Greene, herself, suggested the very simple way out of his dilemma. He had contrived a roller with teeth which would extract the seed from the fiber, but some of the fiber clung to the teeth and clogged the machine. The widow, informed by him of his problem, looked at his handiwork for a few minutes. Then her face lighted up. She went over and picked up a clothes brush. Ah, he got the idea at once. A brush revolving in the opposite direction would do it. He devised one, and, lo, he had the new cotton "gin," a word then applied to the crude rollers then in use, a corruption of "engine."

He had done his favor. He had fulfilled the demands of hospitality. Now he must be off to the wilderness teaching job. Meanwhile, before he had finished his gin, he had received word from President Baldwin that there had been some mistake in the college head's first letter to him about the salary. He would be paid only half the figure originally mentioned. That was unfortunate. But still he was determined to go. He might have got away had it not been for Phineas Miller, who quickly saw the possibilities in the new cotton gin. He importuned Whitney to stay and carry on with his project. There would be a fortune in it. Whitney pleaded he had no money to finance its development on a big scale. Miller thereupon offered to do all the financing, with a fifty-fifty split on the profits. The bargain was made. But Whitney, with his cautious New England instinct, still did not let go of the teaching job. He wrote that he would be detained, but would like the post held open for him. Baldwin agreed. He never got there, of course.

Now he found himself launched in a career and a business, and all so suddenly and unexpectedly. He went off to Philadelphia, the national capital, to see about a patent, though he had little faith in statutory law to protect his gin. Patents were granted by the secretary of state, an office then occupied by Thomas Jefferson. On patent matters the secretary had only a clerk or two to help him. He handled patents directly, himself.

Jefferson, luckily, was sympathetic, being an inventor of sorts himself. He proved open-minded, imaginative, liberal, and he readily granted Whitney a patent on his cotton gin.

Whitney now had the law on his side, but the law meant little those days in the spraddling young country.

While Whitney was in Philadelphia on his patent business, Miller was arranging for the manufacture of the gin. There is a story that the first gin was set up at Smyrna, about six miles from Washington, in Wilkes County.

The secret of the gin leaked out. How this happened has never been definitely established. Whitney, himself, knew there was little chance to keep it a secret long, for the principle was simple, and once someone with a mechanical bent got the idea, a copy would be an easy matter. Mrs. Greene, it was said, showed the model about among friends, proud of the achievement of her house guest which she had encouraged. It may have leaked out in this way. A more dramatic and picturesque story has to do with the gin set up at Smyrna. People were permitted to go by the window and see the clean cotton being thrown out of the gin, but the machine itself was behind a wooden fence so that it could not be seen. These precautions seemed sufficient. But not so. Women were admitted inside the building, on the theory that they would not be able to figure out the machine. But, so the legend goes, a smooth-faced young man, Edward Lyon, who lived at a distance and was not known in the community, disguised himself as a woman and went through one day to look at the gin. He carried a description back to his brother, John Lyon, who had an Irish blacksmith construct a gin for him.

At any rate, copies did appear, here and there, and Whitney began the long-drawn-out process of suing infringers. He and his partner had adopted a policy which opened the way for trouble. Instead of licensing the right to make machines, or licensing for a fee the machines they themselves manufactured, they chose instead to keep ownership in their own hands of all gins they manufactured and to charge a percentage on all cotton ginned. For this they needed large production, and Whitney opened a plant at New Haven to manufacture in quantity. Among other misfortunes, along with his continuous court troubles over patents, this plant burned down and twenty completed gins were destroyed with it. But he did finally produce a large number of gins and scattered them widely in the South.

One of his most trying legal ordeals was with Hogden Holmes of Augusta, who also had a patent on a cotton gin. This case dragged through the courts for ten years. A federal judge finally upheld Whitney's patent and enjoined Holmes from making any more of his machines. Yet by the time this was ended, Miller, who meanwhile had married Mrs. Greene, had died and Whitney was left to carry on alone.

The inventor decided to change his tactics. He would sell the rights to his gin direct to southern states. He appeared first before the South Carolina legislature. It voted him $50,000 for rights to the gin in that state. He got an advance payment of $20,000, but it took years of hovering around the lobbies before he got the remainder. He had similar experiences with other southern state legislatures.

When his patent expired he went to Congress with an appeal for an extension on the ground that he had been cheated of his due returns from his invention. He got a favorable committee report, but southern interests in Congress blocked passage of the bill. They thought he was exacting too high a tribute from the South for his invention.

He found the South most inhospitable where cotton, their new king, was concerned. He had opened a new empire for them, and they wanted to exploit it to the fullest without having to pay toll to a clever Yankee who had come in and showed them how to get something out of it. The court troubles were enough, but, on top of those, his enemies circulated all sorts of false rumors to discredit his gin—to the effect that it put knots in the fiber and made cotton from his gins hard to spin.

He complained bitterly of his treatment in letters to a friend in New England.

"I have," he wrote, "a set of the Most Depraved Villains to combat and I might as well go to Hell in search of Happiness as apply to a Georgia court for justice."

At another time he wailed:

"You know I always believed in the 'Depravity of Human Nature'. I thought I was long ago sufficiently 'grounded and stablished' in this doctrine. But God Almighty is continually pouring down cataracts of testimony to convince me of this fact. 'Lord I believe, help Thou' not 'mine unbelief' but me to overcome the rascality of mankind."

He was well-nigh ready to start a civil war all by himself.

He did get something out of his invention. Altogether he grossed about $200,000 from it, but his net profit was small, because a large portion was eaten up in lawsuits.

The cotton gin was Whitney's contribution to the South. But he contributed something of far more permanent value to his country—the germ of the great industrial expansion to come which would make the United States a shining sun among the nations of the earth. He is the recognized creator of the mass production system. This contribution is often overlooked.

It was developed in the manufacture of arms, where so many other ideas conducive to peacetime progress originate, ironical as that may seem. Around the turn of the century he was awarded a contract by the federal government for ten thousand rifles, a large order. Instead of trying to produce these in the accepted manner, that is, with each workman making a complete gun in the slow and tedious process of hand tooling, he decided to build machines to make the individual parts, interchangeable parts, which then could be assembled, so that great numbers could be turned out quickly. This was a novel idea and was received with considerable skepticism at the start, partly because his manufacture was necessarily delayed for some time by the tooling-up process required. But he eventually proved the value of his idea to the government and delivered the order. He was helped by the faith of President John Adams.

The South ultimately felt the weight of this idea, too, and long after his death in 1825 as a worn-out mechanical genius at the age of fifty-nine. His business, Whitney and Ames, was carried on by his sons, and they made very fine guns. Jefferson Davis, the Mississippi planter who had left his cotton plantation for a military career in the war with Mexico, was highly elated by the performance of some Whitney and Ames rifles which had been procured for his command. It was a new type of rifle with a steel barrel. Colonel Davis said they were "the best ever furnished any regiment in the world." Later, when he was secretary of war in the Pierce Administration, he introduced this gun into the United States Army.

A few years later the cycle of Eli Whitney, which has its tragedy, was complete.

The Whitney gin made cotton a profitable crop. Cotton cultivation needed lots of labor and opened up a new use for Negro slaves. It perpetuated slavery probably much beyond the time when it might otherwise have been peaceably abandoned. Slavery was a contributing element to the Civil War, because it offered an issue to arouse the public.

The Whitney gun was turned on the South.

Jefferson Davis, the champion of slavery which was made profitable by cotton, whose own fortune had come from slave-produced cotton, had recommended the Whitney gun. Now, at Richmond, he sat at the receiving end. And from cotton came the explosives that killed southern men and wrecked southern homes and destroyed southern cotton fields.

CHAPTER THREE

THE MUSIC FROM WHITNEY'S BOX, GAY BEFORE IT WAS SAD

The little box that Eli Whitney fashioned with his clever hands in a big, airy bedroom on the second floor of the widow Greene's mansion along the Savannah River began to make music, both gay and sad. Listen and you may hear it down the years—

The crisp whack of the axes clearing new land in the upriver country, with an echo like the crack of a rifle.

The weird melodies of the Negroes guiding the rafts piled high with cotton down the tributaries of the Savannah and down the Savannah to the sea, a lonesome song across the empty water that lost itself at length among the trees.

The sharp report, like a pistol shot, of the long curling whip over the teams of big horses pulling wagons heavy with more cotton resounding through the streets of Augusta.

The gentle swish of the big fan that the small Negro boy swings monotonously to keep the flies away from the dinner of the white folks in the middle of the day in the Big House.

The high cackle of laughter from the house servants, the aristocracy of slavery, in the roomy kitchen savory with appetizing smells.

The chatter of the low caste, the field hands, as they plow and hoe and pick, with the change of the seasons.

The lilting song of the bobolink in the early morning, and the imitating frippery of the mockingbird, and the warning cry of the blue jay before the rain, and the cheeping in the nest just after dusk as the young birds settle down for the night.

The merry chirping of the fiddle from the Big House for the dance.

The happy jangle of coins in the pocket of the planter in town for the day, standing at the bar.

The excited shouts as the horses plunge down the stretch at county fairs.

The hilarious barking of encouragement to two ruffled gamecocks fighting to the death in the middle of the ring.

The mournful songs from the cabins of the slaves at night, in the moonlight.

The mumble of the slave in his sleep as he twists and turns after a long day, restless from haunting dreams born in some distant jungle.

The lusty singing in praise of a God of Love in the clapboard churches on Sunday, while the slaves sit meekly in the gallery getting grace for Monday morning.

This was the music of the times.

King Cotton waved his wand and this whole south country bloomed white.

It was hard to believe at first, for only so short a time ago, in the memory of older men and women, cotton was only a scraggly plant with a guilty conscience, virtually rejected. Everybody knew about "Cotton" Miller and joked with him. He was a persistent fellow with great faith—they thought him foolish—who for many years had been the only buyer of cotton at Savannah, a curiosity. He bought it in meager lots of twenty to a hundred pounds and assorted it and packed it for market, himself. Everybody, too, had heard the story, whether true or not, how the very first shipment of cotton from Savannah in 1784, eight measly bags of it, had been seized at Liverpool, because it was said that that much cotton couldn't have been produced in the United States. England's industrialists had been leery of cotton. They had big investments in wool, and they didn't welcome a rival.

But now they were accepting it. Big mills had been built and were ready for American cotton. The bales piled up in longer and longer rows along the riverfront at Augusta, carted in by more and more wagons from nearby South Carolina and Georgia plantations, loaded in on more flatboats from the tributaries of the Savannah that reached back, like grasping fingers, into the fertile hinterlands; and transferred to more and more big cotton rafts—cotton boxes, they were called—which bore them down to the big sailing ships tied up at Savannah for shipment to England. By 1805 Savannah was shipping 27,600 bales to Liverpool, over one-fourth of all the cotton sent to that English port from the United States. Soon three fourths of all the cotton produced in the United States came out of the fields of Georgia and South Carolina.

There was a temporary halt in the march of King Cotton, but only temporary.

This was caused by President Jefferson's embargo against all shipping from United States ports, the rather dubious measure devised by the chief executive to keep the young republic from becoming embroiled in the titanic war raging between England

and Napoleon that was affecting the whole Western world.
Savannah harbor became stagnant, like so many others up
and down the coast. Depression settled upon Savannah and
Augusta and the river valley which lasted through the war of
1812.

There were hard times for a while. But the war came to its
end and the Savannah River valley recovered quickly and entered an even more prosperous era. Except for the disastrous
effect on trade and commerce, the second war with England
did not touch this section at all. No British redcoats reappeared
in this vicinity. In guerrilla warfare with the Creek Indians on
the frontier three thousand Georgia troops were engaged, but
the war was in Alabama, far from the Savannah River valley.
The Lower Creeks in Georgia remained peaceful.

Savannah moved to first rank among southern ports after
the War of 1812 and held it for a score of years. In 1826 there
were shipped from the port 190,000 bales of cotton, and this

only thirty-three years after Eli Whitney had invented his cotton gin. There was a tremendous revival of trade in Savannah, beginning immediately after the war. The city began to count her merchant princes who were growing wealthy in the cotton business. Many new public buildings and fine homes appeared. The city began to assume the airs of a metropolis. In 1828 a new theater was built. Worldly good fortune produced a more worldly atmosphere.

Sons of wealthy families in the city, well staked by affluent fathers, began to go out to seek their fortunes on the new cotton frontier, and put up nice colonial homes in the still rough up-country. They acquired wives and children and slaves, and became gentlemen in the new plantation aristocracy. The focus of their lives thereafter was the "city"—Augusta.

Augusta was the pulsing, vivid capital of this new cotton empire, one that radiated from it on all sides into Georgia and South Carolina. Especially was this evident for the week or two during the fall when the cotton came pouring into market. The big wagons loaded high with cotton, drawn usually by six stout horses, would come rumbling into the city all day long, with a continual jingling of bells—since a necessary part of a properly harnessed team was a chime of bells attached to the horses' collars—and a constant loud crack of the long whips. It was the custom of the drivers, as soon as they had entered the city, to begin cracking their long whips, now to one side, now to the other. They kept this up, triumphantly. It was a sort of exultant signal that the heavy work was over for the season. Now a holiday was beginning.

The big plantation owners came riding in on their fine horses alongside their wagons. For them it was a time of relaxation, a mingling of a bit of pleasure with the business of marketing their cotton. They put up at the hotels and devoted their leisure hours to horse racing and cockfighting, to gambling and drinking, to swapping yarns and gossiping, to comparing notes on their common plantation problems. They were sociable and spent their money freely. They came armed, too, as a part of their business on these fall visits, with lists of supplies to be purchased for the plantation and the house. They had errands to do for their wives and daughters.

The hired hands and the slaves who came along had their fun, too: at the horse races and the cockfights, in the cheaper places of amusement, at dance halls and bars. A barroom was always attached to the wagon yards which were headquarters for these menials. And these wagon yards were quite a sight in themselves. They were to be found at various points in the city. They consisted of a row of sheds about a central courtyard. The wagons were lined up in the yard and the animals stabled in the sheds. Buildings at the front provided sleeping quarters for the drivers and helpers. There, too, they took their meals. Usually there was a general store nearby which sold provisions of all kinds for the plantation and forage for the horses.

Cotton spread its civilizing influence in the back country. The new staple crop brought in more money and new settlers. And more money brought more land under cultivation. Comfortable homes began to go up. They supplanted the two-room cabins that had been the standard in the remote regions of Georgia and South Carolina. There was a steady influx of fresh slaves to feed the greedy mouth of cotton. Legal restrictions against trafficking in slaves were not always observed by the big landowners. There was a constitutional prohibition against the importation of slaves after 1808. But boats slipped into the coastal harbors smuggling new black recruits from Africa, who were disposed of quickly and easily in the new cotton empire about Augusta. This sudden uprooting from their accustomed habitats in the jungles and forests of Africa to an alien atmosphere, with the tedious round of work in the cotton fields, invoked melancholia of an incurable sort among some of the newcomers, a few of whom claimed to be of royal lineage in their homeland. There was a wave of suicides. This self-destruction was inspired by their belief that their spirits would return to their native lands.

But these were just incidents, personal tragedies of the helpless and homeless primitive—costly, of course, to the few owners who lost their property in this way—and cotton marched on, spreading its illusive blessings through this country in a prosperity that was enjoyed by a few in a very substantial way, and trickled down, in some degree, to the section as a whole for a time.

Stagecoaches rumbled through this country, carrying in not too much comfort those who would afford the rate of ten cents a mile. They averaged five miles an hour. Social life at the top, among the big plantation owners, was "gracious," with a code of hospitality that invited much visiting about from house to house. For such visitors there were frequent balls in the big houses, not yet, or rarely, on the scale known in Charleston or Savannah or at some of the fine homes on the coastal islands, but entertainment in a more modest and less ostentatious manner. Music was furnished by two or three Negro slaves with banjos and fiddles, while everybody enjoyed himself in a lively and informal manner. It was country house entertainment.

For the ordinary run of folks, the small farmers and those who lived on the margin of this slaveholding civilization in the two-room cabins that had come down from their fathers, there were the simpler and perhaps more hilarious community sports and entertainment. For the men there were occasional horse races and more frequent cockfights. Everybody joined in a strange form of fun, the gander pullings, combining the chivalry of knight-errantry with a bit of crude frontier cruelty. A gander, with its neck greased, would be hung from a pole, head down, and the men would dash by on horseback and try to pull off the bird's head. There was a prize for the successful "knight" at these tournaments, which were always popular. Necessary farm and plantation chores were made the occasion of community gatherings at hog killings and corn-shucking parties. Here, too, the slaves joined the merriment—and the work. In the hog killings each man had the particular job for which he was best trained in experience. At the corn shuckings, to supply the zest of rivalry, sides would be chosen to see which could finish its pile of corn first. Great quantities of food were laid out by the women for these community affairs, which were planned days ahead of time.

There was jollity and merriment, and very often community singing, with accompaniment by the Negroes on their fiddles and banjos. One popular song at corn shuckings, which makes no particular sense and obviously was patched together by the Negroes, was this refrain:

> Did you ever hear the cow laugh?
> Ha, hi, ho!
> And how you think the cow laugh?
> Ha, hi, ho!
> The cow say moo, moo, moo,
> Ha, hi, ho!
> And what you think the cow want?
> Ha, hi, ho!
> The cow want corn and that what the cow want.
> Ha, hi, ho!

Life was very pleasant on the bigger plantations, and there, too, it had other gratifications—of the ego, for instance. There was the comfortable home among the big trees, surrounded by the slave quarters, never more than cabins, sometimes clean and whitewashed, sometimes not. A host of slaves was always at hand to serve the plantation—house slaves, maids, seamstresses, cooks in the kitchen, slave children to do the smaller, easier chores and to run errands, young ones to carry and fetch and be the docile playmates of the white children. There were men slaves who did odd jobs about the house and at the blacksmith shop on the place, tending to the stock and the stables; and the field hands who planted and hoed and picked the cotton. Paternalism offered their masters the natural satisfaction that it always bestows on human beings lifted to the command over less favored human beings who are dependent. There was a sense of well-being and pride, false though it might be, over the possession of such a worldly estate and of power over the lives of so many other people, even though they were slaves. But the management of such a plantation entailed constant and continual worries. These arose partly from the responsibility for control over the lives of a number of other people who were ignorant, though mostly loyal people who required constant supervision.

There was quite a number of large plantations with big, comfortable houses and a number of slaves, but not so many as might be supposed. There were a few fortunes made from cotton, but not many. The plantation system was essentially a way of life, but an extravagant and uneconomic way of life. It

provided for some a pleasant way of living, but was not a profitable business except in rare cases. Bad years came when the price of cotton was down, and the overhead ate up what might have been a small margin of profit. Slaves were too expensive labor, costly both in the original investment and in the upkeep.

Sir Charles Lyell, the English scientist, saw all this quite clearly when he was traveling along the Savannah in 1840. After his visit to a plantation where there were a hundred slaves, he wrote:

> To supply all of them with food, clothes, and medical attendants, young, old and impotent, as well as able-bodied, is but a portion of the expense of slave-labour. They must be continually superintended by trustworthy whites, who might often perform no small part of the task, and far more effectively, with their own hands.

The competition of slave labor drove out the smaller, independent farmers to a considerable extent. Unable to survive, they sold their land to the big plantation owners and moved away, some to the new lands of the southwest—as it was regarded then—in Alabama and Mississippi. Others less resourceful moved to the pine barrens to the south where they degenerated to the level of the "poor whites" who have infested that barren area of earth continually. Not a few migrated to the valleys amid the mountains to the north where it was harder to win a living from the thinner soil.

Life was fairly amiable for the black slaves who remained behind to take the place, in large-scale cultivation, of the once-independent whites with small acreage, although living was hardly on more than a subsistence level for the slaves. If it lacked the joys of freedom, however, it also lacked responsibility and the care that freedom demands. Cruelty among plantation owners was the exception for an economic reason even where kindliness did not motivate. For slaves were valuable property, and as such they were treated well and kept as contented and in as good health as possible to protect the investment in them. Thoughtlessness and occasional brutality were found among overseers. They were usually an inferior grade of humankind by nature, and, if they were not callous to begin with, they were liable to get that way by constant association in the capacity of boss with a still primitive people, unenlightened and lacking a sense of responsibility.

Sir Charles Lyell, who was a very objective reporter, has some interesting comment:

> The negroes, so far as I have yet seen them, whether in domestic service or on the farms, appear very cheerful and free from care, better fed than a large part of the laboring class of Europe; and, although meanly dressed and often in patched garments, never scantily clothed for the climate. We asked a woman in Georgia, whether she was the slave of the family of our acquaintance. She replied, merrily, 'Yes, I belong to them and they belong to me.' She was, in fact, born and brought up on the estate.
>
> After the accounts I had read of the suffering of slaves, I was agreeably surprised to find them, in general, so remarkably cheerful and light-hearted. It is true that I saw no gangs working under overseers on sugar-plantations, but out of two millions and a half of slaves in the United States, the larger proportion are engaged in such farming occupations and domestic services as I witnessed in Georgia and South Carolina. I was often for days together with negroes who served me as guides and found them as talkative and chatty as children, usually boasting of their master's wealth, and their own peculiar merits.

As the Negro woman had told Sir Charles, the master also belonged to them. This is very revealing as to what was happening in this outwardly prosperous region, except that few saw it at the time, a slow process that added up eventually to the tragedy that overtook this land and its people in the bitter end years later.

The plantation owner was tied down to his slaves. They took both his money and his time. They represented an investment that was, in effect, diminishing capital, for it deteriorated constantly and produced nothing permanent; nothing except a crop of cotton to be sold, year after year, so that the planter could meet current expenses to raise another crop of cotton. Thus the planter's talents and his resources were both restrained from being invested in improvements for the section in which he lived. There was neither money nor time for better roads and transport or for better schools; no free capital to invest in local industry, mills of his own to transform the cotton into cloth. So there was little or no progress in these directions. There were a few textile mills, but only a very few. Even though conditions were favorable to their being located here because of plentiful water power, instead most planters sent their cotton to New England to be made into cloth.

Already in the thirties some plantation owners had begun to move away. They went, like some of the smaller farmers who had preceded them, into Alabama and Mississippi. Others emigrated to southwest Georgia, where new lands were then being opened up. But they all left an ominous portent behind them, could it have been read. It was to be found in the ruts and gullies that were beginning to scar the fields. The land was wearing out from overcultivation and careless exploitation; erosion was eating it away. In the earlier days when a piece of land wore out, the plantation owner would merely take up new land in the same general locality. That dodge was no longer possible.

The disintegration of the land and of the plantation system itself was slow, and something hardly apparent to the ordinary observer. A few planters did recognize it and tried to take care of their land. They experimented with fertilizers and the rotation of crops. But most went on unheeding, wrapped up in the crazy game of speculation that cotton farming finally became. The price of cotton would go up. Enthusiastically the planter would buy more land and more slaves. The vicious cycle thus induced is well described by Ullrich B. Phillips, who said that the rise in price "would turn the thoughts of men again to staple expansion—to buy more slaves to make more cotton for the continued purpose of buying more slaves to make more cotton."

Some intelligent and farseeing planters envisaged the ultimate breakdown of this system in its fairly early stages. A few even freed their slaves, from humanitarian as well as from economic motives. Others could see the warning signs in the abolition movement. But they reacted purely defensively to that. Resorting in fear to persecution of the abolitionists, usually they became overzealous in defending slavery. They ranted about abolitionists and passed resolutions. In some of the towns there were citizens who became self-appointed watchers over what they considered to be the public welfare; they set themselves to spy out the community for newcomers or strangers who might be abolitionists. Some abolitionists, zealous and fearless in their missionary spirit, did occasionally turn up. When they were discovered they were treated as criminals and driven away. This nurtured in time a general suspicion of strangers which has extended down to modern times. The significant thing was that many of these self-appointed guardians of the community welfare were not themselves slaveholders at all. They belonged rather to the ne'er-do-well, lazy, loitering element found in the smaller towns, the mischiefmaking, busybody type. Yet this defensive attitude became common to the whole people, so that those who owned no slaves, who never had and probably never would—though always hopeful—rallied about the system jealously against its enemies from the outside. Even years afterward their children and grandchildren would rise up hotly to defend this "way of life," and just as vehemently as the children and grandchildren of those who had had many slaves at their beck and call.

It was an interesting psychological manifestation, but understandable.

Some who lived with the slaveholding system, and some who came in from outside, saw clearly what was happening to the South. The whole people was infected with a guilty con-

science, both humanitarian and economic, and more and more
was there a recognition, whether confessed or not, even to themselves, of the evil they were perpetrating upon fellow human
beings and the losing game they were playing even from a
purely business standpoint. Yet they clung tenaciously to their
error.

What the slavery system was doing to the small, once-
independent farmer was graphically revealed by a young farmer
in South Carolina, Hinton Rowan Helper, in his book *The Impending Crisis*. His book came too late as a warning, breaking
upon the public consciousness only shortly before the Civil War.
The plantation lords dismissed him airily as "a poor white," but
that did not dismiss him.

Long before Helper's book, and long before Harriet
Beecher Stowe too, the evils of slavery were vividly portrayed
from firsthand observation by Fanny Kemble, the famous English actress. Her journals were published both here and abroad
and read widely. Her reporting was of slavery as *she* saw it on
the huge rice and cotton plantations on Butler's and St. Simon's
Islands off the coast of Georgia, plantations which belonged to

her husband, Pierce Butler. A highly emotional and sensitive creature, she was horrified by the filth and squalor in which the slaves lived, by the casual and callous attitude of owners and overseers toward these human possessions; and she was particularly torn by the attempted breaking up of one slave family that was prevented only by her intercession. She became more and more disturbed by the thought that the income that provided such a comfortable life for herself and her children should come from an inhuman business, and to soothe her conscience she ministered to the slaves, seeking thus to alleviate the evil. This effort only caused more trouble. It widened the breach between herself and her husband, one which had already been opened by temperamental differences. Finally she left him and went home to England and back on the stage.

The Butler estate had come down to her husband from his grandfather, the first Pierce Butler, who had fought in the Revolution and sat in the Constitutional Convention. Through generations this estate had exemplified the ideals of southern planters and was typical of the more magnificent ventures of this sort, and of gentle living, which came to be the norm in the romantic fiction that yearning Southerners sat down among the ruins to write in the era after the Civil War, when the dream had vanished and seemed more resplendent in the backward glance. The first Pierce Butler lived in feudal majesty and had six hundred slaves on his rice plantation on Butler's Island and his sea-island cotton plantation on St. Simon's Island. The baronial splendor had tarnished already when Fanny Kemble saw it, and to her it was shabby, more so perhaps because she was accustomed to English country houses which were more comfortable and better kept, with orderly gardens where every flower and every bush and every tree was a special object of special care. Butler's Island was flat, hot and uninteresting, actually sitting lower than the Altamaha River at its high-water mark so that it was protected by dikes. The house here was small and contained as well the office where her husband

and his overseer carried on the business of the plantation. St. Simon's Island, with its giant live oaks and their welcome shades and deep shadows and just a trace of the relics of Oglethorpe's day to give it the flavor of an antique, was much more to her taste, though the once-lordly manor occupied by the first Pierce Butler was falling into ruin and decay and was no longer habitable. It was moldy within, with rotting stairways and leaking roof, she discovered on a visit of inspection. In the passing of its former grandeur she saw clearly, with keen intuition, what was happening to the South and its whole economic structure under the depressing influence of the slavery system.

For this St. Simon's Island estate had once been quite magnificent. Aaron Burr had found it so when he came to it for refuge after he had killed Alexander Hamilton in 1804 to hide away from the public indignation. Here he had lived for several weeks while the Butler family was away in the North. He wrote his beloved daughter Theodosia about the lavish establishment. For his own personal service he had "a house-keeper, cook and chambermaid, seamstress and two footmen, two fishermen and four boatmen always at my command." John Couper, owner of the adjoining estate, sent him over "an assortment of French wines, claret and sauternes, all excellent, and Madame Couper added sweetmeats and pickles sufficient to last twelve months." The Couper estate was still well kept when Fanny Kemble lived here briefly, but it alone approached her expectations of the manner of living she had expected in this lush southern land.

The cotton plantations, in the upriver country as along the coast, revolved about the wife of the owner, who was the mainspring of management of all its multitude of affairs embraced in the housekeeping end of the establishment. This not only included meals, but direction of weaving and spinning of homespun for clothes, sewing by the Negro seamstresses, and care of the health and well-being of the slaves, a constant duty that often took the lady of the manor to the cabins, with her basket of simple remedies, in the middle of the night.

It was in many respects a matriarchal civilization, in its best aspects. But the matriarch always remained unobtrusively in the background, the silent but efficient partner who, among other accomplishments, was the creator of the manners and social customs that made southern life gracious and cultured at its higher levels.

The busy sort of life led by these plantation women is illustrated in the daily round of Mrs. Spalding, wife of Thomas Spalding of Sapelo Island. At nine in the morning, after breakfast was out of the way, she interviewed the plantation nurse, who came to her with a list of the sick. She visited the serious cases at the Negro quarters and, if necessary, called a doctor. Then she had personal interviews with the cook, the butcher, and the fisherman. At twelve she received the three plantation seamstresses with their baskets of completed garments, which she checked and assigned to the various slaves. She had no time for herself until two o'clock, when she got a brief respite, but her time was really never her own, for she was constantly at call to settle this and that problem which came up.

Dinner was at four-thirty in the afternoon, a bountiful spread, and she never knew how many would be about the table. For neighbors dropped in of their own accord and others might be invited by the children or by her husband, who, meanwhile, had been busy on his rounds of the plantation. It was customary for him to invite to dinner any friends he encountered during the morning. One of the daughters said she never remembered sitting down to dinner with less than twenty-four persons present. Mrs. Spalding was busy all this time, too, having babies and caring for them. She had sixteen children, but only six of them lived to maturity.

The Spalding plantation was a big one and living was on a grand scale. But the busy life of the wife was no exception to that on the substantial plantations inland, and even the smaller ones. The woman was, in truth, the center of the plantation.

And, when the hard years came on, when war took the men away, there she stayed. Then she managed it all, not only the home but the fields, through the times when there was not so much food, when life was no longer gracious and pleasant, when the encircling armies got closer, often with heart heavy over the news that the casualty lists brought, on to the end— and afterward, for living must go on.

PART 6

The Transition

CHAPTER ONE

COTTON BROUGHT STEAMBOATS AND RAILROADS

Cotton brought cash into the upper river country. Cash money
makes a market which is quickly exploited by wide-awake
businessmen. There were some of the latter in Savannah and
Augusta and they began to scheme how they could reach into
this market and take some of the money out.

The planters, by and large, were satisfied with their stagecoach economy. They could not see far beyond the cotton at
the end of their noses, and were contented enough with their
lives. They didn't have much left over anyhow after they had
met their bills to invest in improvements, and were too busy
with their plantation routine, including its entertaining and
casual pleasures, to look around and see what might be done
in the way of progress.

But the city fellows had their eyes open.

And so, in time, there were steamboats running up and
down the river, boats which could take a whole heap of cotton

downriver in their ample holds and bring back a whole hull full of "city goods" and, at the same time, provide room above for passengers on a nice, comfortable trip down the river to Savannah and around to Charleston.

In time, too, the railroads came into this country.

It was a rich country, drawing these things to it like a magnet.

How flourishing a market it offered was demonstrated by two simple facts: first, that steamboat navigation developed earlier in a commercial way on the Savannah—it began in 1819— than on any other river with the single exception of the Hudson in New York; and, second, that the first railroad in the United States—and the longest railroad in the world at the time it was finished—touched the river at Hamburg.

Hamburg was the lively little river port just across from Augusta, one which South Carolina fostered as a means of tapping this new upcountry market and drawing this trade away from both Augusta and Savannah by diverting it to Charleston, which was at the other end of the so-called Charleston-Hamburg Railroad.

A series of rivalries was thus set in motion, all emanating at first in progressive minds in the two seaboard cities, Savannah and Charleston. These rivalries in turn created others, so that steamboats were soon sounding their blasts up and down the river valley, and the whistles of railroad trains echoed through the rolling country on either side of the river.

A fight developed first over steamboat transportation. There was, at the outset, only one company operating boats up and down the Savannah. South Carolina interests executed a clever coup by inducing the steamboat company to fix the Savannah rate for the longer haul from Hamburg to Charleston. Thus the rate for the haul through the mouth of the river past Savannah and up the coast to Charleston was the same as that charged for the shorter haul from Augusta to Savannah. And South Carolina could offer plenty of cash freight from her rapidly developing upper country. For a time this played havoc in Augusta and Savannah, and, in the end, broke the steamboat company's monopoly.

Then, in 1833, the railroad was completed from Charleston to Hamburg and South Carolina again got the upper hand. Thereupon Georgia stirred herself again. Work was begun that same year—1833—on a railroad, long agitated, from Augusta to inland Georgia. That same year, too, Savannah woke up to see that this would give Charleston another advantage, since it would now have a railroad link through Hamburg and Augusta with the rich midlands of Georgia. So Savannah interests made plans for a railroad from their city to Macon, in the center of Georgia, to meet the challenge from Charleston. This line was not completed, however, until several years later.

Two interesting and contrasting figures played dramatic roles in the beginning of transportation and commerce along the Savannah and its eventual expansion.

One was William Longstreet, who contrived the first steamboat that operated on the Savannah. The other was Henry

Schultz, the German-born promoter, who founded Hamburg and was the principal agent of South Carolina in this river war in the first half of the nineteenth century.

CHAPTER TWO

WILLIAM LONGSTREET GAVE THE SAVANNAH THE STEAMBOAT

William Longstreet was, like Eli Whitney, an inventor and dreamer. Like the man who gave the South the cotton gin, he, too, grew up in a still primitive American setting. The people he knew were not yet sympathetic to mechanical ideas. They were a pioneer people absorbed in the more immediate needs of life close to the soil and so caught up in stirring events, among them the American Revolution, that they could not be easily excited about visionary industrial development.

Born in Augusta in 1759, Longstreet was seventeen when the Revolution began, and twenty-four when it finally ended. It left the river valley where he lived an almost hopeless shambles of wrecked homes and ruined fields. Reconstruction was the first task to which the people must devote themselves.

But young Longstreet held to his dream, even in the disordered times. He found a counterpart to Whitney's counselor and financial backer, Phineas Miller, in one Isaac Briggs, who teamed up with him. Longstreet's passion was for the steam engine and his consuming ambition was to hitch it to a boat. He, and Briggs his partner, appealed to the Georgia Assembly, and in 1788 it passed "an act to secure Isaac Briggs and William Longstreet, for the term of 14 years, the sole and exclusive privilege of using a newly constructed steam engine, invented by them."

Their difficulties, both in enlisting public interest and in getting necessary materials, are revealed in a letter Longstreet wrote in September, 1790, two years after applying to the legislature, to Governor Telfair of Georgia. It is a most illuminating document, as to both the man and his times. Here is what he said:

> Sir: I make no doubt you have often heard of my steamboat and as often heard it laughed at. But in this I have only shared the fate of all other projectors, for it has uniformly been the custom of every country to ridicule the greatest inventions until use has proved their ability. In not reducing my scheme to practice has been a little unfortunate for me I confess, and perhaps the people in general; but until very lately I did not think that either artists or material could be had in the place sufficient. However, necessity, that grand science of invention, has furnished me with an idea of perfecting my plan almost entirely with wooden materials, and by such workmen as may be got here, and from a thorough confidence of its success I have presumed to ask for assistance and patronage.
>
> Should it succeed agreeable to my expectation, I hope I shall discover that source of duty which such favors always merit; and should it not succeed, your reward must lay with other unlucky adventures.
>
> For me to mention to you all the advantages arising from such a machine, would be tedious and indeed quite unnecessary, therefore I have taken the liberty to state in this plain and humble manner my wish and opinion, which I hope you will excuse, and I shall remain either with or without approbation, your Excellency's most obedient and humble servant.

A cocky and confident fellow he seems to have been, despite his assumption of humility.

It was about this time, probably after the letter, since he didn't mention it, that he is reputed to have hitched a steam engine to a small boat and used it successfully in propulsion on the river. While keeping an inner eye on his steamboat dream, and figuring out ways and means of realizing it, he applied the steam engine to other practical uses. He produced both a steam cotton gin and a steam sawmill. Whether he ever met Whitney is not known, but he helped to improve the usefulness of the cotton gin by the application of steam. Like Whitney, he had his troubles from fire. The building housing his steam gin was burned down in 1801. Destroyed with it was a new boiler he had constructed, one which he believed would make possible an increase in the amount of cotton that could be cleaned in a day.

His steam sawmill was termed a success in the Augusta *Herald* of June 30, 1802, which said:

> This mill, though in miniature, appears to have all the necessary machinery for saw-mills, and strikes out one hundred times per minute, without the aid of any wheel whatsoever.

His tinkering with a steamboat seems to have been generally known and, as he had written to Governor Telfair, "laughed at." For tradition has it that his fancy was the butt of a comic song of the day which ran:

> Can you row the boat ashore,
> Billy-boy, Billy-boy?
> Can you row the boat ashore,
> Gentle Billy?
> Can you row the boat ashore,
> Without paddle or an oar,
> Billy Boy?

Time remained in which to wonder and applaud.

There's a legend that Longstreet operated a steamboat successfully on the Savannah in 1806, but this undoubtedly was an interpolation after the fact made by loyal Georgians who would give Longstreet precedence over Robert Fulton, whose *Clermont* made its first voyage up the Hudson on August 7, 1807.

Over a year later, however, in November, 1808, Longstreet's dream finally did come true. The Augusta *Herald* of November 10 attests his success, formally and without the intimate detail that we would like:

> We are happy to announce that Mr. Longstreet's experiments with his new invented steamboat have answered most sanguine expectations. The lovers of the arts in this place, and the spectators who have been extremely gratified by the different essays he has made, and no doubt remains in their minds, but his labors will be crowned with success, and that it will, were it necessary, add another proof that Americans are endowed with genius.

We have no adequate description of this first steamboat to cleave the waters of the Savannah, except that it was an "odd-looking craft with heavy oak boilers banded with iron." It was obviously a rather crude affair. But it did prove itself, and much to the amazement of a flock of doubters who followed it downstream in a fleet of skiffs, ready to scoff. But lo and behold, it turned back upstream and came puffing along under its own steam power!

Many people lived to see steamboats come and go regularly on the Savannah. But not the inventor. He died only six years later. The inscription on his tombstone in St. Paul's churchyard in Augusta reads:

> Sacred to the memory of William Longstreet, who departed this life September 1, 1814, aged 54 years, 10 months and 26 days. "All the days of the afflicted are evil, but he that is of a merry heart hath a continual feast."

But others already had begun to capitalize upon the genius of the man whose life plainly had not been "a continual feast." Samuel Howard, who is responsible for the first practical commercial operation of steamboats on the Savannah, got a patent from the legislature the year that Longstreet died. It gave him exclusive rights to operate a steamboat line, not only on the Savannah, but on all the waters of Georgia. The South Carolina legislature concurred in this patent shortly afterward, but limited the exclusive right to twenty years.

Conditions were attached to the rights granted Howard. He must have one vessel in operation within three years, and one on each river in Georgia within ten years. The grant would lapse if operations were suspended for longer than a year at a time. Howard's idea at the outset was not so ambitious as a regular steamboat line for freight and passengers. His object was an auxiliary service for other craft in keeping with the legislative grant for steam vessels for "towing and warping the ships, vessels, boats, and rafts, in and upon which the same may be laden, by means of other boats or vessels impelled by the aid of steam."

Howard immediately ran into difficulties. It was three years before he even got his company organized and he had no boat operating on the river as specified. But the legislature renewed his exclusive charter, and with more generous terms. This time he was allowed seven years in which to begin operations. The capital stock of his company was fixed at $200,000. This could be increased to $800,000 by a two-thirds vote of the stockholders. Governor Rabun of Georgia advised the state legislature in 1818 that he had bought, for the state, two hundred shares of stock in the company. As security there was a mortgage on the company's real estate for $100,000 at eight per cent interest.

By the next year, 1819, he had a steamboat on the river and four years later the line was in complete operation. Not only were there vessels running from Savannah to Augusta and return, but also from Charleston to Hamburg and back. South Carolina, having received its favorable rate from Hamburg to Charleston, pushed and protected its advantage by special favors to Hamburg in the way of tax exemptions and a $100,000 bonus to encourage its competition with Augusta.

Savannah and Augusta were sorely hit. Business interests complained in a flood of memorials to the legislature. That body met the clamor by appointing a special joint committee to investigate. In its rather voluminous report the committee drew a grim picture. The trade of Savannah and Augusta had fallen off woefully, rents had gone down, half the houses in Augusta were standing vacant, real estate had dropped one half in value, and the income of all the people had suffered. As one cause it cited the steamboat monopoly of Howard and his associates.

But they enjoyed their monopoly only a little while longer. In 1824 the company lost the protection of Georgia and South

Carolina statutes. In that year the United States Supreme Court, in a decision written by John Marshall, declared such a monopoly of river transportation contrary to the Constitution. This was an interesting story that had a direct link with Savannah in that one of her former citizens was a major figure in the famous case.

This was Thomas Gibbons, to whom we have been introduced previously in connection with Anthony Wayne. He was now a wealthy man.

Gibbons had become interested in starting a steamboat line in New York, but ran head on into the monopoly granted in the waters of New York by the state legislature to Robert Fulton and his father-in-law, Robert Livingston. He decided to fight it. The captain of Gibbons's boat, a combative Dutchman by the name of Cornelius Van Der Bilt, was game for this business war. Eventually Van Der Bilt got himself and his boat arrested. This took the case to the courts, the famous suit of *Gibbons* v. *Ogden.* Ultimately it got to the Supreme Court where John Marshall was waiting, his pen literally aching for a broadside against monopoly. Daniel Webster, who represented Gibbons, did himself proud. It was just such a case as to suit his fancy. And John Marshall did himself proud in his decision, a constitutional landmark. He said the monopoly conferred by New York State was "repugnant to the Constitution and laws of the United States."

There was another episode in this fight against monopoly which was more amusing than significant. The Georgia legislature subsequently regretted its exclusive grant to Howard and, just the year after it extended his exclusive franchise, it chartered another company, the Savannah River Navigation Company, to provide cheaper transportation between Savannah and Augusta. Everybody wondered what sort of power would be used, since Howard had a monopoly on steam. It all came out when a boat called the *Genius of Georgia* moved slowly up the river under power supplied by nineteen horses walking on an endless belt. This treadmill contraption was advertised as a "team-boat." It did not last long and the Supreme Court's mandate in *Gibbons* v. *Ogden* made it no longer necessary.

In time competing companies did establish themselves on the Savannah and the river was lively with the passage of steamboats. These went through an evolution from the little ugly duckling of Longstreet into big and graceful swans with luxurious appointments for passengers and plenty of room in the hold for cash freight. As many as fifteen river steamboats a week would move in and out of Savannah and Augusta. There are records for forty-five years which tell an interesting story. Between 1820 and 1865 some seventy different vessels operated between the two cities.

They had their troubles with the river. River navigation always was attended with hazards because of the tricky currents that changed their course, shifted the channel, and built up sand bars. Often there were periods of low water that brought traffic to a standstill. Many boats were ensnared by the fickle river which so often turned vampire. Of the seventy that served her whims for shorter or longer terms from 1820 to 1865, thirty were destroyed: thirteen by fire, six by explosions, while eleven sank.

CHAPTER THREE

HENRY SCHULTZ BUILDS HIMSELF A CITY

Henry Schultz, who created the town of Hamburg across the river, the town that became such a competitor of Augusta for a time, was a boatman, too, at the start. He was a river boatman, but not for long.

He had come over from Germany in 1806 when the up-river country was still a pioneer region. He came in the role of young man-adventurer, apparently with nothing in the way of worldly goods, but footloose and fancy free. Work was not hard to find for one of his kind. He got a job on a boat on the Savannah River, presumably of the smaller cargo kind, perhaps a Petersburg boat. Later he became a "patroon," which, in the parlance of the times, meant master of a vessel. Possibly he made a little money for himself; though, knowing his ways— he was not at all the thrifty or saving sort—it couldn't have been a great deal. Anyway, he decided to change his business seven years after he arrived on the Savannah.

A career on the river was too placid for one of his energy and talents. He was brimming over with the instinct and vitality of the promoter, and was endowed with the necessary qualities of vision and salesmanship. He was, too, a man of big heart as well as big ideas. Possessed of some engineering talent, he had the fancy of a toll bridge over the Savannah at Augusta. There a fellow might really make some money.

He needed a partner. This he found in a man by the name of Lewis Cooper. They secured from the legislatures of Georgia and South Carolina the right to build a bridge across the Savannah. It was completed a year later, in 1814. Meanwhile Cooper had sold his interest in the bridge to a prominent merchant, John McKinne. The project turned out handsomely. There was plenty of traffic over the bridge with the development of the upcountry. Soon Schultz branched out into the banking business, which also proved to be a profitable venture. He issued bills from his bank secured by the bridge. This way of creating currency was common in those unstable times, not only by banks, where it was more or less orthodox practice, but also by commercial houses. All sorts of bills were in circulation. Schultz went in rather heavily. His issue was $500,000.

After a few years Schultz had built himself up a fortune for those times and decided to sell out his business and go back home to Germany. He disposed of his interest in the bank to Barna McKinne, a brother of John, under an arrangement by which McKinne assumed a $63,000 debt to the bank and Schultz took a bond of $500,000 by the McKinne brothers to guarantee him against loss through his liability on the bridge bills.

Schultz might have gone on back to Germany and passed out of the history of the Savannah, leaving only a bridge behind him, had it not been for the depression that struck the river valley in 1819, an embezzlement by which the McKinnes tried to tide themselves over, and his own integrity. Hard pressed, the brothers dipped deeply into the bank's funds to support their tottering mercantile business, and eventually they were forced to suspend redemption of their bills for lack of "hard" money. Schultz knew that the bond could not protect him now, so he bought back Barna McKinne's interest in the bank and paid off depositors with his own money.

But the McKinne brothers had become otherwise involved. This, in turn, involved Schultz, since he had honestly decided to stay behind to try to straighten out their tangled affairs. They had mortgaged the bridge to the Bank of the State of Georgia, an institution in which the state had acquired stock, just as it had purchased stock in many others in a wave of banking investments that preceded the 1819 bank depression.

In 1821 the state foreclosed on the bridge mortgage as one of the steps it was taking in every direction to get out from under its ill-advised foray into the banking business. Thus Schultz found himself implicated on another front. He challenged foreclosure of the mortgage in the federal court. So began the famous Augusta Bridge case, which meandered in and out of the courts, coming three times before the United States Supreme Court, before it came to an end. Finally, it was thrown out of the highest tribunal in the land unceremoniously on the ground of lack of jurisdiction. But this was in 1855, thirty-four years later, and four years after Henry Schultz's death.

Schultz was well entangled. He resorted to tactics familiar to military men—and promoters. That is, he started an offensive in another direction in order to recoup himself. He determined upon a most ambitious project. This was to build a town across the river from Augusta to capitalize on the rich market that cotton was creating in the surrounding section. He got hold of three hundred acres of land as a site and on July 21,1821, began to build the town. He named it Hamburg after the German port. There is a tradition that the town was thrown together in one night. Schultz, at least, would waste no time once he had an idea. Whether the town actually was raised in one night or not, it was, when finished, a complete town, with stores for trading and warehouses for cotton. He bought himself a steamboat and began trade with Charleston. South Carolina interested itself officially in the project, for it was just what the state needed to jack up her own port of Charleston and meet the rising threat of the young and more aggressive neighbor state in the latter's combination of Augusta and Savannah.

South Carolina was generous with encouragement. The legislature advanced $50,000 to the city, secured by mortgages on property, and voted a five-year tax exemption to attract business and industry to Hamburg.

The city grew and prospered and Henry Schultz prospered with it, at least for quite a time. He became a widely known figure in the whole region. Once again the favored of fortune, he indulged himself in good living and plenteous hospitality. Every year, so long as he was prosperous, he gave a dinner to a great number of friends on the anniversary of the founding of Hamburg.

Ten years after it was established Hamburg was the center of a flourishing trade with the upcountry. Between 35,000 and 70,000 bales of cotton were brought there for marketing every year and there was a brisk business in supplying the cotton planters with sugar, salt, coffee, iron, cotton goods, wines, and slaves. Hamburg developed into a busy slave market. There, after the importation of slaves had been legally stopped, planters across the river in Georgia come to replenish their supply of black labor. This market was active until a few years before the outbreak of the Civil War.

In its general trade the town reached far into the back country over wagon trails that brought it business not only from upper South Carolina, but also from western North Carolina and even as far as Tennessee and Kentucky. When the construction gang that had been building the Charleston-Hamburg Railroad finally completed their work by laying the tracks into Hamburg, they had thus opened another and faster outlet to Charleston and the sea. Hamburg then boomed to the peak of its brief but glorious career as a rival to Augusta, assuming what then looked like a permanent place in the rich upland cotton empire of South Carolina.

But its founder, who saw his dreams coming true, was running into bad times again. As the town's fortunes went up, his went down. His troubles were both of a personal and a business nature, the second growing partly from the first.

His personal difficulties came from getting himself involved in what began as a rather trivial and not uncommon incident in rural communities. Two young women who had moved into Hamburg from the upcountry lost a trunk on the way. They accused the Negro boy who had been driving the wagon carrying their baggage. The boy confessed to stealing the trunk, but he said it was at the instigation of a young white man, one Joseph Martin. The two were arrested. Schultz injected himself into the case, assuming a sort of proprietary interest in anything that happened about Hamburg, and, being present when the arrests were made, he lost his temper and threw the young man into a ditch. He also beat the young fellow severely to try to make him confess.

Schultz's insensate German rage turned him into a veritable wild man. Young Martin fainted several times. Schultz, ultimately regaining control of himself, became contrite. He hurried the boy off to his house and called a physician. Martin's father came to Schultz's home and removed his son to another house nearby. There he died. Schultz was arrested, along with another man, Alexander Boyd, who had become involved with him. The two were tied up with ropes and taken to the jail at Edgefield, the county seat. A third man who had joined the two, David Lynar, was not arrested, yet he went to jail voluntarily to stay with his two friends. He died in jail before the trial.

Schultz and Boyd were indicted for murder by the Edgefield Grand Jury. The trial at Edgefield a few weeks later attracted the wide attention that such affairs do in a rural and frontier community. But the usual interest here was greatly enhanced by the prominence of Henry Schultz. The two men were found guilty of manslaughter and sentenced to prison until the next term of court, when, it was ordered, they should be branded on the thumbs of their left hands with the telltale "M." Both were pardoned several months later and released from custody January 14, 1828.

Henry Schultz's personal fortune was drained severely by legal fees and by the neglect of his business while he was in jail. When he was freed he found his affairs in a bad way. He was heavily in debt. A few months later he became hopelessly insolvent and was taken in custody by the sheriff of Edgefield County until he should turn over his property to a trustee who was delegated to satisfy his creditors. Two years later the state foreclosed its mortgage on Hamburg for the money it had advanced, and Henry Schultz lost still more property. A few years later he was able to get hold of some lots that had not been sold off, but not long afterward he was again sold out by the sheriff.

Even during his adversity, however, he seemed to keep his buoyant spirits, and to sustain faith in the town he had created. Still he burned inwardly with intense hatred for Augusta across the river. It became a deeply personal grudge.

For instance, in 1839, when the Savannah River was in one of its periodic low stages and river traffic suspended, he showed his scorn of the rival city which depended so on the river—"her river," he sarcastically termed it—by planting a garden on a sandbar which had appeared in the channel because of the low water. He went through the formal motions of having the "island" surveyed and planted corn, rice, and turnips. This garden was inundated and swept away not long afterward when the river rose again. But it had served Schultz's purpose, and he pointed the moral in a communication to the newspapers, in which he said boastfully:

"Money will buy rice and turnips for me to eat, but money

will not buy water for them to run their steamboats on. I therefore readily yield my private loss for their benefit."

But there came a time when Henry Schultz did not even have money to buy food for himself. From about 1843 on he was compelled to live on the charity of his friends.

A decline had set in, too, for Hamburg, which he watched, no doubt, with the philosophic sorrow of the old and beaten. Augusta had not been conquered so easily as he had imagined, while a series of developments had contributed to the downfall of Hamburg. Building of railroads in upper South Carolina diverted trade toward other cities, such as Greenwood, Newberry, Anderson and Greenville. Also Augusta's access to the upriver country by way of the Savannah had been improved by the construction of a canal around the rapids and falls. That way navigation of this stretch of the river was made much easier. Likewise, the Charleston-Hamburg Railroad was now extended into Augusta, and the completion of railroad lines from Augusta into the Georgia midlands, and from Augusta to Savannah, gave Hamburg's erstwhile rival valuable new outlets that made her no longer dependent on "her river."

With all this, the river herself became secondary, as the main highway of commerce and civilization, though it was to be many years before she retired almost completely into her "primeval privacy" to become a somber spinster of the wilderness, bent only on picking her way undisturbed to the sea.

She was still a grand lady, though more reserved and less boisterous than in her gorgeous youth, when Henry Schultz died along her banks in Hamburg in 1851. He was buried, so tradition has it, with his head facing toward Augusta, still defiant, so that he could stand guard for the once-proud rival town he had created. That, so the story goes, was at his request.

But "her river," Augusta's river, had the last word. Hers was the ultimate revenge.

She rose up mightily in one of her worst floods in 1929

to wash from the face of the earth, with one tremendous gesture, the last remains of Henry Schultz's Hamburg, then a village of squatter shacks housing about a hundred indigents. They were finally moved by the Red Cross up into the hills to try to start a new, perhaps even a better and drier, life.

PART 7

The Irrepressible Conflict

CHAPTER ONE

STATESMEN ARE SCHOOLBOYS FIRST

Among the still primeval forests along the banks of the Savannah, on the Carolina side about forty-five miles above Augusta, there was a school for boys which once became famous in the region—though its career was relatively brief—because of the distinction achieved by a number of its students and their influence on the course of events that culminated in secession and the Civil War.

Willington School, so named from a nearby settlement, got its character from its founder, Dr. Moses Waddel, sometimes proudly called by local historians "the Carolina Dr. Arnold." He later became an outstanding educator in the South as president of the University of Georgia.

Dr. Waddel was a Presbyterian minister who first entered the educational field as a side line. He was a born educator, a veritable champion of learning in a community still emerging from the pioneer stage. It was in the year 1801 that he started his Willington School and at a time when education was not generally regarded in those parts as an essential. Most of the local farmers' families had more practical uses for strong youngsters with sturdy arms and legs. Simple reading, writing, and arithmetic in the Old Field Schools was held to be enough. Often they could not be spared even for that.

Dr. Waddel, however, had two schools across the river in Georgia, rather informal affairs, before he established another at Willington. This was just after the turn of the nineteenth century, and the institution that he founded was to leave his name forever as a shining mark of progress in the history of the Savannah River valley.

The school was favorably located. It was about six miles from Willington, one of five nearby towns along the river, and situated at a sort of river crossroads. For here the Broad River joined the Savannah from the Georgia side, and a wagon trail led off into South Carolina. On the Carolina side was Vienna, while the other three towns, Petersburg, Lisbon and Southampton, were in Georgia. They had grown up here and thriven on the tobacco trade. But the whole community was then hesitating uncertainly and in a state of transition. Tobacco culture was beginning to dwindle; soon it was to yield entirely to cotton. The growing of wine grapes, which had been introduced by Huguenots, was languishing too. In fact the people of this vicinity were faring none too well.

Despite obvious financial handicaps from the poor economy of the region, students came flocking to Dr. Waddel's school, some at great sacrifice. But the minister seemed to inspire this whole countryside with a yearning for education. As the fame of the school spread, it came to be the ambition of an industrious boy to go to Dr. Waddel's school. In time there were two hundred and fifty students. Some came from far away. Many were from families in good circumstances. Others were from poor families who somehow made provision for educating their sons.

The school consisted of a central hall, or "academy," built of logs. About it were several other cabins, also built of logs and chinked with clay against the chill winds that blew off the river now and then in the winter season. It was a combination boarding school and day school. Some students who lived nearby came for the day's sessions and went home at night. The board students lived in the log cabins, which had been built by the students themselves. The food was plain, mostly corn bread and bacon. Plain living, devotion to study, and high thinking formed the credo of Dr. Waddel.

It was, in many respects, quite an unusual educational institution. For one thing, the boys were turned loose in good weather in the woods along the river for study periods. There, scattered about under the oak and hickory trees, singly or in groups, they conned their Latin and Greek. The classics were the bases of Dr. Waddel's curriculum, which seems to have been an innovation in educational methods for a secondary school. His formula and methods attracted interest among educators all over the country.

The routine was simple. In the early years of the school Dr. Waddel used a horn to arouse the students in the morning and to start the day's work. It was also sounded for changing classes, and as a signal at night for shutting out lights. These were provided by pine knots rather than candles, then a rarity. Later a bell was substituted as a signal. But the doctor often disregarded these signals and would merely step out of the central schoolroom and call the boys from their sylvan study periods with a loud "Books, books, young men!" He was a stern disciplinarian and believed firmly in frequent application of the birch rod for violation of the rules. He inculcated a certain amount of self-rule and democracy by holding court every Monday morning to try offenders of the previous week. He acted as judge but the jury was made up of a panel of five students. His tongue had the acid bite of the legendary country schoolmaster, and most of the students preferred a whipping to one of his tart lectures on the error of their ways.

"It was a kind of rural republic, with a perpetual dictator," one student described it afterward. "The scholars were enthusiastically attached to their school. After they had become grandfathers they still talked of it in raptures."

One of his students who later became famous, Augustus Baldwin Longstreet, describes Dr. Waddel for us as a man of medium height, about five feet nine, inclined to rotundity about the waist, with an "uncommonly large" head, covered with a heavy coat of dark hair, and with gray eyes overshadowed by thick eyebrows. The general impression was one of extreme austerity.

To his school here in the woods there came from the Long Cane section about Abbeville, only a few miles away, the almost equally austere John Caldwell Calhoun, a humorless sort of fellow, straight out of the rugged, God-fearing Calhoun clan of Scotch Covenanters. Patrick Calhoun, John's father, had settled the family here about half a century before, had founded a church, and had seen his family and numerous relatives through various hardships, including a Cherokee massacre which it survived with only a few losses. The founder of the Carolina clan, James Calhoun, the father of Patrick, had landed with his wife and four sons at New York in 1733, the same year that Oglethorpe had brought his first boatload of colonists to the mouth of the Savannah. They had lived for a while in Pennsylvania and then moved to Virginia. There James had died and his wife had later been killed by Indians. The family had then migrated to Waxhaw, South Carolina; finally, they moved to Little River in the Abbeville district, where John was born.

John C. Calhoun came a bit tardily to his education at Dr. Waddel's school. At nineteen he was a grown-up young man for those times. But he came fully aware of what he wanted, and he was energetic about getting it. Dr. Waddel was related by marriage to the Calhouns. His wife was an older half sister of John. As a boy of thirteen John Calhoun had spent a year at the Waddel home, then across the river in Georgia a few miles from Augusta. There he had gorged himself on the minister's library, reading so much, as a matter of fact—and reading very well, too—that his health had suffered and he had gone back home to take up an outdoor life, working on his father's farm, to regain his strength. He liked the farm life and might never have left it had his family not recognized the intellectual endowment of the young man and insisted that he should continue his schooling. He agreed, but only on condition that he should be given the best, that he should go to college and then to law school. To prepare for entrance to Yale it was decided that he should go to Dr. Waddel's school. So he took up his studies there, a tall and spare figure of six feet two, who towered above the other students. He was somewhat set apart, not only because of his age but because of an earnestness of purpose that contrasted with the still mischievous impulses of his younger companions. Already he was beginning to look the statesman, thin and gaunt of frame, but sturdy and tough from his hard physical labor on the farm. He was dignified, though of kindly disposition, with that startling mass of brown hair which was parted on the side and drooped "like an errant cloud, about the shining sun of his high forehead." He had deep-set eyes that now seemed blue, now gray, and the thin face and regular features of the ascetic.

He also had the confident manner of his proud Scottish background. And he had grown up, unlike many of his fellow students, in a frame house rather than a log cabin, for the Calhouns had the first frame house in their community. John Calhoun entered Willington school at its start and had the benefit of the personal attention of his kinsman-educator in directing his studies to the necessary requirements for his entrance two years later at Yale.

Just after John Calhoun had left the school for Connecticut, the same neighborhood sent another promising youngster in James L. Pettigru, who as a boy had been given to mooning along the green paths of the fields and forests that stretched about his home. He came from a comfortable home, though it was not strictly his own. His parents had moved in to live with his mother's brother at "Badwell." The house had been built by her father, Jean Louis Gibert, a Huguenot pastor, who had brought the last group of the refugees of his faith from France to South Carolina. James went to Willington School at a sacrifice, for he was relied upon by his mother to help about the farm at Badwell. It was she who carried the burden of the family rather than his father, William Pettigru. The school was only twelve miles from Badwell and the boy came home on weekends.

To young James, who was fifteen at the time, Willington School was a dream of high adventure which should lead to great things. The day he entered he wrote solemnly in his diary: "This day I am to go to Willington; with joy and fear I view the vast design." His innocence offered the usual temptation to inborn schoolboy cruelty. His homespun clothes and rusty, rural manners were ridiculed by some of the students from wealthier homes who sported broadcloth and fine linen. In desperation he fled from the study group in the woods one day and sought refuge in his own cabin, there to study alone. He was sitting with his back to the wall when, suddenly, he felt a burning sensation in the seat of his pants. One of the students had stuck a lighted pine stick through a crack in the wall. Enraged, James rushed outside and caught his persecutor. The two fought like young demons. Pettigru came off triumphant finally. But fighting was against the rules and both boys were convicted by the court on the following Monday morning—though James made a good case for himself—and both were whipped by Dr. Waddel. The new student had now proved himself. Thereafter he was accepted and life became more pleasant.

From really straitened and impoverished circumstances came another student who, like Calhoun and Pettigru, was to play an important role in the prelude to the tragedy of 1860. This was George McDuffie, who, even as a youngster, and despite his penurious background, carried himself with a proud and defiant face to the world. Leaving his home in Georgia, across the river, George McDuffie took literally to the road, a counterpart of Dick Whittington, with his few personal belongings and all his worldly possessions in a box. He wandered to the Long Cane country about Abbeville and there became a protégé of the Calhouns. They arranged for him to go to school at Willington.

An entirely different background in coastal Charleston contributed another student a few years later who was to join that group of outstanding Willington alumni, men who figured so prominently in the slowly developing crisis that came to its climax in the Civil War.

Hugh Swinton Legaré came from a Huguenot family endowed with culture and property, one that had been established in Charleston a century before his birth by his great-great-grandfather. Young Legaré, thirteen at the time, was impulsive, brilliant and headstrong. He at once disliked the unfamiliar rural backwoods and bitterly resented the unaccustomed discipline of Dr. Waddel. But long and imploring letters to his mother in Charleston were to no avail. She would not accede to his pleas to come home. She was a Scotchwoman, shrewd and of good judgment. She had sent him away just for what he was getting, a course of discipline to tame his wild spirit. He subsided after a few weeks and found contentment in his discovery of the classics under Dr. Waddel's skillful guidance. He stayed the necessary year to round him out for his entrance, at the age of fourteen, to the University of South Carolina. There he left behind a legend of intellectual versatility for being at once a thorough classical scholar and one highly accomplished in modern languages. French, Italian, Spanish, German, history, and philosophy—he was good in all alike. He had a voracious and consuming mind and developed a fine English style. His was, perhaps, the purest intellect of all that glittering array of South Carolinians who created the legendary golden age before the descending catastrophe.

Another figure who came under the influence of Dr. Waddel, but at an even later age than John C. Calhoun, was William H. Crawford, who barely missed the White House some years later. He was twenty-four, a giant, shambling, awkward fellow, when he won his heart's desire for a thorough grounding in the classics under the direction of Dr. Waddel. He had his early education in one of the Old Field Schools, with its sing-song recitations in unison in the three R's. Subsequently he conducted one of those schools in the Georgia backwoods not far from Augusta. He did not go to the Willington School, for it had not yet been established. He attended a school which Dr. Waddel held in Georgia, in Columbia County, some years before founding of the larger and more permanently organized school across the river in Carolina. To help pay his tuition he took a job as an usher in the earlier Waddel School in which capacity he was a sort of supervisor over youngsters. Like Calhoun, he also was Scotch. His family, like the Calhouns, had passed through the migration familiar in those years. They came from Virginia, where the first of the Crawford line in this country had settled in the back country in 1643, to South Carolina, thence to Georgia. There they joined other former Virginians who had followed the back trail and crossed the Savannah to the fertile midlands some years before.

Many other students of Dr. Waddel distinguished themselves later in their several communities and states, many as doctors and lawyers and legislators. But they did not, so directly as these already mentioned, affect the course of political events that rumbled on from Nullification to Secession to Civil War, nor move so markedly in the stream of national and international affairs.

To two of those who were educated at Dr. Waddel's school we are indebted for shrewd and revealing pictures of the kind of people who then lived about the middle and upper Savannah. One was George R. Gilmer, later governor of Georgia, author of many sketches of the period. The other was Augustus Baldwin Longstreet, who came from among those of New England extraction who had migrated to the Savannah. Longstreet, preacher, editor, and writer, was author of *Georgia Scenes*, delightful satirical sketches of the raw and gusty life of the period. He ably portrayed the poor whites and the lower middle classes, gander pullings and political meetings. In his pages the dramas of the courtroom and the circuit-riding lawyers—who traveled about in troupes, from court session to court session, eating, drinking and sleeping together, often in close confinement in the cramped and crude quarters of country inns—come memorably to life.

Thus Dr. Waddel's school, with its emphasis on mental discipline, on the classics, and on history and philosophy, provided a cultural incubation for the politicans and statecraft to which some of its more promising students turned in after years. Its curriculum was conducive to the development of fine, flowing oratory, to the elaboration of closely drawn distinctions about the rights of the states versus the federal government. Its graduates went naturally from the law into politics.

Dr. Waddel taught his students how to think, how to use their minds, how to reason. But he did not teach them *what* to think, and quite evidently he did not try to impose any hard and fast theories of government upon them—nor, as a matter of fact, had the issues about federal and state government developed much during the student days of those who later became such great figures in the impending conflict. For there does not seem to have been a pattern of thinking inculcated among students of this notable school, only a method. Many of its graduates took different sides in the years to come.

Calhoun, an extreme nationalist in his early political career in Washington, one of the "War Hawks" who decried New England's threat of secession over the War of 1812, later moved far over to the opposite side and became an inflexible champion of state rights. He even carried this theory to its ultimate in the doctrine of nullification. A state, he held, had a right to disregard federal laws that it did not approve. This thesis set him off on his memorable contest with Andrew Jackson, the stanch Unionist. Thus began the chain of reasoning, developing into a chain of action, that inevitably brought on the trial of arms in the Civil War.

George McDuffie fought beside Calhoun in Washington, in Congress, winning the title of "the orator of nullification." Like Calhoun, he did not see the tragic denouement of their philosophy, dying as he did in 1851, a year after Calhoun.

But Pettigru lived to see the Union torn asunder. It was the climax he had feared and had predicted. Pettigru stood resolutely against nullification and for the maintenance of a strong federal union. For his convictions he was denied political preferment and advancement. While he served one term in the House of Representatives, he was defeated by the nullificationists in two attempts to win a seat in the U.S. Senate from his state legislature. When he died, three months before the battle of Gettysburg, he was lauded at meetings of both the New York and the Massachusetts Historical Society, to which he had been elected, for his unwavering championship of the Union. Legaré could not swallow nullification, though he wrote and spoke constantly in defense of state rights. Nor could Crawford go all the way with Calhoun.

Dr. Waddel could not have foreseen the heights that his students attained—Calhoun the magnificent, southern pride and willfulness personified, dominant in several administrations as senator and cabinet officer, more than once a candidate for the presidential nomination; the gawky Crawford, senator, secretary of war, secretary of the treasury, the chosen candidate of the caucus for president before that institution passed from history. He lost the prize when a stroke of apoplexy paralyzed his huge body and made him a hopeless invalid for a time, though receiving quite substantial support nonetheless in the election in the House in which John Quincy Adams triumphed over him and Andrew Jackson and Henry Clay in 1824. And McDuffie, eloquently defiant for many years in Congress; Pettigru, who stood up so manfully to take his whipping for his first boyhood fight against injustice, and who stood up for his principles to the bitter end at the cost of political advancement and popularity; Legaré, the impulsive, who won his first battle with himself at Willington and later went on through a distinguished career as lawyer, orator, and writer of brilliant articles in the *Southern Review*, which he helped to found. He become attorney general of the United States.

These men were stars in the South Carolina galaxy when South Carolina shone so brightly in national affairs.

Dr. Waddel must have thought of them, as he saw them move forward to strut upon the stage of state and nation, as the boys he had known as students, with their little vanities and prejudices. For so it is with teachers. And so, too, with the long objectivity of history it is possible to look back upon them as boys parading about proudly, with their manners and their mouthings, playing with fire, and making themselves a war with the blithe blindness of youth—or so it seems as we look backward.

They were a high-tempered and stiff-necked generation. They destroyed themselves with their own pride, refusing to accept the logic of history, but they destroyed themselves right gallantly, and with many a fine phrase and hairsplitting and defensive rationalization; many of them persisted with the bravado of the self-appointed cavalier.

Pride wore itself into the thin and taut fabric of zealotry; honor, which they so often insisted upon, was strained into a hypocritical pose, an empty and silly gesture that was serious only to themselves and a mockery to others. Their so sensitive "honor" could smart from a phrase thrown in jest, from a word spoken in heat, or from the slight difference over the fine shading of a political issue. And so the challenges were sent, the seconds were appointed, and two proud men stood a few paces from each other in some quiet glade and shot for their honor as gentlemen.

Crawford killed a man, one Peter Lawrence Van Allen, in a duel over a political difference. The encounter took place at the famous dueling ground along the Savannah, the site of old Fort Charlotte, about twelve miles below Petersburg on the Carolina side. It was a favorite spot for such affairs. Another was Sand Bar Ferry, in the middle of the river, about four miles below Augusta.

The hotheaded George McDuffie fought two duels with a political enemy, William Cumming. In one he incurred a serious wound that constantly harassed him thereafter, shortened his life, and embittered his last years. Yet, how they loved to flaunt their "honor" on their sleeves in public, and amuse the populace with their gay bravado, as on the occasion when McDuffie, shown a placard which Cumming had tacked up on a tree impugning his honor, walked up and read it slowly and then stepped back and sprayed it with tobacco juice.

John M. Dooly, a wit of the day, ridiculed the code duello, though without much appreciation in his time. Then he, too, became embroiled in an affair of honor through his friendship with General John Clarke, the son of Elijah Clarke, who was constantly mixed up in political feuds, a true chip off the rugged old block.

The challenge to Dooly came from Judge Charles Tait, a friend of Crawford, and leader of the anti-Clarke faction. Crawford served as Tait's second. When the latter two reached the dueling ground they found John Dooly sitting placidly on a stump. General Clarke, his second, was nowhere visible. Crawford asked Dooly where the general was. Dooly replied that he was in the woods looking for a "gum." [1]

"May I inquire, Colonel Dooly, what use you have for a gum in the matter under settlement?" asked Crawford.

"I want the gum to put my leg in, sir. Do you suppose that I can risk my leg of flesh and blood against Tait's wooden one? [The judge had a wooden leg.] If I hit his leg he will have another one tomorrow, and be pegging about as usual; if he hits me I may lose my life by it, but almost certainly my leg, and be compelled, like Tait, to stump it the balance of my life. I could not risk this, and must have a gum to put my leg in; then I am as much wood as he is, and on equal terms with him."

"I understand you, Colonel Dooly; you do not want to fight?" asked Crawford.

"Well, really, Mr. Crawford, I thought everybody knew that."

"Very well, sir, you shall fill a column in the newspaper in no enviable light."

"Mr. Crawford, I assure you I would rather fill two columns than one coffin."

This was too much. Crawford and Tait marched from the field of honor in disgust. Dooly sat on his stump, grinning.

But he was an exception, and usually honor was served.

Long before the test of war finally came, gentlemen's nerves truly were strung tight over the fear of losing the comfortable servile civilization they were creating and defending about the middle and upper Savannah River in both South Carolina and Georgia. This was also true throughout the Georgia midland country across the river and for its heroes and statesmen. They, too, we shall see rising as shining stars high in the dark skies of

[1] Colloquial for a section of bark from the indigenous gum tree which is thick and tough.

the Confederacy. The ugly fact that slavery was the basis of this vaunted civilization hung heavier and heavier on their secret consciences, while shriller and shriller rose their voices in its defense, and more and more righteous were the reasons they dug up to scream from stump and pulpit. More and more uncomfortably the nice cherished rewards of this cotton civilization sat upon their souls—their broad acres, the obeisance of many black men. Their culture of a special kind, their lavish hospitality, even the books in their libraries where they searched for arguments to hush the still, small voice within and the loud accusing voices without—all weighed against them.

One of the still, small voices from without was a constant irritant, that of Pettigru. He was one of the few who saw clearly what was the real issue under all the frothing couched in classical quotations and pronounced with pious and heroic attitudes. It was the losing battle of the southern land against the northern factory, an agricultural economy against an industrial economy. The South, he saw, must yield its political domination of the national government to the North, for the North was now the stronger section economically and would not stop until this strength was reflected in its control of political power from Washington. That it was as simple as that, Pettigru saw clearly. For himself he was willing to have the South take its natural and lesser role, to have it recognize the inevitable, gracefully and graciously, without the ultimate clash otherwise so certain. Sorrowfully he saw the uneven contest go on.

For the South continued to fight its sham battles. It beat off the inexorable decision through a series of compromises starting with the Missouri Compromise, drawing lines below which slaves would be allowed and above which they would not; fighting, fighting, fighting to hold enough slave territory so Southerners could keep their power in Congress and in the national government. Never would they brush away the subterfuges, the specious, high-sounding arguments, and go directly to the issue, as Lincoln did finally, and see it clear and plain, as the simple choice of slavery or no slavery. So the moral issue eventually became paramount, as it was bound to do.

Just after his election in 1860, Lincoln wrote to his old friend, Alexander H. Stephens, whom he had known and admired and loved years before in Congress, and put the issue frankly: "You think slavery is right and ought to be extended; while we think it is wrong and ought to be abolished. That, I suppose, is the rub."

It was.

CHAPTER TWO

THE SAVANNAH VALLEY GAVE STEPHENS, TOOMBS, AND COBB

Alexander Stephens was a child of the fertile cotton country across the Savannah River in Georgia. He became, for history's sake, one of that brilliant southern triumvirate which included, besides himself, Robert Toombs and Howell Cobb, both also from this same region. Consequently this middle Savannah area, when you consider South Carolina's contribution already mentioned, was comparable in the creation of the Confederate States of America to the James River and Chesapeake Bay country in the formation of the United States of America three-quarters of a century before.

The Savannah River valley was, in truth, the Mediterranean of the Confederacy, providing it with men and ideas.

The South Carolinians evolved the philosophy that came into full bloom ultimately—after most of them were dead—in the Confederate States, and the Georgians were the legatees of that

philosophy, accepting its rational deductions belatedly and re-
luctantly, but carrying it forward to reality in the new, separate
government that was its inevitable outgrowth. Two of this triumvirate sat in its councils.

When Stephens, Toombs and Cobb left Georgia for the
convention at Montgomery from which the Confederacy was to
emerge, full blown, it would have been a very safe forecast that
one of these three would become the head of the new government, for they were the acknowledged three leading candidates.
But Toombs and Cobb, both strong and outspoken characters, had
made too many enemies, and Stephens, who had the most support of any one figure at the convention, yet hung back and refused to accept a condition that the South must strike the first
blow. He would not compromise his principles to be head of the
Confederate States of America. Out of these circumstances Jefferson Davis of Mississippi was selected president and Alexander
Stephens vice-president.

Howell Cobb presided over the Montgomery convention.
Later he took the field in Georgia when war surged over its borders toward the end. His brother, Thomas R. R. Cobb, was dominant in framing the constitution of the Confederate States, in
which Stephens also shared. The latter had become a delegate
to the convention from Georgia with the condition that Georgia
would go on record officially for a constitution modeled after
the United States Constitution. That model was followed to a
large degree as he had hoped. Thomas Cobb was killed in the
fighting in Virginia. Toombs became secretary of state in the
Jefferson Cabinet for a short time, resigning to enter the service.
His military career was distinguished.

These men represented, at the same time, the best and the
worst of the society that had developed about the middle Savannah, its culture, its easy friendliness, and its philosophy rationalized to accommodate it to an economy based on slavery. They
represented, too, a cross section of the sort of people who had
been thrown, from various backgrounds and antecedents, into

that melting pot, to come out, so many of them, and in a comparatively few years, in the patrician mold.

Stephens was the son of a poor and pious father who earned a sparse living by farming and schoolteaching. "Alec," as he was called, was only two generations removed from the Battle of Culloden. His grandfather was a soldier under the Stuarts and fled Scotland immediately after that catastrophe and took passage to the New World. He lived for a while among the Indians in western Pennsylvania and fought under George Washington in the French and Indian Wars. Later he was a captain in the American army in the Revolution. He moved to Georgia in 1784 and settled on Kettle Creek below Augusta.

The year before his arrival there, the grandfather of Howell Cobb and the father of Robert Toombs had taken up land in this same middle Georgia section. Both of these forebears of the Cobb and Toombs families had come from Virginia. Howell Cobb's grandfather, John Cobbs, had acquired large acreage in Jefferson County, become a planter of substance, and a leader in local affairs. He served in the House of Representatives for six years and also on the Executive Council of Georgia and was a member of the state constitutional convention that had drafted the 1795 constitution. His son John, Howell Cobb's father, who dropped the "s" from the family name, improved upon his heritage. He likewise was active in public affairs and a member of the legislature and when Howell was a child had moved the family to a big house in Athens. The Cobbs were thus established as a leading family of the state.

Robert Toombs also was born into a family that was in very comfortable circumstances when he arrived. His father, Major Robert Toombs, had led American troops against the British in the fighting on the Georgia front. For his services, he was awarded three thousand acres near Fort Washington, about which the town of Washington was then beginning to grow as one of the centers of that flourishing section.

Both Cobb and Toombs were thus well established in the planter background, the aristocracy of that place and time. Consequently they were the natural heirs of its social and political advantages as well as of its prejudices and predilections. They were confident always of their positions in the scheme of things. Howell Cobb was the wealthiest man in this region, with bounteous plantations tilled by a thousand slaves. Toombs also was affluent for the times, with his broad cotton fields cultivated by a host of Negroes and a fine colonial house in Washington, where he was always a hospitable and engaging host. His attitude was neatly put when he disdained a proposal of local citizens to build a hotel in Washington, saying: "If a respectable man comes to town, he can stay at my house. If he isn't respectable, we don't want him here at all."

Alexander Stephens, who possessed probably the finest mind of the three, was a vacillating soul, constantly torn between an inherent belief in the federal Union and a love for his native South. He was, in fact, the Hamlet of the Confederacy, its guilty conscience personified, and is perhaps the most sympathetic character of the whole cast in the short-lived drama of the Confederate States of America. We suffer with him as he went through his soul searching. He tortured himself continually.

His, too, was a tortured body. He was an invalid most of his life, so frail as a boy that his parents never expected him to grow to manhood, though he lived to be seventy. He suffered from colds, neuralgia, and fearful headaches. Familiar to the House of Representatives in Washington was the thin, emaciated figure, with the large head and penetrating eyes, sitting shrouded in a shawl that he threw across his shoulders to protect him against drafts. Yet he was figuratively a giant when he rose to speak. For magnetism flowed from his slight body and compelled attention, while his sincerity transformed his high-pitched voice into thunder. There was a spiritual quality about him that was lacking in the more vigorous and fleshly Toombs and Cobb, both giants physically, full of animal spirits, rugged, and down to earth.

As a boy, "Little Alec" performed the lighter chores about the family farm, a small farm, such a contrast to the sweeping acres where Cobb and Toombs grew up. He went to school for a time to a Catholic priest, afterward at the Academy at Washington, and took his college course at the University of Georgia, where he was quiet, studious, and a model student. He became an orphan in his boyhood and lived with relatives after the deaths of his father and mother. He never married. But he had two strong devotions in his life, his half brother, Linton Stephens, and Bob Toombs. He mothered the former as a youngster and nurtured his career later in life. Linton was his confidant. To him he poured out his soul in long, numerous, and revealing letters.

Bob Toombs was hardly more than a boy when he entered the University of Georgia, a bubbling youngster of fourteen, incorrigible, independent, and full of mischievous energy. Nevertheless, he wanted to be treated as a man of dignity and mature years. He chafed under the discipline for three years. He never bent his imperious will as had Hugh Legaré at Willington, and so was marched repeatedly before the authorities for infringement of the rules and regulations. Finally he had to leave college when his antics could no longer be tolerated.

There is a legend which persists at the University of Georgia with which every succeeding generation is acquainted. This is to the effect that, after his dismissal, Bob Toombs turned up before the chapel on Commencement Day while graduation exercises were in progress, quite intoxicated, took his stand under a huge oak tree that stood nearby, and began to deliver an oration. Gradually, so the legend goes, the chapel was emptied, until practically the whole Commencement audience was outside listening to Bob Toombs. The Commencement ceremonies proceeded in a cheerless vacuum. "Bob Toombs' Oak," as the tree was called, stood there for years. It finally withered away with old age and had to be cut down and a sundial was placed there to mark the historic spot.

Later he finished his college course at Union College in Schenectady, New York, and took his law degree at the University of Virginia. He was admitted to the bar in 1830, being examined in open court, as was the practice in those days, by no less a personage than William H. Crawford, then a circuit court judge. Toombs married and settled down to the practice of law at Washington, a brilliant and promising young man at twenty.

He had left the university before Alexander Stephens entered, and the two young men met later as fledgling lawyers. They took to each other at once, and a friendship developed that lasted all their lives. It persisted even through serious political differences. These, however, never became bitter. They were a strange pair seen together, the big boisterous Toombs, convivial, fun loving, a man's man, a natural-born hero to political crowds, and the wraithlike Stephens, quiet, shy, extremely temperate, ethereal rather than physical. They rode the circuit together, and always roomed together. In his simple home at Crawfordsville, Stephens set aside a room for his friend.

Stephens, Toombs, and Cobb, who also went to the university in his home town, drifted naturally into public affairs and politics, then the accepted career of men of their training, background, and abilities. Stephens and Toombs were Whigs, Cobb a Democrat. Stephens and Cobb went to the House of Representatives. The latter was elected speaker at the age of thirty-four. Bob Toombs went to the Senate, where he became an outstanding figure and one of the most effective orators in the history of that body. He had a sharpness of wit that was a constant joy to his fellow senators and a buoyant, radiant personality that made him a popular figure on Capitol Hill and in Washington society.

Howell Cobb also was a strapping fellow, tall, with broad, overwhelming shoulders, and a great mass of hair that floated about his head even more effulgently than did the ponderous shock of Bob Toombs about his great head. Cobb had the well-fed, sleek look of the plantation owner, and a double chin that was constrained by his high collar. In temperament he was even and moderate, calm of manner in speaking, not given to invective or tartness, as was Toombs.

These three men were, at the outset and until a decade before the war—Stephens even up to the war itself—effective brakes against the hurtling weight of emotion and passion that was hurrying the South toward the brink. All three had aligned themselves against the nullification movement, its philosophy and its motives. Cobb had won a reputation as a man who had stood up boldly against the South Carolina giant, John C. Calhoun. He stood solidly behind Andrew Jackson and the Union. All three were against secession as a principle. The movement for separation grew naturally out of nullification.

One of the most dramatic and amazing political campaigns that ever occurred in Georgia was when Cobb, Toombs and Stephens created the Constitutional Union Party in Georgia in 1850 and stumped the state in every direction, up and down and across, to cry down the doctrine of secession and plead for the Union. They were completely successful if their campaigns represented a mandate, for all three were elected: Cobb, governor; Toombs, senator; and Stephens, a member of the House. They had entrenched and fortified Georgia against the flood of separation sentiment that was running at high tide all about the state's borders, particularly in South Carolina. Cobb made a great political sacrifice, for he was a member of the regular Democratic Party. It had honored him with what was then regarded as the second highest office in the land, speaker of the House. He left this post to run for governor as the candidate of a new party, deserting the Democratic Party which had so honored him. His name had been mentioned prominently as a likely candidate for the nomination for president of the United States. In the face of all these allurements he bolted to follow his convictions. The enmities he thus incurred probably were among those which kept him from being chosen head of the Confederate States later.

But the valiant effort of the three men to check the rising tide was short-lived and unavailing. The truth was marching on, the bitter truth. Slavery must go. It was as if Joshua's hosts were stamping about the walls of the southern Jericho. In defense every Southerner, with few exceptions, went streaming to the ramparts. The trumpeters of the North blew their angry and penetrating blasts with Harriet Beecher Stowe and her *Uncle Tom's Cabin* to provide an exaggerated but devastating manifesto, while John Brown became a martyr before the horrified nation, North and South, and Abraham Lincoln gave the crusade its compelling truism: "This government cannot endure permanently, half slave and half free."

And Abe Lincoln—Honest Abe—was elected president of the United States.

Cobb and Toombs, themselves, were engulfed by the swelling tide. Cobb became a hopeless and disgusted man. He left Buchanan's Cabinet, where he was serving as secretary of the treasury, and went back to Georgia to await the certain event. Bob Toombs became embittered. He ranted in the Senate like a madman, pouring out a stream of subversive vitriol: "black Republicans—Lincoln an enemy of the human race—the Constitution of the United States a mistake—the Declaration of Independence, glittering generalities." War, it must be, and he welcomed it—"The Union, Sir, is dissolved—You see the glittering bayonet, and you hear the tramp of armed men from yon Capitol to the Rio Grande. It is a sight that gladdens the eye and cheers the hearts of other men ready to second them—Come on and fight.—Georgia is on the warpath! We are as ready to fight now as we ever shall be. Treason? Bah!" So he declaimed as he marched defiantly up the center aisle of the Senate and with a lordly gesture pushed open the doors and stalked out from the chamber and from the United States of America forever. However, he went to the Treasury, collected the salary due him and his mileage back to Georgia. Thus with his fare paid, he went home "to take up the sword."

Only Stephens of the three still stood firm, a frail reed waving and bobbing in the wild torrent, but still with his head above water. His battle with his conscience was like that of so many other thoughtful and patriotic people of the South. He still stood stanchly for the Union and the Constitution on which it was founded. Surely it would not be wrecked on the issue of slavery alone. That certainly could be compromised. Stephens rationalized himself, as did so many others, into a defense of slavery as a righteous institution. It was approved by the Bible, he insisted. And the more it was deprecated from the North, the more holy it became in his speeches. Listen to him: "Until Christianity be overthrown and some other system of ethics be instituted, the relation of master and slave can never be regarded as an offence against the divine law." Furthermore, subjugation was the natural order of the Negro! He was being civilized and Christianized through slavery! Alexander Stephens had become a crusader in a strange crusade. At his own home he had only two or three slaves to look after his personal needs. He was very kind to them, and they were devoted to him. So were all the Negroes in the village of Crawfordsville, where he lived. He was no plantation owner, only a squire without acres. Essentially he was a man of public affairs, one whose profession gave him a comfortable living, for he was an able lawyer.

Also Alexander Stephens was a sensible man, not given to rash judgments. Yet he could build up this kind of rationalized defense. If this could happen to a man of his sensitive and honorable character, it is easy to understand what was happening in the South. For there was great provocation, and there was hypocrisy on the northern side, too, arrant hypocrisy, as the abolitionists themselves had discovered.

These earnest souls had battered for years in New England at the hard crust New Englanders had baked about their consciences in defense of those profits which slavery had supplied in the form of cheap cotton that was going into their mills and making millionaires. Furthermore, the South asked another question, and not an unfair one. It was whether the "white foreign slaves," who were toiling from daybreak to dusk at a mere pittance for wages, were as well off as the Negroes of the South.

Stephens weighed all this, still clung to the Union. It must be saved!

He refused to accept the easier way out of Cobb, Toombs, and the others. So when Georgians gathered in a tense convention to pass on secession from the Union, Alexander Stephens stood up against both his friends. He pleaded against separation. His persuasive logic had won a minor preliminary skirmish in the Taliaferro County convention. He had convinced his neighbors there, and they had voted against secession and had sent him as a delegate to the state convention. He knew full well of the wrath to come, for he wrote the next day: "Revolutions are much easier started than controlled." He felt, too, the temper of the state convention. He could sense the ultimate decision. But he made his fight. The vote was close when the temperature of the times is considered, 164 to 131 for secession, not at all an overwhelming triumph for Cobb and Toombs and their like.

Stephens adopted the logic that Robert E. Lee later followed. He was against secession, but if his state decided upon that step, then he felt he must follow his state. And so he did, and went to Montgomery and was elected vice-president of the Confederate States of America. For the following four years he still fussed with his conscience, and with the course adopted by Jefferson Davis. To Davis and to many an outsider observer, Stephens was nothing but disloyal. But to himself he was the true voice of the southern people and their better instincts. He spent a good deal of his time at Crawfordsville, promoting dissension, promoting peace propaganda, and never—until his private peace mission in January, 1865—was he consulted by Davis after the capital was moved from Montgomery to Richmond. For Davis knew his real views, his secret hostility, and he knew, too, Stephens's rather low opinion of him as the president of the Confederacy. It was better and safer, he thought, to let the tortured philosopher keep to himself.

So Stephens was left to concentrate all his antagonism to the war, all his doubts of himself and of the role he had accepted outwardly and officially, into a fervid campaign to preserve civil liberties. He struck out against conscription, suspension of habeas corpus, martial law. These were symptoms of an autocratic central government, despotic and dictatorial. They were what the South was fighting against, weren't they? Yet he knew full well, for he knew his history, that a nation battling for the right to be born cannot ask such nice questions. Still in such crusades on side issues he sought refuge from the realities, and found salve for his inner wounds.

Also he talked peace. He prayed for peace. He had high hopes that Lincoln would be defeated for re-election, and that this might bring peace. He constantly schemed to arrange peace negotiations. Finally, when it was too late, he met with President Lincoln on a ship in Chesapeake Bay. It was a dreary January day, when the wind cut to the bones. Stephens was all wrapped up in a big coat plus several layers of shawls, and there were numerous lengths of muffler about his vulnerable scrawny throat. Lincoln, watching him unwind himself, smiled his slow, sad smile and said: "Never have I seen so small a nubbin come out of so much husk."

Personally, it was a friendly meeting. They spoke with pleasant recollections about their days together in the House, so long ago now. But it was nothing more. Lincoln would not recognize Stephens as an envoy, nor the Confederacy as a government. So nothing could be done on the ship in Chesapeake Bay.

Actually the Deliverer had arrived at the mouth of the Savannah a few weeks before. The whole world heard of his victory. Lincoln knew the end was near. With a sweeping gesture of the bayonet he had uprooted the civilization that Stephens and Cobb and Toombs had tried to preserve, had cut loose the bonds of the black people upon whose backs it had rested so tenuously. Now it was falling with a great roar in which were mingled strangely the lamentations of many widows and the jubilant, exultant shouts of many more Negro slaves.

General William Tecumseh Sherman was at Savannah!

CHAPTER THREE

General Sherman had marched his legions across Georgia and now they were encamped about Savannah in a great semicircle, their campfires gleaming above the city like a halo from the river to the beach below, hedging in General William J. Hardee and his army of fifteen thousand Confederates and a population of some twenty thousand civilians.

We can see Sherman on a moonlight night, the vigilant soldier, as he risked his personal safety to go forward and take a look to size up the situation.

"Wishing to reconnoitre the place in person, I rode forward by the Louisville road, into a dense wood of oak, pine and cypress, left the horses, and walked down to the railroad track, at a place where there was a side-track, and a cut about four feet deep. From that point the railroad was straight, leading into Savannah, and about eight hundred yards off were a rebel parapet and battery.

"I could see the cannoneers preparing to fire, and cautioned the officers near me to scatter, as we would likely attract a shot. Very soon I saw the white puff of smoke, and, watching close, caught sight of the ball as it rose in its flight, and, finding it coming pretty straight, I stepped a short distance to one side, but noticed a negro near me in the act of crossing the track at right angles. Some one called to him to look out; but, before the poor fellow understood his danger, the ball (a thirty-two pound round shot) struck the ground, and rose in its first ricochet, caught the negro under the right jaw, and literally carried away his

head, scattering blood and brains about. A soldier close by spread an overcoat over the body, and we all concluded to get out of that railroad cut."

Day and night Sherman was busy at his soldier's business, again the tactician after his long march across country. He arranged to make contact with the Federal fleet that was lying outside Savannah in order to advise Admiral Dahlgren that he had reached the city and was investing it, also he ordered General Hazen to move a division and take Fort McAlester, below Savannah on the Ogeechee. Sherman got on his horse and rode down to watch this action. In the late afternoon, as he perched with a group on the roof of a rice mill, tensely waiting for the assault, a wisp of smoke appeared over the trees down the river, and presently a steamboat appeared. Joyfully they saw the United States flag whipping in the breeze. Signal flags began to wigwag back and forth.

"Who are you?"

"General Sherman."

"Is Fort McAlester taken?"

"Not yet, but it will be in a minute."

It was not quite that quick. But this conversation was hardly over when General Hazen's troops began to appear from the woods across the river, marching in precise company front, flags flying, almost like toy soldiers they seemed at a distance, a beautiful sight to the eye of the general sitting on the roof on the other side of the Ogeechee. He watched them proudly. They had been with him at Shiloh. They knew their business. Immediately they disappeared, swallowed up in a cloud of smoke pouring from the angry mouths of the guns of the fort. When it cleared, the bluecoats could be seen scrambling and tumbling over the parapet, leaving their quiet bundles of dead and wounded strewn across the fields.

Thus it was done. This was quite a prize. For Fort McAlester had stubbornly repulsed assaults of Union troops who had tried to subdue it a year before, trying to approach

Savannah from the south. Fort Pulaski had fallen the year before that. But Union gunboats and troops had never been able to subjugate the other defenses that protected the mouth of the river and the city. They were well placed strategically and well constructed. General Robert E. Lee had seen to that. Lee had spent some months in and about Savannah in the early part of the war on an engineering mission, before he had been called to command the Army of Northern Virginia.

While on this mission Lee had visited the grave on Cumberland Island where his father was buried.

Light-Horse Harry Lee had died there, far away from Wakefield in Virginia, while on a visit to the daughter of General Nathanael Greene. He had paused on his way north from a trip to the West Indies at the thirty-two-room mansion that General Greene had built on the site of the old hunting lodge erected by Oglethorpe. Thus the generations of the Savannah River came together when Robert E. Lee stood by the grave of his famous father, who had fought along the Savannah under General Greene to free that colony which Oglethorpe had founded.

Sherman's arrival at Savannah must, then, have awakened personal recollections, beyond their distressing military implications, in the harassed man who was fencing skillfully, but against such great odds, far off in Virginia against General Grant. Lee was well aware of the portent of another aggressive foe at his back, ready to close in behind him, and squeeze his hungry army between two walls of steel. Even then, though he did not know it, Grant was sending word to Sherman to load his army on transports and bring them up the coast for such a pincer movement.

Sherman received these instructions with disappointment, for he had planned to capture Savannah and then march up through South Carolina to give that fomenter of rebellion her full measure of vengeance, the Georgia treatment with trimmings. He still thought he might have time to take Savannah

before the transports were ready, even though it was surrounded
by those bastions which Lee had prepared so effectively. He had
spent his time well in the intervening period before the change
of plans had come in the letter from General Grant. After the
fall of Fort McAlester, he arranged to visit the fleet outside Savannah. He was rowed down the river from the rice mill where
he had watched the battle and stopped for supper at Fort
McAlester, leaving us in his memoirs one of his grim sentences
that later were concentrated in that expression "War is Hell"
and revealed, in odd moments, the real human heart that beat
beneath that seemingly rough exterior.

"Inside the fort lay the dead as they had fallen, and they
could hardly be distinguished from their living comrades, sleeping side by side in the pale moonlight."

Outside the moonlight was as bright as day, and down the
river, not long afterward, General Sherman was taken in a skiff,

searching for some units of the fleet. He finally sighted a gunboat and went aboard. From the captain in command, the general learned that Admiral Dahlgren had been notified that his army had reached Savannah, that the South Atlantic Squadron which Dahlgren commanded was blockading the coast from Charleston southward, that General J. G. Foster, in command of the Department of the South, had his headquarters at Hilton Head, and that large stores of supplies for the army were waiting on vessels lying nearby.

Everything was ready, then, for the siege of Savannah.

General Sherman returned later that night to Fort McAlester. Hardly had he laid himself down on the floor for some rest, alongside General Hazen and the other officers at McAlester House, when he was awakened by a messenger with word that General Foster would like to see him that night. The general apologized for not being able to come to General Sherman, but he was incapacitated by an old wound incurred in the Mexican War.

So, weary as he was, Sherman arose, walked the mile to the fort and there boarded a boat for the trip down the river to the steamer where General Foster was waiting. He got from General Foster a picture of the military situation in the adjacent South Carolina region across the Savannah River, and was told about the Union supplies, including heavy artillery, needed for the siege of Savannah. From there, General Sherman was taken down the inland channel to Wassaw Sound, where the flagship *Half Moon* was anchored, and there he conferred with Admiral Dahlgren. The two made arrangements for moving the food and guns to the army, after which General Sherman returned to Savannah, without sleep, and immediately outlined the general situation to Generals Slocum and Howard. He ordered them to be ready to receive the siege guns and to emplace them preparatory to a bombardment of the city.

It was when he returned to the city that he received instructions from Grant to move his army promptly northward along the coast, as soon as the transports arrived. Still, he thought, there might be time to take Savannah. He sent a demand for surrender to General Hardee, who defiantly rejected it. These usual formalities over, Sherman decided he would try to close the one gap in the steel line about Savannah. That was an old plank road leading into South Carolina which was still open to General Hardee and his Confederates to receive supplies and reinforcements, or an exit if they desired to escape.

Already Hardee was in sore straits, for two Confederate gunboats which had attempted to get down the Savannah from upriver to his relief had been sunk by Union artillery, and the river was fairly well blockaded from the north.

The Federal plans for closing the gap across the river by the plank road required personal conferences with General Foster, since the operation would have to be initiated from the Carolina side. Accordingly, General Sherman again was off down the Ogeechee for the circuitous journey by sea around the mouth of the river to Hilton Head. Before he left he gave orders that the attack should be held up until his return two or three days later.

When he did return he found that General Hardee had slipped out of the city by the plank road, with his army of fifteen thousand ragged veterans, and that he was off into South Carolina beyond successful pursuit. So Savannah was Sherman's without a fight, and some of the army was already in the city.

"On the morning of December 22nd," he writes, "I followed with my own headquarters, and rode down Bull Street to the custom-house, from the roof of which we had an extensive view over the city, the river, and the vast extent of marsh and rice-fields on the South Carolina side. The navy-yard and the iron-clad ram *Savannah*, were still smouldering, but all else looked quiet enough."

The Union general has left us a description of the city of that day.

The city of Savannah [he wrote] was an old place, and usually accounted a handsome one. Its houses were of brick and frame, with large yards, ornamented with shrubbery and flowers; its streets perfectly regular, crossing each other at right angles; and at many of the intersections were small inclosures in the nature of parks. These streets and parks were lined with the handsomest shade trees of which I have knowledge, viz, the willow-leaf live-oak, evergreens of exquisite beauty; and these certainly entitled Savannah to its reputation as a handsome town more than the houses, which, though handsome, would hardly make a display on Fifth Avenue or the Boulevard Haussmann of Paris. . . . Outside of Savannah there was very little to interest a stranger, except the cemetery of Bonaventure, and the ride along the Wilmington Channel by way of Thunderbolt, where might be seen some groves of majestic live-oak trees, covered with gray and funereal moss, which were truly sublime in grandeur, but gloomy after a few days' camping under them.

In making the rounds of the city, General Sherman was irritated to find that an agent of the Treasury had arrived in the city ahead of him and had seized the large stock of cotton there, first estimated at 25,000 bales, later found to amount to 31,000 bales. The general quickly and characteristically told the gentleman off, and took over the cotton in the name of the army. One happy event came out of this conflict of authority, however, which may account for Sherman's description of the agent, A. G. Browne, of Salem, Massachusetts, as "a shrewd, clever Yankee." Browne advised him that a boat was leaving for Fortress Monroe and suggested that General Sherman might send with it a message to President Lincoln about the capture of Savannah which probably would reach the president by Christmas Day. The general wrote out the message which was filed at the telegraph office at Fortress Monroe and actually reached

Lincoln propitiously on Christmas Eve. It was a message which rang through the North like a peal of Christmas bells:

"I beg to present to you as a Christmas gift the city of Savannah, with one hundred and fifty heavy guns and plenty of ammunition, also about twenty-five thousand bales of cotton."

This message was truly a great relief to the anxious president, for he had had no word of Sherman since he went "into one hole" at Atlanta—as Lincoln had put it, expressing mystification at "what hole he would come out of." All the news that was available had been rumors printed in southern papers that Sherman had been repulsed; that he would be swallowed up in Georgia by the angry civilian population. And southern newspapers had stopped mention of his army a month before on word from Richmond that they might give valuable information to the enemy. So Sherman was during this time in fact "lost." The "lost army" was much on Lincoln's mind and heart and one day, while shaking hands with visitors, he was so completely preoccupied that he did not respond to a caller who stood waiting patiently for recognition. Finally, coming back to earth, the president apologized. He said he was thinking "of a man down South."

Once in the city General Sherman had new problems, problems of administration, of feeding a population shut off a long time from supplies. They could not eat the cotton piled up in their warehouses. He enlisted the co-operation of the mayor, retained the regular civil government, and gave the city during his stay probably the best government it ever had; or so it has been stated. He let the congregations of the churches continue to pray for President Davis and the success of Confederate arms, with the quip, "Yes, Jeff Davis and the devil both need it." He was besieged by women who wanted all sorts of favors and handled them exceptionally well, though they became a nuisance.

His chief annoyance, however, was from outside meddlers, agents from the North, the forerunners of the pestiferous army of carpetbaggers that swarmed into the South in the next few months and years. Some were sincere and fervent, but narrow-minded, zealots determined to impose salvation as decreed by the abolitionists upon the Negroes; many were greedy and unconscionable rascals bent upon seizing political power and grabbing the pennies off the southern corpse. Sherman, who had lived for many years in the South in the past, knew its people, liked them, and understood them and their problems. He could see dimly the wrath to come and tried in vain to warn of it and to avert it.

He divined the developing purpose of the Radicals in Congress. It became apparent in the attitude suggested in hints let out here and there by the chief of the northern agents who descended upon Savannah while Sherman was there. This was none other than Secretary of War Stanton, who hurried down by boat at the first opportunity to look the ground over. Stanton was fussy about many things, peeking here and there, prying, asking questions, seemingly deeply concerned about the Negro and his future, but in reality carefully measuring the political potentialities in this southern tragedy, thus foretelling his action, a few months later, in joining the Radicals openly in their desperate and vicious Reconstruction program.

Sherman was most resentful when Stanton revealed his intention to quiz the Negroes about the commanding general's own policies and actions. But he complied and rounded up a group of twenty Negro preachers, Baptist and Methodist, for an inquisition by the secretary of war. At one point the general was asked to leave the room, and he found out later that the reason was that Stanton wanted to ask directly about him. The general came off with high praise from the Negroes, and the witnesses upheld Sherman also in the firm policy he had adopted against recruiting Negroes for his army by state agents who rushed into Savannah and were trying to enlist Negroes right and left. Sherman had a well-organized pioneer corps which went along with the army to open up roads and to bridge rivers and creeks. It was a work corps, in which many Negroes were used. But he did not want to enlist any Negro soldiers, not only because of the bother of handling such unseasoned troops, but also because he had smarted under the taunts of Confederate General Hood at Atlanta to the effect that the North had to use the South's own Negro slaves to defeat the Confederacy. He had been made touchy by this, even though such a charge was untrue and unjustified.

During these days, sensing the motives that governed Stanton, Sherman saw how difficult would be the adoption of the moderate course for the South that he, himself, favored, one which he knew Lincoln favored, too. Punishment for the leaders, yes, that was necessary, as Lincoln already had outlined in his Proclamation of Amnesty, but no more punishment for the common people than what they had already suffered from the ravages of war, devastations such as he had spread coming down through Georgia, and the ruin he intended to continue to spread going north through South Carolina. When the South laid down its arms, then the people should be permitted to return peaceably to the Union, to elect their officials, locally and to Congress, and go about their business normally again. That was his idea.

In order to provide the southern farmers with money to buy food and clothes and to subsist, he devised a plan for the government to buy the cotton seized at Savannah, not at the full price, but at three-quarters of the quotation on the New York Cotton Exchange. But Stanton squelched this and had the cotton shipped north.

Stanton also wanted to set aside a vast section along the coast and the coastal islands for the Negroes. Sherman worked out a plan for settling the Negroes, temporarily, on the abandoned farms and plantations, where they could raise food crops, until some permanent solution could be found. But the general was stoutly opposed to any policy of wholesale confiscation of southern land to be turned over to the Negroes under any such scheme as the "forty acres and a mule" program adopted later. Nor did he think that the Negroes should be permitted to vote until they had proved themselves qualified to exercise the franchise, after a period of education and training.

Stanton left Savannah with most of the problems arising from the freeing of the slaves still unsolved—for nobody could do that in a few days or a few years—but he left behind enough clues as to his attitude about such matters. Sherman realized that this attitude was representative of many who had sat out the war in Washington. It disturbed him because he knew so much more about the many problems of the South and the instincts of the people who lived there, and must somehow continue to live there.

But now he had to be about his principal business, which was to bring an end to the war. So he turned his attention to that immediate project, and organized his army for the invasion of South Carolina across the Savannah River. He was weary of inaction, weary of the necessary civil problems he had to meet, and so, too, were the boys from the Midwest who made up his army. They were surfeited with this semitropical land, with its moss-draped trees, the gloomy shadows they spread, and the depressing spirit of a defeated people.

Sherman now had authority to carry out his original plan. This was to proceed north across the Carolinas in order to take Lee in the rear and thus furnish his half of the pincers that finally would crush that elusive general between two powerful armies. It had been discovered that it was impossible to get together quickly a fleet to move his troops north, as Grant first had instructed.

So Sherman threw his armies across the Savannah, happy to be on the march again, confident of the fighting spirit of his troops. The commendation for his great achievement, figuratively speaking, was shouting from well-creased letters in his pockets from Grant and from Halleck, the chief of staff in Washington. Grant described the Georgia campaign as "the like of which is not read of in past history" and confided to his friend and lieutenant, now that it was all over, that he "would

not have intrusted the expedition to any other living commander." Halleck commented, "Your march will stand out prominently as the great one of this war."

"I do not like to boast," Sherman replied to Grant, "but I believe this army has a confidence in itself that makes it almost invincible."

What South Carolina was going to get, and what we know this birthplace of secession did get—for we have heard the stories from generation to generation—was forecast in the exchanges of correspondence between Sherman and Halleck before the movement northward began. With gentle irony Halleck wrote:

"Should you capture Charleston, I hope that by some accident the place may be destroyed, and, if a little salt should be sown upon its site, it may prevent the growth of future crops of nullification and secession."

"I will bear in mind your hint as to Charleston, and do not think 'salt' will be necessary," Sherman replied, after explaining the "wonderful effect" of his march through Georgia upon the people of that state in showing them what war was really like, and he added, "To be sure, Jeff Davis has his people under pretty good discipline, but I think faith in him is much shaken in Georgia, and before we have done with her South Carolina will not be quite so tempestuous."

He said, "The truth is, the whole army is burning with an insatiable desire to wreak vengeance upon South Carolina. I almost tremble at her fate, but feel that she deserves all that seems in store for her."

He had support, too, from the people of Georgia, so he recorded, for giving her neighbor harsh treatment.

"Many and many a person in Georgia asked me why we did not go to South Carolina; and when I answered that we were en route for that State, the invariable reply was, 'Well, if you will make these people feel the utmost severities of war, we will pardon you for your desolation of Georgia.'"

Sherman did not attempt to capture Charleston, believing it

hardly worth while, since it was now isolated and of no strategic value and was no threat to his army. Instead, he moved northwest across the state toward Columbia, the capital. This, his opponents thought, would be practically an insuperable project, especially in its earlier stages, because of the swamps and network of streams. But Sherman knew this country as he had known the Georgia country. He had ridden over it with his military eye always alert, as a young soldier years before, and he knew how he could follow the ridges to avoid the quagmires. This he did most adroitly.

We leave him as he heads his legions northward for the conquest of South Carolina.

The people he left behind in Georgia knew very well that this was the end.

The Savannah had drunk of blood and was sated.

CHAPTER FOUR

THE SAVANNAH SAW THE END OF THE WILD DREAM

A few months later a considerable band of horsemen in grimy and discolored Confederate gray pulled up at the banks of the Savannah near the now dilapidated town of Lisbon in the neighborhood where Waddel's school once had stood. They had clattered slowly through the woods green with May and sweet with the perfume of wild flowers and cheerful with the songs of birds. But the spirit of spring was not among them. Their faces were drawn and weary and shadowed with overgrown beards.

One among them was more impassive than the rest. He

sat his horse easily, for he was an accomplished rider, and with the dignity of one born to rule. Jefferson Davis was in flight for his life, but he exhibited none of the outward signs of anxiety. He was distinguished among the horsemen for his aloofness, as for his civilian attire. He was still the acknowledged leader, "the president," to himself and to his companions. In his mind he refused to accept that the cause was lost.

As he had fled south ahead of the armies, from Richmond when Lee was forced to yield up the capital, from Danville, the capital for a few days, from Greensboro, on across South Carolina, he had mulled over in his mind a plan for continued resistance in the West. This meant a stand first in Alabama and Mississippi, where there were still scattered Confederate forces, or, if not there, across the Mississippi in Arkansas and Texas, where the gallant Kirby Smith was yet at large at the head of a small but effective army.

Philosopher though he was, it is probable that his mind was concentrated now on his immediate problem of escape and his danger, with lapses into daydreams of continued resistance, rather than upon the meaning of this spot where he now stood on the banks of the Savannah. Yet it did have deep symbolism. For here, in another month of May, three hundred and twenty-five years before, De Soto the Spaniard had passed up this river, the first white man to see this virgin wilderness, known then only to the Indians. Along here, too, had come Dr. Henry Woodward to open this river and this country to the English. Here, too, had marched the brave little army of Colonel Maurice Moore into the very den of the Creeks and Cherokees to stave off, by a show of force and diplomacy, the red hordes that were about to sweep the English settlement in the lower valley about Charleston clean off the continent. Here, too, among the trees through which the Confederate cavalry had passed, were the ruins of Fort Charlotte, which had been a bastion against the Indians and a center of activity in the Revolutionary War.

Along the road he had followed had come the thousands of immigrants from Virginia and North Carolina, yes, even from far New England. Here, where he was about to cross the Savannah, they, too, had crossed into a fertile, rolling country and had established their little agricultural empire with its slowly developing prosperity, with its peculiar social customs and its ways of thinking that had bloomed eventually into the philosophy behind the Confederate States of America, the Confederacy that was now falling apart even as he fled through it.

Here in Georgia he had his own roots. His grandfather, Evan Davis, had come from Pennsylvania to start a new life in the colony Oglethorpe had started. His father, Samuel Davis, for his faithful service in the Revolution, had been given land across the river near the town of Washington. There Samuel Davis had farmed for nearly ten years, though on a smaller scale than the forebears of Robert Toombs and Howell Cobb in this same region. Then he had moved on, restless with pioneer fever, first to Kentucky, where his son Jefferson was born—not so many miles from that log cabin where Abraham Lincoln had first known life.

Jefferson Davis's doting elder brother, a successful Mississippi planter, had taken the younger member of the family under his wing and educated him to be a gentleman; first at Transylvania College, at the time one of the finest institutions of learning in the country, and later at West Point. Then he had given Jeff a plantation next to his own in Mississippi, well stocked with slaves. For this the younger brother had finally given up his military career and settled down with his charming second wife, Winnie, to be a Mississippi squire.

While Jefferson Davis's course of life had thus taken him south, Abraham Lincoln had gone north from Kentucky to Illinois, struggling up the hard way in poverty in a new country.

Both, as young men, had served in the Black Hawk War, Davis with some distinction, Lincoln with none. Davis later became a hero in the war with Mexico, an experience which so convinced him of his ability as a soldier that it left him with the firm belief that he was a military strategist of parts. The Confederacy and its generals had suffered from that.

Now the man who had learned to be a gentleman the easy way, and had learned too much statecraft from books, saw the end of the dream of southern empire as he crossed the Savannah River on that May morning. He was now a fugitive from the armies that had been set against him by that other man born in Kentucky. Abraham Lincoln was a victim of the tragedy, too. Perhaps he was better off now even in a martyr's grave.

Less than a month before, in Charlotte, North Carolina, Davis had been told of Lincoln's assassination. He did not gloat.

"I am sorry to learn it," he said. "Mr. Lincoln was a much better man than his successor will be, and it will go harder with our people. It is bad news for us."

And indeed it was. Davis had sensed the wrath to come.

Now he was fleeing for his own life and had reached the banks of the Savannah, deep in the South.

"I crossed early in the morning of May 4th, with a company which had been detailed as my escort, and rode some miles to a farmhouse, where I halted to get breakfast and have our horses fed," he wrote afterward.

Four members of his Cabinet still were with him when he reached the Savannah. There, at the river, he left Secretary of War Breckinridge, and most of the force of two thousand cavalry which had escorted him south to Georgia. Breckinridge was instructed to join him later with this force. Secretary of State Benjamin, who had been riding in an ambulance with three or four other members of the party, left the president after breakfast at the house where they stopped the first morning in Georgia. He now took another route, with the idea of joining Davis later in the West. But subsequently, after the whole plot for a western adventure blew up, Benjamin escaped to England. There he settled down and became a famous barrister, piling up another fortune in a new career. Secretary of the Navy Mallory departed from the presidential party when it reached Washington, Georgia, also with the intention of joining the president later in the West; Postmaster General Reagan, alone of the Cabinet, remained with Davis.

In Washington Davis tarried at the old Heard house. It had served in the Revolution as the capital and refuge of the harried Americans during those desperate days when the British overran the whole Savannah River valley. Bob Toombs was not at his home in Washington to welcome the president of the Confederacy. He had fled to Cuba. Davis was described by someone who saw him at Washington as "worn and jaded." He looked "pale and thin, but was plucky to the last."

In vain he now waited here for Breckinridge and the cavalry. There were repeated rumors of marauders on the loose in the neighborhood, bands of Union soldiers as well as looting gangs of Confederates. The cavalry did not show up, and Davis could not afford to wait longer. Two messages to Breckinridge brought no reply. So he headed south. His purpose was to go far enough south to avoid Federal troops, and then turn back west in keeping with his plan to get beyond the Mississippi to continue the war there. He still clung to this vain hope although he knew now that General Johnston also had surrendered to General Sherman in North Carolina, eliminating his army, as well as Lee's, from further combat. He was most angry at Johnston. He was convinced that this Confederate commander could have escaped into the mountains and saved his army. He never forgave him all the rest of his life.

Davis rode out of Washington, Georgia, with an escort of only ten men. The whole company of his escort had volunteered to follow him, but he feared that a larger guard would be too conspicuous riding through this country, so he insisted that only ten should accompany him. He lost four of these after two days. Overtaking a quartermaster train which had valuable papers in its possession, he discovered that it had no expert woodsmen and insisted that they take four of his men who were qualified as woodsmen.

As he rode south through the fine spring nights, with a full moon overhead to light almost like day this flat, wire-grass country of few habitations, he got reports of marauders in this area. He had learned previously at Washington that Mrs. Davis and the children were traveling through this vicinity, headed for a destination in Florida, where they might escape by boat. Fearing that they might be troubled by the wandering, lawless gangs, he decided to overtake them if possible. So he changed his course directly to the east and thus rode toward his doom.

His private secretary, Burton Harrison, was in charge of Mrs. Davis's party, which had a guard of seven troopers. From Charlotte, Davis had sent Harrison to Abbeville, where he had heard that his wife and the children had taken refuge.

He changed course for this mission, only to encounter more bad luck. The horses of his cavalry escort gave out, yet he pushed ahead with Postmaster General Reagan and his personal party. Early one morning toward daybreak, after riding all night, he met a group of soldiers from an Alabama regiment who told him of a party of women and children not far off. Soon the Davis family was reunited in the Georgia wilderness as fugitives and outcasts. The father rode south with them for three days, when he decided that he should leave them and take his intended and determined course to the west.

He refused to drop this project.

His plan was to depart about nightfall. This was abandoned, however, when one of his officers returned from a survey of the neighborhood to tell of a party of marauders, supposedly Confederate soldiers, which intended—so he had been advised—to attack the Davis encampment that night.

So the ex-Confederate president again changed his mind and decided to remain to protect his family. He went to bed in his wife's tent, fully dressed. Nothing occurred during the night. But just before dawn a Negro coachman, a freeman, who was in

Davis's own party, came and woke him to tell him that he had heard firing beyond a nearby stream.

As Davis stepped out of the tent in the dim light he saw some horsemen whom he recognized at once as Federal cavalry. They were deploying to encircle the camp. When he stepped back into the tent and told his wife, she urged him to go at once. He reached out in the dark inside the tent and picked up what he thought was his raglan, but which he discovered later was his wife's raincoat. He hastily threw it over his shoulders and stepped outside again. Still he hesitated, unwilling to leave his wife, and thus, as he says in his own account of this night's adventure, he "lost a few precious moments."

Mrs. Davis continued to implore him to go and finally he turned to go and she threw her shawl over his head. It was a damp morning.

He was ill equipped for escape. He had neither mount nor arms. His horse with his holster and pistols had been tied a short distance away along the road up which the Federal cavalry were now advancing.

He now began to walk away from the tent and had gone fifteen or twenty yards when a Union cavalryman dashed from the woods and ordered him to halt. He did not stop. The horseman shouted again, drawing his carbine. Davis stopped, threw off the shawl and coat, and advanced toward the Federal soldier, his purpose being, he explained later, to try to unhorse the trooper, get on the horse himself, and escape. At this moment, Mrs. Davis rushed out to her husband and threw her arms around him to protect him.

There was nothing to do but surrender.

The president of the Confederacy was a captive.

Alexander Stephens was at his home in Crawfordsville when the Union soldiers came to arrest him. He went willingly, asking only a few minutes to arrange his affairs and get a few things together to take with him. He was spirited away on the train from Crawfordsville. The soldiers were still looking for Bob Toombs, and Stephens waited expectantly for his friend to be brought to the train to join him. But they could not find Toombs. He had, as a matter of fact, already escaped to Cuba.

Stephens was taken to Atlanta, after a change of cars at Barnett, where there was a wait of an hour. He was surrendered formally to the Union authorities at Atlanta. All about him there he beheld the destruction and havoc wrought in the siege and by the fires. He saw the ruins of landmarks that he had known for years, associated many of them with vivid chapters of his own life: the Atlanta Hotel, where he had sat in many conferences in the troublous days trying to find some way out of the catastrophe of war; the Trout House, where in 1860, on the eve of election, Stephen A. Douglas had spoken in his campaign against Abraham Lincoln for the Presidency.

He was put back on the train again and, once more, the train stopped at Barnett on its way southeast. This time Jefferson Davis and his wife and their baby girl, Winnie, came aboard. Along with the ex-president as fellow prisoners were General Joseph A. Wheeler, whose cavalry had annoyed Sherman's legions as they marched across Georgia to the sea; C. C. Clay, who stood charged with participation in the plot to assassinate Lincoln; Postmaster General Reagan, and a number of others, including four private soldiers of the Confederacy. Stephens was not pleased when Davis got on the train. The two did not meet on the railroad trip.

The train stopped at Crawfordsville. There a large crowd was gathered, and there Stephens was permitted to visit his home again in order to make final arrangements for he knew not what; imprisonment surely, execution perhaps. He was allowed to take along two Negro servants, one Anthony, and a boy Henry, who had been with him at Richmond. When he was on board again the train moved on through the pleasant Georgia countryside, here smiling and untouched by war.

At Augusta all the prisoners were taken from the train and

conducted to carriages which took them to a tugboat tied up at the dock. Davis and his wife nodded to Stephens as they passed him in the station. The white nurse who carried Winnie Davis in her arms rode, at her own request, in the carriage with the now deposed vice-president.

Stephens was in a wretched state. He was weary, distraught, and plagued with a nauseating neuralgic headache and a sore throat. Two soldiers assisted him up the gangplank. There were only a few bunks in the vessel. Davis went below to these meager sleeping quarters with the women. Stephens and the other prisoners slept on deck. Mrs. Davis kindly sent up a mattress for Stephens and General Wheeler gave him a blanket, which he shared with Clay. He passed a miserable night. They had had no food all day.

That night, all the next day, and most of the next night too, they spent in the trip down the river. It was one of the saddest flotillas that ever passed down the Savannah in all its long history. This was the end of a civilization. Truly, the Savannah was once again the river of frustrated dreams. From the pleasant country about Augusta, once so hopeful, they passed, symbolically, into the dark and unfriendly caverns of the wilderness along the lower reaches of the river. Here, like the end of all happy living and hopeful dreams, was a nightmare of muddy water, running red as if with the blood of all those who had suffered and died in this mighty tragedy that Davis and Stephens had managed. All around stood the forbidding jungles, like the walls of an eternal prison.

Against this background the two men who had been at the head of the Confederacy met on deck and shook hands. They talked in the polite southern manner, concealing behind masks their bitterness of soul and their mutual dislike for each other.

The tugboat reached Savannah at four o'clock in the morning and the prisoners straggled off disconsolately in the wan dawn. They were taken aboard the steamer *Clyde* for the trip north.

Here was one sorrowful scene that must have lingered long in the memories of all who saw it. It was the final parting between two seven-year-old youngsters, one white, the other black. They had had nothing to do with all of this tragedy and could not understand it. But the little Negro slave Jimmy and his white playmate Jeff Davis must inexorably go their separate ways now. Both wept unashamed, both protesting, as the Negro boy was taken away. Jimmy's plaintive cries got fainter and fainter as the *Clyde* pulled out into the river, a veritable last desolate symbol of all this strange era of slave civilization with its human loyalties and its inevitable tragedy for white and black.

The steamer headed north. At Hampton Roads the first and last president of the Confederacy was taken off, a prisoner of war, to be locked in a cold cell at Fortress Monroe.

A few days later, the *Clyde* steamed into Boston harbor still carrying its other chief prisoner. Stephens was taken to Fort Warren in Boston harbor, to another chill and drear cell whose doors locked out the world and his friends. He took up his pen and began to write furiously against his loneliness.

CHAPTER FIVE

AFTERMATH

Through the late spring and early summer of 1865, after their tragedy of Appomattox, the Confederate soldiers wandered back to take up life again. From the armies of Lee and of Johnston and of Hood, from the many smaller commands that were scattered across that vast southern battlefield from the Atlantic to Texas, they straggled home.

They came back to the valley of the Savannah too.

Except for the country about the mouth of the river, which had been plowed over by Sherman's army on its victorious march north, the valley was spared the physical damage that had been visited upon other parts of Georgia and South Carolina. It was not like the barren desert, with lonely chimneys standing like leering outlaws among the ravished farms and pine forests, that had greeted the soldier who went back home after that first civil war along the Savannah more than three-quarters of a century before. Yet the souls of its people were seared if not warped and thwarted as they set about to begin life anew.

Despair truly haunted the land. In its somber mood and desperate problems, the Savannah River valley was a replica, in miniature, of the whole South in these desolate years after the Civil War.

Listlessly its people took up life again. They had no standing as citizens for some years. They were reminded of their crime against the Union by the Federal armies that encamped among then to supervise and enforce the horror known as Reconstruction which Sherman and Lincoln had so wanted to avoid. They had to stand by as outcasts, without the privileges of citizens, and watch their political institutions being taken over by the army, the carpetbaggers, and the "scalawags." This last term was a designation for ex-Confederates who agreed to co-operate with the carpetbaggers and were rewarded with restoration of citizenship. These three combined groups manipulated the Negroes, now freely given the franchise, and they controlled local government, such as it was.

Bitterly, as is the way of a conquered people, the disfranchised whites struck back. Their vehicle of vengeance was the Ku Klux Klan, that hooded order which galloped through the night, like ghosts, to terrify and intimidate the

Negroes. On the Carolina side of the river another vengeance corps sprang up, the notorious Red Shirts. Soon there were riots and bloodshed along both sides of the river. By force and by threats, the whites gradually regained control of the government, frightening the Negroes away from the polls, or buying them up in droves, so that in Columbia County, for example, the number of Republican votes was reduced from over a thousand down to a single ballot in successive elections held within the period of a few months. This was too much for the military government in Georgia, which hurried troops into this section, reoccupying the territory and ruling by military force. In South Carolina, across the Savannah, nine counties were taken over by Federal troops under orders from President Grant.

Gradually, however, the whites recovered their government, at first by force, and later through the process of amnesty restoring civil rights.

This, however, was little help for their economic difficulties. Local civil government could do nothing about this. Other influences, cumulative in effect, governed the economy—and tended toward gradual misery. The whites literally became slaves to forces they could neither understand nor control. Theoretically the Negroes were free, but only by legal fiction. For in physical and economic fact they were still slaves. At first, immediately after the end of the war, they roved about, many of them, from one place to another. The Freedmen's Bureau set up to arrange their salvation fed them and clothed them for a while. But this was no answer, no remedy. Good intentions of northern humanitarians who came into the South, so full of noble ideals and starry eyed with visions, availed little. This problem was beyond simple charity.

The people of the Savannah River valley could get little help from their old political leaders. Alexander Stephens was released from his damp cell in the fort in Boston harbor in time and came back to his home at Crawfordville, a spent and weary old man. Bob Toombs returned, too, in time from his exile in Cuba. But he still flaunted his personal rebellion by refusing to take the oath of citizenship to the United States so that he was barred forever from participating in the affairs of his state, and could only stand about and relieve his ancient bitterness with his bellowing voice to any who would listen, and many did. For it was a solace to hear old Bob, still a man among men, still an idol and a god but slightly tarnished, as he recalled the glory that was and damned the degradation he now knew.

All up and down the valley the stump orators cried out against the new oppressor, harking back to the old tradition, calling upon the people to rise against their masters from the North. But these were personal devils only.

The real devils were economic forces spawned during the years before the avalanche, such as land grown wan and wrinkled with gullies from continual planting of cotton and improper care; dependence upon a single crop; the waste of slavery which broke down the planter's fortitude and independence like a drug and at a terrible cost that was not recognized at the time; the failure to build up a compensating industry to process their cotton at home instead of sending it away to the North, to New England. Textile mills might have absorbed the excess of labor, both white and black, and provided a regional income to be spread locally, thus improving the lot of the people.

Stephens and Toombs had no ready solution for these accumulated ills. They thought too much in the old patterns. Theirs was still the old-fashioned creed that called for a contented and prosperous agricultural society, for sane living and integrity, for honesty and idealism in government. There could now be no contented and prosperous agriculture. And honesty and integrity and idealism in government likewise were becoming outmoded.

The political regime that had taken over in Georgia after the war had made its compromises with the carpetbagger politicians and was intensely practical and grasping. The state was going through a noisome era of corruption. The regime bargained with northern capital, particularly with the railroads, which had money to invest, and this resulted in exploitation and political corruption. For the new Georgia political dynasty took its own cut in the profits. It had all the instincts of the brash nouveau riche.

The economic-political movement fostered by the new political leaders, hand in hand with business promoters, that beckoned to northern capital so invitingly, was known as "the New Departure."

The lesser favored along the Savannah, people in the small towns and on the farms back from the river, began to hate this shoddy new industrialism. They resented the false and showy pride of the new masters who controlled the state lawmakers in order to build into the economy legal artifices to protect and nourish the new industrialism. It was a system that penalized agriculture more and more and made living all the harder for the farmer. The grim factories that marked its "prosperity" began to draw behind their grimy windows a gradually increasing horde of folks who came out day after day more pasty faced, more like pale ghosts. They became stringy men, weary women, and pale and forlorn children. That, it was plain to see, was no way for people to live, not even poor people.

And these factory hands could hardly live on the wages, which were so pitifully low. In the cotton mills in Augusta the weekly pay was only $4 or $5, often less, for the toil of long hours, even so late as 1890.

Basically in theory this industrialization of the South was a sound idea, but being brought about at too great a cost to human values. Those who accomplished it pointed to the glistening surface of things, to the goods that came out at the doors, while they resented bitterly even a peek into what was happening to those who did the work inside.

Across the river in South Carolina, quite in contrast to Georgia, the old Confederate regime had assumed control after a disturbing era of Reconstruction. It managed to hold on until 1890. It was unprogressive, old-fashioned, and lacked the ideas necessary to meet changing conditions. But it remained honest over-all and was without the corrupting influence that pervaded politics in Georgia when the New Departure made its bargain with northern capital. South Carolina had finally risen up and thrown off its Reconstruction government under the leadership of a Confederate hero, the tall and handsome Wade Hampton, that dashing cavalry officer upon whom had fallen the mantle of Jeb Stuart in Lee's army.

But throwing off the yoke of Reconstruction, the political yoke, did not bring the millennium either in the Savannah River valley or in other parts of the state. Far from it. It did ease the temper of the people. It relieved the tension caused by their subjugation to outside masters by removing constant reminders of their defeat. But they were still vassals economically. The departure of the troops, the disappearance of the strange and alien figures in their governing bodies, including Yankees and Negroes, could not solve their problems. It did not make their lands any more fruitful nor reduce the debts of tenants, white and black, to landowners or town merchants, or cancel the debts of landlords to the banks.

In the midst of this decay, the old order passed away in Georgia. Alexander Stephens, who never lost his yearning for public office, became governor in a compromise with the New Departure in 1882, much to the outspoken outrage of his old crony, Bob Toombs. Previously he had served again in Congress for a period. He did not live out his term as governor. His last public speech was at Savannah, at the sesquicentennial of the founding of the Georgia colony. He traced the history of the colony and of the state that succeeded it, closing on a high optimistic note for the future of Georgia. A few days later he died, not at his home in Crawfordsville, but in the governor's mansion in Atlanta. There in his last days he had lived in Spartan simplicity, sleeping on a cot in a room shared by his Negro

servant, Aleck Kent. He had ordered out of his bedroom the
Louis XIV bed in which other governors of Georgia had reposed.
That for him was too much luxury.

In his last delirium he was making a speech back in Congress again in the days before the war, pleading for a course of
moderation for the South, trying to hold off the catastrophe. His
last words were:

"Get ready—we are nearly home."

Bob Toombs wept openly at his grave, choking with sobs.
He was almost blind. His great voice broke from time to time as
he delivered the funeral oration over his beloved friend.

"He was more the child of his country than any man that
ever lived," Toombs said of his companion of many years.

Toombs did not long survive him. On his deathbed the with-
ering giant was told that the legislature, which had been
dawdling for weeks, was still in session.

"Send for Cromwell," he mumbled hoarsely.

Then he died.

The effects of the war in which the two had played leading
parts lingered on still, long after they were gone.

Economic forces moved in a cycle. Each time around they
left more victims in their wake. There was nothing to do when
everybody took stock for himself, both whites and blacks,
after the war, but to pick up and go on again from right where
they were. There was no easy way out. But there was still
cotton. In the South there's always been cotton. All they knew
was cotton. They must go on planting and selling it.

The Negroes moved back into the cabins in the cotton country along the middle Savannah, on both sides of the river. Life then went on about as it had before the war, except that it was not laid out for them so easy and simple. Now they had become day laborers working for a wage. In some cases it was fifty cents a day, in others a dollar with "deducts." That is, they were fined twenty-five cents here, a half dollar there for various derelictions; for failure to obey orders or for misbehavior. On some plantations food and supplies were furnished in lieu of wages. It was a hit-and-miss, patched-up system, varying in different localities, not too expensive for the landowner, hardly a living for the Negroes.

At the close of the war cotton was selling for a dollar a pound, a fine price, so life was not so hard for a time. The plantation owners could borrow from the banks. Even in Baltimore and New York they could get credit to carry them until the end of the crop year.

But the boom was short-lived. The price of cotton began to drop. It kept on dropping until finally, in the early nineties, it was selling for four cents a pound. Cotton was sensitive to outside influences far away from the Savannah River valley. It reacted to the great depression of the seventies, from 1873 to 1879, and to other economic developments that the small white farmer and the simple Negro could not be aware of, and certainly could do little about.

The only answer was to plant more and more cotton; to "try to keep up." But planting more and more cotton wore out the land so that production became more expensive. Less cotton grew on the same land that required more and more money for fertilizer. So the smell of guano pervaded the middle Savannah River valley. While the land became more pockmarked with deepening gullies, raw wounds in the dying earth.

Slowly changes occurred. The wage system was replaced by the sharecropper system. Yet few fared any better. The landowner took to renting out sections of his land to tenants. This did away with the necessity of having paid overseers to watch and direct the hands. Overseers were hard to get. Many of them were lost in the war, killed in the fighting, or shifted to other means of livelihood. Simple cabins were built in the fields. There the sharecropper, white and black, lived with his brood that might often be a big one. He gave part of his crop in exchange for his rent and his "furnish," which last included some items of food and all his tools. He usually had no equipment of his own. As the price of cotton dropped, the sharecropper got further and further behind. His crop was mortgaged before it was picked, and he still owed some ahead which must come out of the next crop.

Many of the croppers seldom saw cash money, others became virtual slaves. Sometimes they were forced to move when they were unable to make a go of it. Then the landowner would look for new tenants. Some who could move voluntarily did so, hoping for better luck elsewhere. Consequently, they took no particular pride in the little homes they had but did not own, and these deteriorated. In time many plantation owners moved to nearby towns, handling their properties by absentee ownership. Then the tenants would move out of the comfortless and tumbling cabins into the big house that slowly fell into decay through lack of care. Some of these people became entirely shiftless.

The landowners, being influential in the legislatures, got laws passed to protect them in their relationship with tenants. The sharecropper's rent now became a first lien on his crop. This was followed by another protective law which also provided security for advances and supplies. In time a new class developed in the towns that lived on the sharecropper. This was the "time merchant," as he came to be called. He was a merchant who would furnish supplies on time and credit, just as the landowner had formerly. These merchants largely took over this former function of the landowner. They, too, got their protection from the law in the form of a second lien on the crop.

Often enough, through agreements with the landowners, they held a first lien too. Some of them became wealthy and they lived in the finest houses in town. Meanwhile, the sharecropper, with little protection, slid slowly downward to a state of further degradation.

The continual drop in the price of cotton coupled with the increasingly smaller return on the land in time hit the big landowner, who borrowed from the banks to carry his part of the burden. Some planters thus got deeper and deeper into debt and finally had to sell their lands. Many of the smaller independent farmers also lost their lands, being likewise unable to survive.

By the early nineties all these factors combined to create a situation that was becoming intolerable in the cotton country along the middle Savannah. The farmers big and little, the sharecroppers white and black, were ready for anybody who would deliver them from their bonds. They were ready, in short, for revolution.

Two movements swept into the South from the West, symbolizing the uprising of the farmers against conditions which were grinding them down. First was the Farmers' Alliance. On its heels came the Populist movement, a political crusade seeking to change the attitude of voters at the polls and, through them, to influence state legislatures and Congress toward rural relief. The farmers, for the first time as a class, raised their voices threateningly to the national government, for the evils were nation-wide and required national treatment.

Two deliverers, two leaders of this revolution, appeared along the Savannah, one in Georgia, the other in South Carolina. One was Thomas E. Watson, who spread the Populist revolt up and down the Savannah on the Georgia side, and then over the whole state. Ultimately he became a formidable national figure in the Populist movement as its candidate, first for vice-president, and then for president. The other leader was Benjamin R. Tillman, "Pitchfork Ben," as he came to be called. He became the particular champion of sharecroppers and millworkers in South Carolina, who sent him first to the governor's chair at Columbia and afterwards to the United States Senate.

The revolution in which Watson and Tillman were caught upward is still going on.

The Watson and the Tillmans were typical of the society created along the Savannah midlands out of a mixture of the diverse backgrounds and traditions of people who had come from the north along the back-country trails three and four generations before. They had put down their roots into the soil and produced a type with a character all its own.

The Watsons originally were Quakers and had been part of the colonial migration from Pennsylvania that had established the town of Wrightsborough along Little River, a tributary of the Savannah. These Quaker settlers were a quiet, earnest, and industrious people. Peace loving, they had refused to take up arms in the American Revolution. This had set them apart from their neighbors in that region. Later they alienated themselves still further by their antagonism to Negro slavery. Some among them were fearful of a slave insurrection and eventually moved back to Pennsylvania. Thus Wrightsborough gradually disintegrated and disappeared to join the roll of vanished towns. The Watsons, however, remained in Georgia and in succeeding generations gradually accommodated themselves to the prevailing manners, customs and thinking. They left the Quaker persuasion to become Baptists, and they acquired slaves.

Tom Watson's grandfather owned a big farm. The house, once plain and primitive, was gradually added to until it assumed the rambling proportions of the manor house of the time and place. There Tom Watson was born. He remembered his grandfather in his early childhood as a splendid old gentleman, a personage with an air, who carried a silver-headed cane as he walked about surveying his acres.

The Tillmans came from Virginia, where the family, which earlier spelled its name Tilghman, traced back to 1638. The

South Carolina branch was founded by George Stephen Tillman, who settled in the Savannah midlands in 1750. He was killed in South Carolina at the siege of the town of Ninety Six in the American Revolution. His three sons likewise fought in the Revolution. Among them was Frederick, Ben Tillman's grandfather, who was rewarded for his services by a grant of 681 acres of land in the Edgefield district. This military grant along the Savannah became the hereditary nucleus of all the Tillman holdings in this fertile farming country.

Out of these similar backgrounds, veritable crucibles of pioneer hardships, Indian fighting, and white men's wars, came the two fiery-tempered and vigorous spirits who helped engender their own peaceful revolution in the Savannah River valley, one that eventually merged with the upheaval of the whole nation as it struggled with the new forces of a machine civilization.

PART 8

Another Revolution Rises From the Ashes of Chivalry

CHAPTER ONE

TOM WATSON DIRECTED IT IN GEORGIA

Tom Watson was a child of the turmoil and turbulence of the Reconstruction era. He was nine years old when the Civil War ended. As a youngster of seven, he had stood at the station at Thomson, his home, in the Savannah River valley, where he had gone to get the mail, and had seen a freight train come in loaded with Yankee prisoners. They were cheerful and gay, and sang "John Brown's Body" lustily and triumphantly. He knew they knew the end was in sight, that their side was going to win. He felt it. Young as he was, he could sense that. For he could also feel the pessimism and despair that the older folks in his community could not conceal.

And he had seen the realities of war and smelled its smells

and heard its sounds and seen its ultimate tragedy. A favorite uncle had come home from the war, a desperately sick man, to die. The little boy had wandered with his mother to some misty and vague battlefield, to some dim camp, to find his father, who twice had been wounded. That was a memory that remained with him always.

His father had survived it all and come home, one of the vanquished, but not in the spirit of the vanquished. He did not seem to realize, as so many others did not, that the war was the end of many things. He came home to find his slaves scattered, his fields forlorn and fruitless. But, instead of recognizing the passing of a regime, he was buoyantly optimistic and built himself a big, new house in place of the simpler farm home he had left behind when he went off to the war. It was an ironic whim. For he could get no help, and his farm soon became a barren habitation. Finally he had to sell it to meet his debts. The family moved to a smaller farm for a time but, in the end, drifted along the Savannah to the city, to Augusta, following the pathway of decline so common to so many along the river.

Here, instead of the big house Tom Watson vaguely remembered as a child, there was now, up the dirty street and around the corner, the boardinghouse and bar that his mother was trying to make a paying venture. His father had wilted under the pressure of misfortune and had become a listless and disconsolate figure, his ambition draining away into idle dreams distilled by the whisky from the bottles on his own shelves with which he solaced himself.

But Tom, now approaching manhood, spent little time in Augusta. He did not like the city. His favored domains were the small town and the country. He had been educated at country schools, and, to help pay his way at Mercer University, a Baptist college at Macon, he taught in country schools in his summer vacations. His mother saw in him, among all her children, the one shining talent who might go far, and it was she who insisted that he should go to college. While he was unable to complete his course at Mercer, he discovered there his gift for oratory. During these years of early manhood his was a vagrant life. As he moved from one country school to another, he mixed into the life of the small town and rural community. He made speeches occasionally at the temperance rallies popular at the time; he played the fiddle at country dances, making love somewhat indiscriminately to country maidens with a painful platonic ardor; he wrote bad poetry; he kept a diary in which he solemnly recorded the somber meditations of one of his years.

Eventually, through the influence of his mother, he got an opportunity to study law at an office in Augusta, and at the age of nineteen was licensed to practice. Since there was no propitious legal opening at the time, he went back to teaching for another year, back to the country folks among whom he delighted to be. But this nomadic life, pleasant as it was, must end, he decided; so he borrowed some money for his board and keep from one of his former schoolteachers, hung up his shingle in the town of Thomson, and became a full-fledged lawyer. He was twenty years old. In his first year he took in a grand total of $212. Thomson, then a town of seven hundred, became his home for the rest of his life. He had found his niche.

Young Watson now traveled the circuit, even as Stephens and Toombs had done, and so many other lawyers before them. He also visited often at the Stephens home at Crawfordsville. There the aging statesman of the mansion was still his idol, just as he had been when as a small boy Tom had sat in the chimney corner at his grandfather's house and listened to the ex-Confederate vice-president talk. He also loved the belligerent Bob Toombs.

In those years of riding the circuit Tom Watson learned people and human nature. He learned also about the economics of this farm country. He began to discern the forces responsible for conditions and to ponder in his mind how they might be changed and improved. Also he pondered on how, capitalizing on all this, he might advance his own career and become somebody in his own little world; perhaps later on, somebody in the bigger world outside.

It was still a rough-and-ready community in which he lived. Passions ran close to the surface. They bubbled up hotly at minor insults and affronts. Many a social occasion, a picnic, a barbecue, a political meeting, ended in a shooting affray. Murder was not infrequent. Tom Watson developed a peculiar skill as a defense lawyer in murder trials. He was so successful that his business began to flourish and his reputation to spread all through his native region. Tom Watson was much in demand. His rival in this field of criminal law was a local lawyer by the name of W. D. Tutt. More and more frequently the two were compared, with the result that a personal rivalry grew up. Each had his own champions. They naturally became enemies, and Tom Watson, following the custom of the times, began to carry a pistol.

One day he and Tutt got into a heated argument in another lawyer's office. Watson accused Tutt of taking a case during his absence, one that Watson thought should have come to him. He insulted the older man. Tutt struck at him. Watson pulled his gun as Tutt picked up a chair to defend himself and shot Tutt in the hand. Watson was taken into court on a charge of assault with intent to murder. The trial had run along for three days when friends of both men tried to bring about a settlement. Watson refused until he had been given an opportunity to state his case in his own defense. This he was permitted to do, after which the case was dismissed. This was strange procedure, but typical of the times.

Watson, indeed, was becoming quite a figure in the Savannah midlands and, at twenty-six, he decided to try his fortunes in politics. He entered the race for the state legislature. Despite the fact that advancement in politics in such a community was then often settled by the leaders, by an easy and simple agreement, Watson had become such a controversial figure that he attracted an opponent. He made his race an exciting event, dramatized it, and it became the chief center of interest in politics, though more important offices were at stake in the election.

Negroes were voting then and Watson appealed to them. He had many friends among them, because he had defended Negroes in court. Already he was beginning to stand out as the champion of the downtrodden and the dispossessed, both white and black, the people he knew and understood so well. He appeared before the Negroes in their Republican convention. So successful was his speech that the meeting ended with an endorsement of his candidacy, more than he had expected or wanted. The word also got around that he had endorsed the Republican platform. This was not true, but it proved embarrassing. For the resentments of Reconstruction still prevailed, though there was an acceptance of the participation of Negroes in politics at that time on both sides of the river in Georgia and South Carolina alike. Among the ordinary people this acquiescence disappeared later.

Tom Watson endeared himself to the Negroes by his advocacy of free schools for them and by denouncing the convict-lease system under which unfortunate blacks, caught in the toils of the law, were put into "chain gangs" to work out their time. His campaign generally was a foretaste of the liberal political program he expanded later to win the hearts of the poorer elements in this region and beyond it. He explained away the dilemma of Republican and Negro support by pointing out how respected state leaders, hang-overs from the old regime, also were supported by Negroes and readily accepted their votes. So he won his election, but by a narrow margin.

During this first campaign he established the "Tom Watson" character and caricature for all time in its several physical, mental and spiritual aspects. He became the great original of the nervous and angry redheaded Jeremiah, fussy, temperamental and full of furies, who wins the common people by his plain and simple talk and homely illustrations in their own vernacular; who builds up a bitter flock of enemies by prying out the foibles and tricks of the well-to-do, and then by his shrewd methods thwarts them, for he is always what is known as "a smart feller."

In the state legislature Watson shone naturally, but only by contrast to the stupid and ignorant fellows who for the most part made up the general assembly of Georgia. They are described by Woodrow Wilson, who then having time to spare from a meager law practice in Atlanta, occasionally joined the crowd in the galleries. He spoke of the legislators as "country lawyers, merchants, farmers, politicians, all of them poor, many densely ignorant. . . . As different as the poles from the British Parliament, wherein a class of men from leisured families, disciplined for leadership, ruled the state." Wilson then was enamored of the British ideal, a bookish fellow, supercilious, unrealistic, and somewhat snobbish.

Watson lost no time in presenting a program directed to the ills from which his agricultural constituents, white and black, were suffering. He introduced bills to protect the rights of farm tenants; he supported a bill permitting counties to tax railroads which operated across them; he sponsored bills fixing responsibility more directly upon the railroads for accidents on their rights of way; he supported an investigation of the convict-lease system. In every particular he was unsuccessful. The convict-lease investigation whitewashed the evils of that system. The bills he sponsored and supported got nowhere. He saw how hard the battle was going to be.

Georgia wasn't anxious for reform. At least so it appeared to be represented in its legislature. This only spurred him to delve deeper into the ills of the economic and social system, however, and to join with movements from outside the state aimed at the elimination of the abuses he was fighting.

He gave his support to the Farmers' Alliance, which was spreading into the South, although he did not become a member.

But he joined with the Alliance in open warfare on the jute-bag trust which was charging extortionate prices to farmers for their cotton bagging. The trust came to terms. The Alliance recognized his help.

Then he threw himself on the wave of Populism as it swept in from Kansas and across the South. He linked arms with such economic evangelists as Sockless Jerry Simpson, General John A. Weaver, and L. L. Polk, all of whom came to Georgia on a crusade, preaching similar doctrine. He went off to Populist conventions to join with these determined folks in plotting against the existing order.

To carry his own crusade and that of this new revolution to the national field, Watson got himself elected to Congress in 1891. Before he took his seat he had broken openly with the Democratic Party and, in keeping with the Populist mandate, fought the election of Charles Crisp of Georgia, a champion of conservatism, as speaker of the House. Watson opposed Crisp at first in the Democratic caucus, where the little band of Populists in the House failed, as they were doomed to fail, and subsequently in the House itself, where they supported Watson as their candidate for speaker. He got eight votes.

None of them, however, was from his own state, though eight members of Congress from Georgia, including himself, were swept in on the Populist wave in that state. Populists also won the governorship, many members of the legislature, and numerous local offices. The Savannah River valley especially was a hotbed of Populism. The conservative interests in Augusta and Savannah watched this new movement with increasing anxiety. They were up against a revolution.

Watson laid the Populist program before Congress in a series of bills designed to break the strangle hold of moneyed and corporate interests on the instruments of government. He fought the control of credit, which made money for agriculture so tight and expensive. He fought high railroad rates. He sought to break the monopolies that made farm implements and fertilizer so costly. He assailed high taxes on land. His program, which was expanded gradually to embrace even more deep-seated reforms, was not so revolutionary, except for the times. In his day, however, it provoked the outcry of "communism."

Most of the measures Watson espoused have long since been enacted in one form or another in the Theodore Roosevelt administrations or in those of Woodrow Wilson and Franklin D. Roosevelt. There is quite an astonishing list of such measures: a graduated income tax; postal savings banks; government insurance of bank deposits (this finally sponsored by a regular Republican); issuance of fiat currency by the federal government, regulation of the practice of transporting hired thugs to break up strikes (sponsored by a southern conservative senator of the thirties). This last was a practice then made notorious by the Pinkerton Detective Agency, which Watson had denounced in Congress. His original proposal for subtreasuries was later broadened by Woodrow Wilson in the Federal Reserve System, and Wilson likewise struck at monopolies, the evils of which Watson had dramatized many years earlier, by sponsoring the Clayton antitrust and the Federal Trade Commission acts.

Only one of his bills was passed in his time, that creating rural free delivery. His bill was selected for enactment out of eight that had been introduced on this general subject. Only one other of his bills ever got out of committee. Congress was no more receptive than the Georgia legislature. But, nonetheless, he had become a very devil to the conservative overlords of his own Congressional district along the Savannah and throughout all Georgia. He was a symbol of revolt, a figure that must be struck down at all costs. His campaign for re-election became the chief political interest of his own state and, as a matter of fact, it even won him national attention. Business interests in Augusta appealed for campaign funds to New York financial interests, and $40,000 was raised in the East and sent to Georgia, according to the New York *Tribune,* which remarked at the time that "insurance and railroad companies responded liberally."

Watson's opponent was a professional Southerner of the old school, "Major" James Conquest Cross Black, a conservative and eminently respectable lawyer of Augusta. He was also a deacon in the Baptist church, one who taught a big Bible class and he had likewise been a private in the Confederate Army. His title of "major" was purely one of civil courtesy.

Grover Cleveland, that apostle of conservatism and sound money, who was running again for president against President Harrison, also had an eye on this Congressional race in Georgia. He was quoted afterward as saying he was "almost as much interested in Major Black's campaign in the tenth district" as he was in his own election.

Never was there such a political campaign in the valley of the Savannah. There were fist fights, gun fights, murder even, before the ballots were cast.

When Watson got home from Washington to begin his campaign he was met at the border of his district by a great throng and escorted to his home at Thomson. There he harangued his noisy cohorts for two and a half hours. Thereafter he was constantly on the go. He and Black met a few times in public debate. On the trains going to these events the supporters of each candidate were compelled to ride in separate cars to avoid public brawls. Once, as Watson himself was leaving Thomson on a train, a passenger shouted, "Hurrah for Major Black! Watson is a deserter from the Democratic Party and sold out." Shouting "You're a God-damned liar," Watson climbed over other passengers and attacked his detractor, beating him to the floor.

Everywhere Watson went, in the small towns, at the crossroads, he was welcomed by mobs of raving enthusiasts who carried huge banners, thirty and forty feet long, made of silk, emblazoned with his picture and Populist slogans. They serenaded

him with a mournful song, a composition of Watson's own,
to the tune of "The Bonny Blue Flag," which went:

> My husband came from town last night
>   As sad as man could be;
> His wagon empty—cotton gone—
>   And not a dime had he.
>
> He sat down there before the fire,
>   His eyes were full of tears;
> Great God! How debt is crushing down
>   This strong man—young in years!
>
> Huzza! Huzza! It's queer I do declare!
> We make the food for all the world,
>   Yet live on scanty fare.

Cotton was selling for four cents a pound in those days, not
nearly enough to pay for the cost of production. Yet Major
Black was saying that the plight of the farmer was exaggerated.
He used the old cry heard before, and so often since, that Watson's campaign was "un-American and un-Christian, arraigning
one class against another."

The whole state was in a furor as people bitterly took sides.
All this was doubly intensified in the Tenth District. Personal
attacks were common. Just the day after Watson returned
home to begin his campaign, C. C. Post, the Populist novelist
who had moved to Georgia with his wife sometime before,
and had become editor of Watson's paper the *People's Party*, was
struck on the head with a rock when he and the Populist candidate for governor were attacked by a crowd at Quitman. Just
a few days before, Governor Northen, who had been elected
by Populist votes and had written the Populist platform but
who now had deserted the party, assailed Post personally as an
"infidel," an anarchist, and an "infamous cur" and then called the
editor's wife "an atheist" for good measure. After the incident

at Quitman, Post left the state and went back home to Michigan.

Southern chivalry, indeed, seemed to be retired for the nonce. General John A. Weaver, who had come to Georgia to promote his campaign for president on the Populist ticket, was subjected to numerous indignities, and at Macon he and his wife were showered with rotten eggs, one of which hit his wife in the head. The general cut his campaign short and left the state.

Watson had the support of the Negroes and he addressed meetings attended only by Negroes. One young Negro, H. S. Doyle, a preacher, was one of his most ardent campaigners, and spoke day after day all over the district. One day at Thomson he was threatened with lynching and sought protection from Watson. Enraged by this threat, Watson sent out word to the neighborhood and the white farmers began to rally in Thomson at his call to help protect the Negro preacher, many coming from quite a distance. Some two thousand gathered, bringing their guns with them. These they stacked on the porch of Watson's home. Then Watson and Doyle spoke to them from the steps of the courthouse.

"We are determined in this free country that the humblest white or black man that wants to talk our doctrine shall do it," Watson told them, "and the man doesn't live who shall touch a hair of his [Doyle's] head without fighting every man in the People's Party." Later Doyle said that "after that Mr. Watson was held almost a savior by the Negroes. The poor ignorant men and women, who had been oppressed so long, were anxious to touch Mr. Watson's hand, and were often a source of inconvenience to him in their anxiety to see him and shake hands with him, even to touch him."

This incident, the gathering of white farmers to protect a Negro, was a symbol of the friendly relationships then existing among the poorer classes of both races in the Savannah midlands. They had a community of interest. They were brought together in their common misery in a common cause. It lasted only so short a time, but it did exist, and is a worthwhile footnote to history.

Watson's enemies were quick to make capital of this mobscene incident, particularly the hostile newspapers. They shouted in frenzy that Watson was creating anarchy and bringing communism to the South. They claimed that Doyle never had been threatened with lynching. Yet only a week later he was shot at while addressing a meeting. The bullet missed him and killed a white man. It is estimated that fifteen Negroes were killed during this campaign.

Watson was, of course, foredoomed to defeat. The *haves* could not tolerate such a triumph by the *have-nots*. It was in Augusta that they stole the election. There every sort of political thievery was resorted to. They stuffed the ballot boxes and voted repeaters. They intimidated Negroes who wanted to vote for Watson, while they brought in droves of other Negroes from outside the state. South Carolina just across the river contributed a goodly number. They were given plenty of liquor and run into the polls in long lines.

In retaliation the Populists also used some of the same tactics, but not so successfully. There were twice as many votes cast in Augusta as there were eligible voters. There Major Black got more than half the votes he received in the whole district. Richmond County, in which Augusta is located, was the only county in the district that Watson lost. He carried the other twelve. The fraud was plain and unmistakable. Watson contested the election, but he could get no justice in the House of Representatives, where he had made so many enemies. A quarter of a century passed before he got back to Washington in an elective office, and by then Populism had been long dead and the face of the world had changed. So had Tom Watson, and much for the worse.

His defeat first stunned him, then embittered him. Now he in truth was a political outcast. Only from without the pale could he keep up the fight. But those without the pale were now become a vast multitude of discontent that began to take on the aspects of a mob throughout the whole country. Terrible lean years were upon the Savannah River valley and upon all America. In 1893 depression spread through the land, shutting the doors of factories in the towns and cities, and swelling the number of the destitute and homeless in the farm regions. 'Ninety-four was worse than 'ninety-three. The forces of revolt captured the Democratic Party and William Jennings Bryan became their champion. Thereupon the Democratic Party proceeded to swallow the Populist Party.

The conservative, old-line Democrats won their way back into power in the Savannah River valley, where Populism had for a time burned like a consuming fire, and also throughout the rest of Georgia. The regulars re-established themselves through clever use of the vicious weapon of race prejudice. They renewed and made poignant old loyalties dormant since pre-Civil War days, but still latent through appeal to that pernicious issue —"white supremacy." For a time, in the days of their degradation, the white farmers and tenants had admitted Negroes to political equality with them. They had in effect accepted them as equals at the ballot box. But, when times got some better, the poorer whites succumbed to appeals to their race pride. It was all that some of them had left. So their former allies in adversity became merely "niggers" again.

Watson always had made it plain that he was against "social equality." But this label of "social equality" had been placed on his crusade for the underprivileged whites and blacks by his enemies, and they made it stick. He always had insisted, however, that Negroes were entitled to political rights.

He saw very clearly how the Negro issue could be raised to defeat him. In 1892 he had written:

"You might beseech a southern white tenant to listen to you upon questions of finance, taxation, and transportation; you might demonstrate with mathematical precision that herein lay his way out of poverty into comfort; you might have him 'almost persuaded' to the truth, but if the merchants who furnished his farm supplies (at tremendous usury) or the town politician (who never spoke to him except at election times) came along and cried 'Negro rule!', the entire fabric of reason and common sense which you had patiently constructed would fall, and the poor tenant would joyously hug the chains of an actual wretchedness rather than do any experimenting on a question of mere sentiment. . . . The Negro has been as valuable a portion of the stock in trade of a Democrat as he was of a Republican."

So, to beat down such annoying doctrines as Populism, the old-line Democrats invented the "white primary." It began in Georgia and it extended all over the South during the late nineties and in the early years of the new century. It eliminated the Negroes from successful participation in elections, for in the South the primary was the election that counted under the one-party system.

Tom Watson was the champion of the poorer, ill-favored people of his community in the Savannah River valley, but he was never of them. He was in fact in the best tradition of the educated, cultured Southerner who becomes the natural leader of affairs, though he used his knowledge of the prejudices of the poor whites to advance his cause. He became a person of substance through his law practice and built himself a comfortable home in Thomson. "Hickory Hill" he named it. He finally became one of the largest landowners in the state, and had more tenants working for him than his grandfather had had slaves.

After 1896 he retired from political life to his law practice and his writing. He turned out a popular life of Napoleon, in which he indulged a secret admiration for the French liberator turned dictator; a history of France; a life of Jefferson and another of Jackson, and a novel, *Bethany*, his only work of fiction. These, and his law practice, piled up for him a comfortable personal fortune. He lived virtually a recluse, and during these years he fed his soul with the disappointments of his political failures.

He emerged from retirement to become the candidate for president of the languishing People's Party in 1904, and again in 1908. In the first campaign he traveled all over the country. He got 117,000 votes. That year the discontents flocked rather to Eugene V. Debs, the Socialist, who increased his vote of 90,000 in 1900 to 400,000 in 1904. In 1908 Watson polled a handful of 27,000 votes. Populism was dead.

After that he returned to the Democratic Party and began a retreat from revolutionary political doctrine. He demonstrated this in a bitter series of articles about socialism, which, ironically, repeated some of the phrases that had been used against his once-cherished Populism. In time he had his own mouthpiece, *Watson's Magazine,* which attracted some nationally known writers and some national attention. A large part of each edition was given over to his own editorializing on every passing issue.

Gradually, through the years, he turned into a kind of warped demagogue, with only occasional flashes back to his old self in behalf of some progressive cause. Mostly he spilled forth venom in a strange, distorted bigotry that struck out at religious and racial minorities, at Jews, at Catholics, and even at the Negroes whom he had befriended earlier in life. He closed an editorial attacking Booker T. Washington with the words:

> What does Civilization owe to the negro?
> Nothing!
> *Nothing!*
> NOTHING!

He was wandering off in dark paths, indeed!

Yet Watson was, for all his baleful attitudes and poses, a political factor of considerable importance in Georgia. He maintained a loyal and devoted band of followers whom he maneuvered here and there as a balance of power. The result was that he became a boss with whom the politically ambitious must treat, although he broke afterward with nearly every political leader whose cause he championed and whom he helped to places of power. He was a political sadist. He was mercurial, passionate and unpredictable. He could never abide Woodrow Wilson. He opposed the war and, afterward, the League of Nations. On an anti-League of Nations platform he finally went back to Washington and the United States Senate, in 1918. But he contributed nothing, nothing worth while, in those trying and decisive years.

Still he remained, always, almost a god with a segment of the populace. They were the poor and the ignorant, those who lived in the less pleasant acres of the state, in the Savannah River valley, in the flatlands in middle and southern Georgia, in the valleys of the mountains to the north. To these folks he was still a champion. He knew them well, and he fed their prejudices and their narrow minds and their starved and twisted souls. This in turn fed his own ego until he became a political tyrant of the worst order. The deliverer of the nineties had turned into an evil spirit with a fanatical gleam in his eye and the poison of hatred in his heart.

When he died, in 1922, those who wrote the obituaries found themselves confused and disturbed by his strange contradictory career.

Yet his story tells much of the Savannah River valley.

CHAPTER TWO

"PITCHFORK BEN" TILLMAN STARTED IT IN SOUTH CAROLINA

Equally significant of the saga of the valley was the career of Ben Tillman on the other side of the river in South Carolina from Watson's stamping ground.

The Tillman family farm, where Ben was born and grew up, was in Edgefield District along the Savannah where lived a tempestuous and volatile people. Of this section in the era of Ben Tillman it was said that "one did not have to go far to find either a fight or a frolic." There was much drinking and gambling and much gunplay, the last sometimes of the gentlemanly sort on the dueling ground, but oftener of the more primitive kind, where brawls provoke the quick draw. This was truly a profligate and undisciplined neighborhood. One of its historians recounts proudly that it had "more dashing, brilliant, romantic figures, statesmen, orators, soldiers, adventurers, daredevils, than any county of South Carolina, if not any rural county in America." This estimate may be an exaggeration, but is perhaps not too far afield.

One of the citizens of this section stands out in American history for a single act of violence that displayed not only his hotblooded Edgefield heritage but also the hair-trigger tension in the South at large, an incident that forecast what has been called "the irrepressible conflict" of the Civil War. This citizen was Preston S. Brooks, the man who caned the New England foe of the South and slavery, the crippled Charles Sumner, while on the floor of the United States Senate, in retaliation for Sumner's verbal attack on another Edgefield man, Senator Andrew P. Butler.

Brooks and Butler were of the polite society of Edgefield Courthouse, the county seat and cosmopolis of the local aristocracy. These gentry were the local molds of culture, fashion, and social customs of the times and place. Distinct from this breed were the Tillmans. They were country folks, respectable county farmers, well-to-do, but keeping themselves apart from the courthouse gentry, apparently somewhat jealous in a proud way of the Edgefield clan and its more extravagant living. While Ben Tillman's family was reasonably prosperous for that era, they were also thrifty and eschewed lavish spending and display.

Ben's mother, who was left a widow when he, the last born of ten children, was only two years old, was a self-reliant, hard-fisted and shrewd business woman. She was a "manageress," typical of the matriarchal tradition of the era in the South. She virtually doubled the original inheritance left her by her husband. She became the richest farmer of the whole community and the owner of eighty slaves who worked her 3,500 acres. Yet, when she went to Augusta on business, she left her horse and wagon in Hamburg on the South Carolina side of the river and walked across the bridge to save the toll. But the Tillman home place, called "Chester," was not the southern typical manor characteristic of the times, although it was a commodious and comfortable twelve-room house, the finest in the neighborhood. Nor was it, like others, a center of free community hospitality. Instead, the Tillmans turned their home into a crossroads inn for passengers on the stagecoach from Augusta to Edgefield. It was situated conveniently for this purpose halfway between Augusta and Edgefield, i.e., only about fifteen miles from the river metropolis of the whole middle Savannah valley.

This inn, then, was the childhood and young manhood background of the political leader who left such an imprint on his region and his state. Here he grew up, the favorite of his mother. Figuratively as well as literally he was the "Benjamin" of the Tillman tribe, and yet altogether a normal enough boy. He was adept in boyhood games, fished in the small streams of the hilly, red-clay country. And he was particularly fond of hunting the usual small quarry of youth, squirrels, rabbits, and birds. Often, too, at night he trailed over the hills on possum hunts with the Negroes on the place. Also, in true southern style, we can be certain, he lorded it over the Negroes in a way familiar among young heirs of the manor of that day as a rustic sort of patrician. His early education was at a private school established by families in the community. His mother provided the schoolhouse as well as joining with the neighbors in its financial support. The teaching talent was brought from the North, which was the practice of the times.

Ben's first teacher—it was she who taught him to read—was the sister of a man who later became president of the United States. She was Miss Annie Arthur from New York.

Later Ben went to a school at Bethany conducted by one George Galphin, presumably in preparation for a college course at the University of South Carolina. He never got to the university, however. The Civil War intervened with its confusions and interruptions to normal life. At Bethany he got the usual education of the young man of that time, and of later days, too—English literature, grammar and rhetoric, mathematics, history, and doses of Latin and Greek. All of which, with his wide supplementary reading, contributed to the effective and colorful prose style that he later developed both as a writer and as a political orator.

In all ways, in family background and his education, in his upbringing, and in his general outlook upon the world and its affairs, he was in the tradition of the Savannah midlands. When the Civil War broke upon his part of the world, it was just another reminder to him and his family of previous wars in which his forebears had taken part.

Young Ben had, in fact, grown up in the midst of the memories and traditions of the Revolution. He was familiar in his childhood, for instance, with the "murder field," as it was still called, a spot on his mother's plantation where a Tory had once been hanged. And in the neighboring forest was a large over-hanging rock, "Shelving Rock," it was named, under which a great-uncle had hidden away from the British while he was suffering from an attack of smallpox. Lying there in his forest refuge, he had been nursed back to health by his sister, Annsybil Tillman, Ben's grandmother.

Closer, but not in the immediate memory of Ben, who was born August 11, 1847, was the Mexican War, to which so many of the young men of the Savannah valley had gone. Among them were three Tillmans. One of them, and one of Ben's seven brothers, was Thomas Frederick. He had trooped off gaily with Captain Preston Brooks's "Old Ninety Six Boys," a company of the famous South Carolina Palmetto regiment. Thomas Frederick had been left dead far away on the battlefield of Churubusco only nine days after Ben had been born at home in Edgefield District.

So violence and quick death had followed the generations of Tillmans, in war, by pestilence, and in all the other wild vicissitudes of pioneer living. Rather than diminishing, violence seemed to come to a fine red, full bloom in the family of Benjamin Ryan Tillman the First, for so Ben's father is known in local Edgefield history. This "Benjamin the First" had himself murdered a man, but because of his prominence in the community he was let off scot free. His eldest son, George, who was twenty-one years older than his little brother Ben, was a fellow of wild and ungovernable temper when angered. He was constantly fighting and feuding. One of his more notable encounters was with Preston Brooks. Then in a rage one night over a faro game he had shot and killed an innocent bystander and fled the community. He went first to California but later joined William Walker's filibustering expedition to Nicaragua. Eventually, George returned home, but he was still compelled to lie low. By day he lay hidden away upstairs with his books, for he was an omnivorous reader and student, but at night he would venture out to take walks with young Ben. Finally, however, George gave himself up and was sentenced to two years in jail. There he was treated as a distinguished guest, going and coming almost as he pleased. He left jail to become a successful lawyer and was thereafter much in and out of politics, serving in the state legislature and in Congress.

Then years later, in 1857, typhoid fever took another son of the family, Henry Cummings Tillman. In the following year two others, John Miller and Oliver Hancock, were both killed only eight months apart in scrapes involving women. Oliver died in Florida. Thus when the Civil War broke upon the Savannah valley there were only three of the seven Tillman brothers left. George, the oldest, sagely advised against any rash hurrying into this bloody affair, which he believed would go on for years. He observed that there had been too much of death in the family. Ben, of course, was still too young to go to war. But George and the remaining brother, James Adams Tillman, responded a year later to the call that sounded through the South and joined up.

George seems to have listened to his own advice. He enlisted in an artillery unit stationed at Charleston for a quiet tour of duty, without danger. Even that hazard was cut short by his election to the legislature in 1864. But James got in the thick of the fighting in Tennessee and Georgia with the armies of Johnston and Hood. Young Ben had an experience in the amphitheater of war akin to that of the boy Tom Watson, although Ben was somewhat older when it happened. He went with his mother to Atlanta to look for James, who was wounded in the gory series of engagements about that Georgia city. They found James finally in one of the many field hospitals. He recovered from those wounds, with the help of his mother's nursing, and got up and out to fight some more, and that most gallantly. But he was a hopeless cripple when he returned home after the war. Exhausted by his wounds and privations, he died a few months later.

The time came for Ben, too, to offer himself to the failing

Confederacy. A month before he was seventeen he left school and enrolled his name in an artillery unit operating along the South Carolina coast. But he never got into the army. A few days after he left school he was stricken with an abscess in his eye contracted during an afternoon of swimming. He was ill for months, with complications of convulsions and a brain disturbance. He recovered, long after the war had ended, but with only one eye.

Ben found plenty to do around the farm when he was able to be about again. He helped his mother with management of the land under the difficult conditions caused by the freeing of the slaves. George thought his mother should give up the South Carolina farm and go to Florida. While she refused to leave South Carolina, she did buy a farm in Florida which Ben and one of his three sisters, Frances, took over. But they had bad luck there and after two years returned home to South Carolina.

Ben married when he was twenty. He and his wife settled down on a 300-acre tract allotted to him by his mother out of her still plenteous acreage. His wife, born Sallie Starke, daughter of a Fairfield District farmer, was eighteen when she married Ben. He had met her when he and his sister, Frances, were on a visit to their own mother's family in Elbert County, Georgia, in the last months of the war. The two young Tillmans were taking refuge there from the armies of Sherman that were sweeping down across Georgia. Sallie Starke was also visiting her mother's family in Elbert County at the time.

Sallie was a pretty girl of farm background with no social pretensions or ambitions. She was a proper and fitting wife and a companionable helpmeet for Ben in the rather discouraging conditions the young couple met in beginning life together in those troublous times. Sallie, however, did have a mind of her own. For that reason she proved a good balance for her more temperamental husband when later on he switched to a political career, even though she had no part in his decision to change his course. She was amply satisfied with the life of a farmer's wife.

It was hard and crude at the outset. Ben built a three-room house, the customary L-shaped structure typical of the neighborhood and era. In this house they lived in quarters no better than those of the average tenant farmer, and they lived there for many years without enlarging them. Ten years passed before the couple had a child. Afterward, children came along regularly, and the house grew larger and larger to contain them.

Ben Tillman was not only an industrious farmer, he was also an intelligent farmer. He recognized full well the evils of exclusive, one-crop farming. On his own farm he diversified, not only to provide a rotation of crops that would keep his land fertile but also to supplement his major cash crops with vegetables and produce for his family. He became a familiar figure in Augusta in the crop season, walking up and down the streets selling vegetables, with his wagon and his Negro driver following along behind. He was not too proud to be a huckster. Because of his reputation as a sound farmer, he was frequently the center of an interested group, while he explained about his experiments with new crops, his ideas about diversification, and, at the same time, digressed to talk about the problems of the day.

Ben assiduously read farm magazines and occasionally wrote articles for them himself. He also kept up his reading of literature, and was so fond of poetry that upon occasion he could quote great chunks of it. In his leisure from his problems of farm management he could often be seen stretched out on his back on his front porch with a book. He would read thus by the hour.

He had his ups and downs as a farmer—good years and bad years. He was active in community affairs and altogether a temperate and sober family man. He joined the local military organization, the Edgefield Huzzars, and took a minor part in local politics. But he twice refused to run for the state legislature. Meanwhile, he was a member of the Executive Committee of the Edgefield County Democratic organization and later its county chairman. He was sent as a delegate to the Democratic state convention in 1882.

But as yet he exhibited no appetite for political office. Then, suddenly, his whole career was changed in that very direction by a speech he delivered one hot day in August, 1885, to the ninth annual joint session of the State Grange and State Agricultural and Mechanical Society at Bennettsville. He was just a plain farmer when he rose to speak.

He told this gathering, plainly and courageously, the truth that they all knew, though which few admitted and fewer still could see with such clear perspective, and which none other dared to tell; to wit, that farmers of South Carolina were shockingly ignorant of their own business—farming; that they were bound, like the black slaves that had been freed, in a slavery of their own to the lien merchants of the towns, who carried them from year to hard year, to their own inevitable bondage and to the profit of their creditors; that they had no real voice in their government, which was in the hands of a few, those being the ruling political oligarchy dominated from Charleston, consisting of smart lawyers and members of old families there and elsewhere who passed around the state offices within a closed corporation, and who carried out the dictates of the financial overlords of the state.

"The people have been hoodwinked by demagogues and lawyers in the pay of finance," he shouted.

The solution that Ben offered that day to this assembly of farmers was a simple one, better education for the farmer and direct political action to give him a say in the government. He confined himself at the time to a series of resolutions he offered concerning education, since that was the more fundamental. And he denounced unscathingly the futile lip service that the State University gave to agricultural education—"just a sop to Cerberus, a bribe to maintain the support of the farmers of the legislature." He asked, in his resolutions, that the university trustees be forced to carry out in good faith the purposes of

previously from the legislature by his organized farmers' movement before he became governor.

Generally he freed the politics of his state from the shackles of the tight machine, feudal in management, that had controlled South Carolina so effectively. Though he did not originate the direct-primary system, which had previously existed locally in some counties, he did improve and enlarge upon it, with the result that he left behind an elective system that was more democratic, at least for the white people.

With that end in view he broke the strangle hold of Charleston and the coast on the government, something that had existed since the state was founded. He did this by reapportioning the legislature to give the upstate country more voice in state affairs. He was also the creator of a political feature that is still peculiar to South Carolina. This is the joint-debate system whereby candidates for county and state offices travel around over the state in cavalcades and discuss most issues in turn from the same platform. For this purpose their expenses are paid by the state. This measure he had brought about by action of the state Democratic convention even before he became governor.

But his ideas of more democracy in politics did not include the Negroes. On the contrary, he wanted to disfranchise them entirely. And this was to be put in effect by a mandate in the state constitution, itself. However, he never could get authorization for the state constitutional convention that he desired for this and for other purposes.

In the field of economic reform Tillman met his most formidable resistance from the railroads, which, as so often in our history, were able to enlist the support of the federal courts. It took him four years to get what he regarded as essential in the way of powers for the state railroad commission to examine the books of railroads in making determination of rates.

He also tangled with the courts when he attempted to levy

higher tax assessments on railroads, the levy to be based on higher valuation of their properties. All this was part of a much broader program to make big corporate interests pay a more proportionate share of taxes. A test case wound its way through the federal courts, and back and forth, in many dramatic episodes, before the United States Supreme Court finally upheld his basic principle. So exasperating, however, was this tussle with an entrenched economic interest that finally, after one rebuff, he denounced the "unholy marriage" of the railroads and the courts in a vituperative document of a dozen pages. In this he said in effect that the railroads had become more powerful than the states.

The Tillman administration was also responsible for another reform directly in the field of social welfare, but the governor, himself, did not initiate it. He simply acquiesced, for he still had little interest in those who most benefited from it, the "poor whites" in the factories. He called them "the damned factory class," and his antagonism seems to have been typically that of a farmer toward city workers. Undoubtedly he magnified his own experience with them as part-time hands on his own plantation when millwork was slack.

However, he signed the bill passed by the legislature. It fixed the hours of work in factories at sixty-three a week. This measure, sponsored by an upcountry member who was called "Citizen Josh" Ashley, started out as a sixty-hour a week limitation, but it caused such an uproar among the business and financial interests—one manufacturer exploded that "a ten-hour day law would ruin every mill in the state"—that it was raised to sixty-three hours before it was finally enacted.

But even this measure threw a sudden chill, gray light on the meager lot of another growing class in the state and in the South, namely, workers in the cotton mills.

For at last the cotton mills were really beginning to move from New England to the source of supply in the South. It had taken a long time. But now the mills were coming finally, a century after invention of the cotton gin in the South. Even then this was not due to southern initiative, but to the foresight of shrewd New Englanders who saw the advantages of locating their mills near the cotton fields, instead of paying to transport the raw cotton to their long-established mills in the Northeast.

In the domain of education for agriculture, always Tillman's pet hobby, he accomplished much for his native state, although at the expense of education in the liberal arts. His outstanding achievement was Clemson College. It was, in truth, his child and remains perhaps as his outstanding memorial. Thomas G. Clemson, son-in-law of John C. Calhoun, had become interested in Tillman's ideas for agricultural education, and in particular his suggestion for a separate state college of agriculture. He invited Tillman to visit him at Fort Hill, the Calhoun estate, in the autumn of 1886. There a group, including two of Clemson's neighbors, outlined the project for a separate college of agriculture. To this Clemson then offered to donate to the state the 814-acre Calhoun estate upon his death. He had long been interested in a state college of agriculture, even before Tillman's agitation, but its championship by the Edgefield farmer had suggested a way of practical realization, since Tillman had demonstrated his influence in politics as organizer of the farmers' movement.

Later, with his help, a normal and industrial college for women was established by the state through acquisition and enlargement of Winthrop Training School. It had been established in 1886 by David B. Johnson, a Tennesseean who had been superintendent of public schools at Columbia. Tillman's achievements for agricultural and vocational education were not matched, however, in the field of higher cultural education. As a matter of fact, he was guilty of distinct disservice in that direction. His attacks on the State University weakened that institution and its already small enrollment dwindled figuratively to a handful during his administration.

In the domain of reform affecting the always nettlesome

liquor problem, Ben Tillman had an experience that carried his name far and wide. This came about not only because of the innovation he introduced in South Carolina but because of its bloody climax in what came to be known as "the Darlington Riots." He got through the legislature a law establishing a state liquor dispensary system, unknown then on a state-wide scale though adopted broadly forty years later after the nation's corrupt, costly, and also bloody experiment with national prohibition.

It displeased both the friends and the enemies of prohibition. Rabid prohibitionists were angry because they felt they had been hoodwinked. The law had been rushed through the legislature as a prohibition law, but they waked up too late only to find it was nothing of the sort. The liquor interests resented it because their business now was taken over by the state.

Not long after the law went into effect on July 1, 1893, the governor found that he had a virtual rebellion on his hands. While dispensary stations were established for sale of liquor and constables were appointed to enforce the law, the violations were open and flagrant. Blind tigers continued to operate with the connivance of local citizens. Magistrates, judges and juries refused to convict violators. Newspapers carried on a constant hostile campaign on the grounds of the invasion of individual liberty. All this only aroused Tillman to added fury. He issued orders to agents to "shoot to kill." When local constables were unable to control the lawbreakers, he encouraged spying by citizens by offering rewards for the report of violators.

The inevitable incident eventually occurred at Darlington in the Pee Dee section in the western part of the state. Citizens there had refused to patronize the dispensary. Instead they encouraged and protected operators of blind tigers. The governor dispatched four special constables to Darlington. They were ignored and ridiculed. Then he sent eighteen more, at which angry citizens corralled the arms of the local militia and prepared to resist. The governor's reply was to order in a militia company from Sumter. It remained four or five days and peace and order were seemingly restored.

The special constables now prepared to retire from the scene, four of them heading toward one railroad station, eighteen to another. But a mob of townspeople followed them. In a brawl between a group of citizens and one constable, the latter drew his gun and killed a man.

In the general shooting that followed another citizen and a constable were killed while two citizens and two constables were wounded. Four of the constables escaped on a train bound for Charleston, which left the station amid a fusillade from the mob. The remaining constables who were still whole of body then fled to the woods and swamps. A mob was organized to hunt them down. The town bell rang out ominously to summon the inhabitants to war.

When the news of the Darlington riot reached Columbia a mob also gathered there. Thus Tillman suddenly found himself in the midst of what came to be known to the nation as "the Dispensary War." Newspaper correspondents from all over the country were rushed to South Carolina to cover it. The governor now ordered three companies of Columbia militia to go to Darlington. They bluntly refused to serve. Meanwhile the mob was threatening to burn down the dispensary warehouse in Columbia, and Tillman perforce withdrew to the governor's mansion. He had also ordered militia from Sumter and Manning to Darlington, but these units likewise refused to obey him. Subsequently he got a hotly worded reply from the commander of the militia at Charleston when he ordered that unit out. It was to the effect that the Charleston militia would fight to defend the honor of the state "but will not lend itself to foment civil war among our brethren." Tillman was seemingly blocked. Mutiny was abroad.

But he still had a last resort. He issued an appeal to the source of his power, to the plain people of the state. He called upon them to rise up and help him. They responded. In droves they began to converge upon the capital city, leaving their plows and bringing along their rifles and shotguns. Most of them camped in the grounds of the state penitentiary. Among the volunteer units was his old command, the Edgefield Huzzars. He made them his guard of honor charged with protecting him personally. When some five hundred citizen soldiers had rallied to his defense, he canceled his appeal, saying there were enough, though many others were still on the way.

Meanwhile, two hundred of the organized militia which had not deserted arrived in Darlington only to discover that all the constables had escaped and the posses that had been scouring the countryside for them had returned to their homes in Darlington. The militia, however, remained there five days. Finally, when it was evident that the trouble was over, they were ordered out and the Darlington Riots and the Dispensary War were over. Yet the uprising had created a sensation all over the country, and Tillman became a national figure. For quite evidently in the minds of the public elsewhere than in South Carolina he was regarded as the hero of this state insurrection. The story even got beyond the shores of the United States and the English *Spectator* praised his conduct.

His enemies thought, for a time, that they had him hung high, as the proverbial goose, on his own dispensary system. Yet characteristically he came out of this harassing experience stronger than ever with the rank and file of voters in the state. So much so that he now took the next step upward on the political ladder with ease; namely, his elevation to the United States Senate.

In his campaign for that office he had created his own enemy, a convenient straw man to whip about on the stump. Yet he picked a big one, and, as a diversion, one outside the state. This "straw man" was none other than Grover Cleveland, president of the United States.

Tillman's public crusade against Cleveland was on an issue that lay ready at hand—hard money *vs.* cheap money. He had, indeed, already joined the silver bloc of the Democratic Party, and had won some recognition while still governor by his appearance before the Bi-Metallic Convention at St. Louis in 1893. That had put him into direct conflict with Grover Cleveland, and so in his own peculiar way he now performed as an antagonist of the Democratic president in the grand manner. He resorted to hyperbole to picture Cleveland as a dark and shady villain, one who was allied with the money trust to grind down the common people.

This new crusade had its personal interest. The president had refused to let Governor Tillman handle the federal patronage for South Carolina. Cleveland, in truth, did not care for Ben Tillman. It was during the senatorial campaign that Tillman invented from the language of the barnyard the tag that was forever after to hang on him. This occurred when he cried out one day in a diatribe against the president, whom he had already compared to Judas Iscariot, "He [Cleveland] is an old bag of beef and I am going to Washington with a pitchfork and prod him in his old fat ribs."

So it was "Pitchfork Ben" Tillman who arrived on the national scene to sit in the Senate. And it was as Pitchfork Ben that he was known thereafter, in the newspaper dispatches that went out from the national capital during his twenty-two years in the Senate, and in the frequent cartoons that depicted various stages of his career as a national legislator. His service in the Senate ended only with his death, July 3, 1918.

Though Ben Tillman did achieve something for some of the people of his state, principally by arousing them to the necessity of organizing politically if they wanted to get something for themselves, he is remembered chiefly for sheer personality. In himself he achieved the pattern of the southern demagogue that later became so familiar in those who followed him—the Huey Longs, the Bilbos, the Talmadges, and a legion of minor replicas. Tillman carried with him all through his career as governor, and as United States senator too, that bitter race prejudice which he exploited so callously and so carelessly to advance his own political aspirations. In that, too, he was copied. Thus he left a legacy that has now long contributed to keep the South from realizing its true destiny, and so also did Tom Watson in Georgia.

Fairly early in life, as a young man, Tillman exhibited a cruel streak where race was concerned by his part in one of the most ghastly and brutal episodes in all Reconstruction history. The episode was what came to be known as "the Hamburg Riots," and it, too, is a part of the history of the Savannah and its people in a troublous period. It shocked the nation.

It was the natural but evil fruit of the seed of violent license that flowered, like a noxious weed, from the poisonous soil of Reconstruction. The pattern was fixed in Ben Tillman's own community of Edgefield. It evolved from the idea that the only way to cast off the rule of Republicanism, foisted on the South by military force, was to use counterforce to intimidate the Negroes. They, if properly organized, could always furnish a majority of votes. So the Negroes simply must be kept away from the polls. The way to turn the trick most directly was patently by a combination of intimidation and plain fraud. To this the white politicians soon resorted, and it worked.

To accomplish this purpose the whites formed certain military organizations of their own. This method became known as "the Edgefield Plan." Tillman joined an outfit in his own community in Edgefield County that had the flamboyant name of "the Sweetwater Sabre Club." It was organized in 1873 and numbered forty-five men. The "enemy" in its case was two companies of Negro militia, part of a regiment organized in Edgefield County by the Reconstruction government with headquarters in Meriwether Township. One of these companies was commanded by a Negro named Ned Tennant, described as "a dashing figure" because of his gay airs and grand manner. He affected a plumed hat. So he was particularly obnoxious to the whites in his own community, and the Sabre Club set out premeditatively to provoke an incident about him. Ultimately there were two incidents concerning Tennant, both of which, in the usual course of such inciting events, became a kind of prelude to the ultimate and preordained tragedy staged at Hamburg.

One grew out of an episode in which a group of whites, youths who had become angered over the boisterous drilling of Tennant's company on July 4, 1874, gathered for a demonstration before Tennant's house and fired several shots at the Negro's front door. Subsequently, the word went around that Captain Tennant had ordered his company to assemble because of this insult. Accordingly, the alarm was raised for members of the Sabre Club to converge on his house. He appeared when the company of whites gathered before his home, completely cowed, and sent out orders for his Negro militia company to disperse. Thus the first incident was closed.

The second occurred three months later when the home of General Matthew Butler, a Confederate veteran and prominent organizer of the whites in Edgefield District, burned down. While there was no evidence to link the fire with Negroes, warrants nevertheless were issued for the arrest of Captain Tennant and some of his leaders. Captain Tennant was not at his house when the constable arrived there, so a posse was organized to hunt him and the other Negro leaders, consisting largely of the Sabre Club.

Two Negroes were wounded in an exchange of shots during the chase that followed. A white doctor who was called in to attend the injured blacks was fired upon, and a mob was then organized which spread out over the countryside. The Negroes named in the warrants had fled. None of them could be found. Tennant and his men, it was soon discovered, had escaped to Edgefield Courthouse and had there surrendered their arms to the Negro colonel who commanded their militia regiment. The Sabre Club and its volunteer allies then marched to Edgefield and seized the surrendered arms.

These "victories" in what Tillman called "the Ned Tennant

Riots" crystallized into a fixed formula, as he described it, "of terrorizing the negroes at the first opportunity, by letting them provoke trouble, and then having the whites demonstrate their superiority by killing as many of them as was possible." He spoke from personal knowledge of the aims of the Edgefield leaders, including his own brother George, General Butler, and Martin A. Gary, another Confederate veteran.

A climax to such affairs was inevitable. The inciting incident and the excuse for it occurred two years later, in 1876, on another July 4. This time it was in Hamburg, the town across the Savannah from Augusta that had been established a half century before with high hopes by Henry Schultz. But by 1876 Hamburg was a poor down-at-heels community inhabited solely by Negroes, a refuge for their politicians and some criminals. It was also the headquarters for a Negro militia regiment commanded by a black named Dock Adams. Whites seldom ventured even to pass through the town.

But, on this July 4, two young white men, on their way home from Augusta in a buggy, decided to return through Hamburg. Dock Adams had his company on parade for the holiday occasion and it was spread across the street in platoon front formation, so that the two young men found their passage blocked. The sidewalks were lined with Negroes watching the parade. Captain Adams shouted "Charge Bayonets." The young white men, refusing to turn about and withdraw, pulled out their pistols and threatened to shoot the first soldier who pointed a bayonet at their horse and buggy. The platoon fronts then parted to let them through. Dock Adams had a warrant sworn out against the two young white adventurers for interfering with his drill, and they retaliated with warrants against the captain and his entire company for obstructing a highway.

There was an ominous atmosphere in the courtroom in Hamburg four days later on, July 8, when the Negro justice opened the legal proceedings. He looked down upon seventy armed white men, including the Sweetwater Sabre Club. Ben

Tillman, who was present, said quite frankly, in describing the occasion afterward, that "it was our purpose to attend the trial to see that the young men had protection and, if the opportunity offered, to provoke a row, and if one did not offer, we were to make one."

The Negro judge divined this clearly enough, and ordered the trial postponed. But the whites found an excuse, anyhow, for their vengeance. Dock Adams and his company had taken refuge in the armory. They were ordered by the whites to surrender their arms. They refused. Then the whites, though outnumbered, determined to take the armory.

They were promptly joined by a white mob which came across the bridge from Augusta, and this army surrounded the armory building.

The shooting began at sundown. One white man, McKie Meriwether, was killed by the fire from the armory, which was nevertheless quite desultory. When night came on, the terrified Negroes escaped from the armory and fled for their lives from the besieging white army. Two were killed, among them the town marshal, one Jim Cook. Forty more were captured.

The death of the one white man, Meriwether, had aroused the others to a vengeful mob frenzy. They were prodded on by two cousins of the dead man who wanted to know if the lives of only two Negroes should pay for one white. Consequently, the white leaders designated an execution squad to shoot five more of the Negro prisoners in cold blood. Ben Tillman proudly lent his own pistol to one of the firing squad.

After this gruesome demonstration of white prowess, the Sabre Club and the rest of the mob left Hamburg. They left behind them seven Negro corpses in the street as a grisly welcome to the Negroes when they should come back home there the next day. On *his* way home, Ben Tillman stopped at a neighbor's house and consumed, with relish, a piece of watermelon to top off the night's business.

The Republican regime in South Carolina knew it must do

something about this atrocity. News of it had swept across the nation, calling down condemnation upon its perpetrators and a demand for justice.

But the pressure of local tradition, which it was clear was backed by force, then made of justice the same mockery that it has so often done since in the South, despite its boasted heritage of Anglo-Saxon judicial fairness. The indictment for murder and conspiracy was duly handed down at Aiken, South Carolina, but the sheriff at Aiken followed a well-known southern tradition. Instead of serving warrants upon the accused, he invited them to meet him at a place outside the town and follow him to the Aiken courthouse. The meeting was arranged and the murderers went to the outskirts of Aiken. There they camped for two days to await the trial, which began on September 8. While encamped they hatched a plan for a public display of law defiance which they figured, and correctly, would temper the dictates of justice. They took their cue from the accelerated criticism they had aroused in other parts of the country. This they described as "waving the bloody shirt."

Well, they would wave the bloody shirt, themselves, they decided. So they induced the women of Aiken to make them homespun shirts. These they daubed with turpentine, oil and Venetian red. Tillman, himself, then supervised the construction of a giant effigy of a Negro, a hideous spectacle, with gun wounds in it. Then they staged a parade in their red shirts, carrying the effigy before them. The procession went first to the homes of the women who had fashioned the shirts, cheered them, and then paraded through the city. The Negroes hid out while a white federal military garrison cheered on the gruesome parade. Thus was created the costume, the bloody shirts, which thereafter became the uniform of those who rallied behind Wade Hampton to sweep the Republican carpetbaggers out of office, in a combination of Negro intimidation and vote stealing which gave Hampton the disputed victory over Republican Governor

Daniel H. Chamberlain and sent that Reconstruction executive back home to Massachusetts.

When the defendants marched solemnly into court for the trial they sat down with the thud and thump of weapons that did not need to be concealed. Court officials did not take long to find a way out of their dilemma. They decided to let the culprits out on bail bonds. It was first decided to go through with the bonding procedure the following morning, but the sheriff stepped in to advise that it be done now, "right now, to get these men out of town." His advice was followed. The bonding was, of course, a joke. One man who was known to have virtually nothing signed bonds for $20,000. Tillman frankly told of the determination of himself and his colleagues on this occasion.

"If they had attempted to put us in jail," he said, "I am sure few or none of us would have acquiesced; and we would have probably killed every obnoxious radical in the court room and town and gone to Texas or to some other hiding place."

This was the end of "justice" in the Hamburg riots—nothing further was done. But it was not the end of violence. For there was more of it in Edgefield and along the Savannah River in the years immediately following, and in all of it the Sweetwater Sabre Club and Ben Tillman had a part.

CHAPTER THREE

OF THE NOBLE PROFESSION OF RAFTING

The story of the Savannah, its valley, and its people is told in the changing commerce of the river. The change was slow, almost imperceptible to any one generation, except for those who lived for a very long time. But it is clear to us who can look back across the span of the centuries.

We have seen it unfold before our eyes. First were the Indians with their periaguas. Then, to tell of the coming of the white man, there coursed down it boats piled high with deerskins from the wildernesses about its headwaters and tributaries, once alive with these stately animals. The advent of the first crude, settled civilization was denoted by the boatloads of tobacco, the first substantial cash crop of the fertile Savannah midlands. This gradually gave way to cotton, and so the river was flecked with the famous "cotton boxes," those slow-moving rafts like white clouds, significant of the prosperity of the midlands at their zenith, symbolic of the broad plantations and the comfortable farmhouses, of the rarer fine mansions with fluted pillars, and of the wagon trains converging upon Augusta with its busy streets and carnival atmosphere during the marketing season.

This prosperity was what made possible the handsome steamboats that for a time traveled the river, with elegant and commodious accommodations for passengers, with roomy hulls for transporting cotton and other products to Savannah, and ample room for bringing back manufactured goods for a people who could now afford luxuries.

Then progress brought the railroads, and they in time supplanted the steamboats.

There was, however, still another form of traffic, quite active for many years, to tell of another era along the Savannah, a traffic that lasted well into the twentieth century. This was the rafting of lumber down the river to the sea. Lumbering, to be sure, had gone on intermittently from early times, but it became a large industry toward the latter part of the nineteenth century when the demand for timber made it profitable to cut into the thick forests in the swampy lowlands below Augusta, and that on a big scale.

Lumbering, too, created its own craft and its own traditions and legends.

Along the Savannah the rafting of lumber was all done by Negroes, and they made it a proud and noble profession, with its own code and standards and regulations. Curiously enough, the rafting of lumber on the neighboring Altamaha was entirely in the hands of white men.

The master of the raft, by tradition and in practice, was the pilot. Not only did he have charge of the raft in its journey down the river to Savannah, but also superintended the building of the raft itself on which the lumber was piled. Likewise, it was he who contracted for the whole job, selected the crew, received the pay for the entire transaction and from that paid off his helpers.

Each raft carried a crew of three, the pilot, the assistant pilot, and the roustabout, as the third man was called. He was also the cook. The first job was building the raft, which was quite a task and done according to a prescribed standard.

The typical Savannah River raft was about 6 feet across at the bow and sloped back on each side at an angle until it reached a width of about 25 feet. It continued then at that width to its end. Its length was about 175 feet. No nails were used. The raft was fastened together with wooden pegs which were cut with an ax of razor-edge sharpness. No saws were used.

All the work was done with the ax, which was the universal handy tool. A small piece of iron, known as a "dog," was inserted in each log in the cargo, at the rear, to hold the next log back. The oars or sweeps were usually made of hickory or maple, because of the resilient quality of these woods. They were about 50 feet long.

After it was built, the raft was floated. The logs were rolled on lengthwise from behind, with the Negroes standing on them in the customary fashion of loggers everywhere. This required considerable skill. When the raft was finally loaded and ready to go, the pilot would take his place at the stern with his oar ready at hand for pushing when needed, while the assistant pilot took his post at the bow to guide. The roustabout would ride at any convenient place on the craft. Aside from cooking the meals, which was done on a piece of sheet

metal set up in the middle of the boat to keep from setting the
lumber on fire, the roustabout was in charge of docking operations when the raft was tied up for the night along the river.
Docking was quite a trick. When it came time to tie up, the
pilot would pick out a tree along the bank to which he wished
to tie. The roustabout would then take the bateau, which was
always carried on the raft, row ahead to the bank, land, take his
position near the tree, and then catch the rope thrown by the
pilot and tie it to the tree. The raft was then eased up to the
shore. Skill was required in handling the raft in all of its operations, as it usually weighed around 360,000 pounds, or about
eighteen tons, when loaded. The usual load was 30,000 feet of
lumber.

Ordinarily a raft traveled about eighteen hours a day, tying
up at night for only six hours. The crew would snatch sleep by
turns in quiet stretches of the river. The speed was about four
miles an hour. In lumber rafting the old custom was preserved
in which the pilot would shout "Georgia" if he wanted the guide
at the front to steer toward the right and "Car'lina" if he desired a course to the left. These orders, echoing along the river,
were a familiar sound of the rafting era.

Directing the raft into a slip at Savannah was a delicate
maneuver, because of the tide that comes about twenty-five
miles up the river. In the early days the crew would return
to Augusta by steamboat, always taking their bateau along
with them. Later they used the ramshackle automobile—a jalopy
—that belonged to the pilot, stowing the bateau on that. The
round trip from the region around Augusta would take about
ten days, according to John P. Mulherin of Augusta, a veteran
lumberman, who graciously supplied the facts about rafting
operations.

He was very high in praise of the rafting crews, lauding
their efficiency, their faithfulness, and their loyalty to their
tradition. In forty years of operation along the river, in which
he shipped thousands of raftloads of lumber—chiefly white cane

ash—Mulherin said that only three raftloads of lumber were broken up. During off seasons, when there were floods, or when there was a cessation of activity for other reasons, the Negroes often ran out of money and would come to him for a loan to tide them over.

"I never lost a dollar to any of the Negroes on my rafts in forty years," he said. "They always paid."

Mulherin was full of the lore of rafting, as are other rivermen of their particular interest.

A Negro who wanted to be a rafter would start as a roustabout and work his way up, learning all the tricks of the trade and the quirks of the mischievous river. It was a special redletter day when he became a pilot in his own right.

These pilots knew the river like a book, its every crook and turn and whimsy. They had uncanny eyesight at night, and they could see—so Mulherin said—where a white man was unable to pierce the darkness. Some rafters, strangely, never learned to swim. They didn't even bother to acquire what would seem almost a necessary accomplishment.

The average pay of a pilot was $5 a thousand feet of lumber. This would thus bring him about $150 a trip, the load being around 30,000 feet. From this gross he would pay his two crew members and buy their provisions. His net would usually be between $50 and $75 per trip.

The lumber was cut in June and July ready for rafting down the river in the winter months. Sometimes the timber was taken far back from the river but, as Mulherin pointed out, you had to take it where it was. In such operations away from the river, a flood was helpful in getting out the timber, as the logs could be floated on the floodwaters out to the channel proper ready for rafting when the waters receded. The river was a scene of great activity on such occasions. All the Negroes in the neighboring community would rally for flood operations, since, in their terms, it meant considerable cash money for a short period of work.

Four logs would be tied together in what was known as a "bull" and two Negroes would ride this small raft, the man at the rear poling and the one in front guiding, as on the regular rafts. The Negroes were familiar with the terrain and were skillful in guiding their bulls where they knew there were hollows and depressions where the water would be deep. This "drifting," as it was called, was paid for at an hourly rate, and, by working all day and night, which most of them did at such times, a man could make $10 a day or about $40 or $50 for the four or five days of floodwater. That was big money for the backwoods, enough to last for quite some time, a true windfall.

CHAPTER FOUR

"IT IS A VERY WIDE HARBOR"

For many years after the end of the rafting era the Savannah was a lonely river. It offered little service to the tremendous territory that is its domain and the many people who live there. But a new destiny seems now, 1950, to be in prospect. The river is on the verge of what can be another glorious era as this chronicle is brought to its conclusion. The story of this drawing era must be recorded in a later history, but it is possible perhaps to foresee some of it in general outline.

For the Savannah, which has been a wild and profligate hoyden of a stream, is now being tamed and brought with control. Great stretches of its swampy lowlands between Augusta and Savannah, lands which have long lain idle because of frequently recurring floods, may soon be reclaimed. Again

timber can be cut and the rich bottom lands thus cleared can be turned into farms and pastures.

Thus the potentialities of the Savannah, like those of so many other rivers, are to be utilized by man-made dams, vast works in the modern manner, by which the waters will be controlled and regulated and transformed by the same means into electric energy from which so many benefits flow. This will be the fruition of the dreams of many forward-looking and public-spirited men all up and down the Savannah valley, but particularly of the men of Augusta. That city always has had the river in its mind. Living beside the water highway as it does, it looks up and down it like an old familiar street, and not outward to the sea and the world beyond, as does Savannah near its mouth. But it was the vision of men far away from the river that finally brought this dream, too, to the Savannah. They were modern and scientifically minded men who saw in the rivers of America general sources of blessings, not only for the people who lived directly along their banks but for those who lived far away from them as well.

A farseeing president of the United States, Theodore Roosevelt, first recognized that rivers must be included in any thorough conservation policy of the United States—and it was he who inaugurated a great water-conservation policy. It was his conviction that these natural waterways belonged to all the people and so must be used for all the people. He saw, too, that a river must be developed in its entirety for all the purposes of which it is capable. There must be integrated development. The conditions under which river systems were exploited must be fixed by the national government, as the representatives of all the people. Rivers knew no local boundaries or state lines.

A senator from Nebraska, George W. Norris, saw the possibility of utilizing plants built by the government during World War I at Muscle Shoals, Alabama, on the Tennessee River. He sought for years to get approval by Congress for government operation of these plants for the generation of electric power and the manufacture of nitrates for fertilizer. Private interests resisted, seeking to get their hands on them. But ultimately, in the administration of another Roosevelt, Franklin D., this dream of the persistent Nebraska senator was realized.

It was realized even far beyond his dreams when the president espoused the utilization of the whole Tennessee River for power development, navigation, flood control, and the conservation of water resources through a government corporation. This was the Tennessee Valley Authority, or the TVA, as it was popularly called.

For many years men with vision in Georgia and South Carolina had also dreamed of a similar development of the Savannah. The success of TVA gave them at once a living and working text. So, in time, there was evolved the project for a great dam across the Savannah. Eventually, it was authorized by Congress. This dam was projected at Clark's Hill, twenty-one miles above Augusta. It was strategically located for the control and regulation of the river below that city. The whole project embraces a series of eleven dams upriver, with Clark's Hill at the base of these watery steps. The concrete dam at Clark's Hill, 351 feet high and more than a mile across—5,680 feet—will back up the waters of the river for forty miles to form a great lake covering 78,000 acres with a 350-mile shoreline. Across the top of the dam is projected a four-lane superhighway connecting South Carolina and Georgia.

Its benefits for the whole valley and its people are manifold. There will be cheap electric power, which can be widely distributed from the seven units of 40,000 kilowatts each, or a total of 280,000 kilowatts, in the power plant at Clark's Hill. Control of the river flow will stop recurrent floods, of which there are now an average of four a year that regularly inundate some 263,000 acres of bottom lands between Augusta and Savannah, according to a survey of the Soil Conservation Service of the United States Department of Agriculture. Major floods, which have swept into Augusta, occur every fifteen or twenty years, and these will be obviated. The great expanse of lowland between Augusta and Savannah now lying idle can be converted into useful purposes—farming, dairying, woodland. Considerable clearing will be necessary to make this land suitable for farming, but it is estimated that a large part of the cost of conversion to agriculture can be met by marketing pulpwood, saw logs, and fuel wood. This would mean a reopening of timber operations suspended now for many years along the river.

Recreation benefits for the people of the Savannah valley are also a part of the Clark's Hill project, as they already are a reality in TVA. Some 16,000 acres is set aside for parks in the region surrounding the lake that will be formed above the big dam at Clark's Hill. This will be used to create a woodland and lake playground for the whole middle and upriver sections of both Georgia and South Carolina.

The over-all Savannah River development likewise envisages the reopening of navigation on the river on a fairly large scale. A twelve-foot channel from Augusta to Savannah is planned. This should open the way for further industrial enterprise by making available low-cost water transportation for raw materials.

After the end of World War II the river began to come alive again, not only with preliminary work on the Clark's Hill development, the biggest thing that ever happened to this river, but with a tiny trickle of navigation to recall the heyday of steamboating. This traffic may be an augury for a return of the prosperous old bustling life of the river, once it is controlled and its channel is deepened sufficiently to permit a passage from Augusta to Savannah that will be easier and more dependable than the tricky adventure that the navigation of the river is under at present.

During World War II the river was a deserted highway

above Savannah, though the port itself was overbusy with the war. But, after the war, there was another cargo boat left plying the river. It was the *Merry Maid*, a successor to *Merry Queen*, which, as we saw in the first part of this story, had been transferred to coastal war service by the government, an act that removed the only boat that had been navigating the river.

Reggie Dales, to whom we listened as he thought out loud about the prostrate state of river traffic and the loss of the *Merry Queen*, which he had once managed, now has the new boat, *Merry Maid*, under his charge as director of river operations for the Merry Shipbuilding Company and the Merry Brothers Brick and Tile Company. This vessel, built at St. Louis, carries brick and tile products of the company on its downriver voyages to Savannah, and down coast to Fernandina, Jacksonville, Sanford, and Palatka, Florida. It brings back a cargo of oil, gasoline, and oil products.

One boat, however, does not make a busy river. But it is a beginning and, for those who love the river, hopeful.

The waters at the lower reaches of the river, in Savannah harbor where it meets the sea, were periodically churned up in recurrent wars by urgent boats at their chores, as they have been down through a long history. At the turn from the nineteenth to the twentieth century, there was the Spanish-American War, in which the lusty new world power took its first timid, faltering steps into the adventure of world politics. After a lapse of nearly three centuries, Spanish war vessels were back in the Caribbean where they had once been a familiar sight. But they were a different kind of vessels now, trim and streamlined, yet far less beautiful to behold than the much smaller and more stately ships that were part of the armada that had been turned back by Oglethorpe in his victory at Bloody Marsh on St. Simon's Island.

In the Spanish-American War there was no actual threat to the Georgia coast, though there were constant rumors and people lived in anxiety, especially over the erroneous report at one time current that the Spanish fleet was headed north. It was a war in the neighborhood, for the Caribbean was in the marine neighborhood, and most of the major battles at sea and on the land were fought not so far to the south.

Young men from the Savannah valley trooped off gaily to this war, only to suffer and die from disease, as so many of them did, or to be killed in battle, as far fewer of them were. They were commanded, in some cases, by men who had fought under another flag, the Stars and Bars of the Confederacy, and who now were fighting for the first time under the Stars and Stripes. This fact was much exploited for its national propaganda

value in sentimental poems and songs. Also the exciting tune of the Spanish-American War, "There'll be a Hot Time in the Old Town Tonight," echoed through the streets of Augusta and Savannah as it did elsewhere.

Across the span of forty years, there was a connecting link between that amateurish, melodramatic little war and World

War II. This was a tugboat, *Cynthia Second*. During the Spanish-American War, this little vessel, new then, was diverted from her ordinary and peaceful routine of guiding big ships in and out of Savannah harbor, and, under charter by the Associated Press, was used to ferry war correspondents back and forth in Cuban waters and to deliver copy to cable offices. After that war experience, she returned to the Savannah and for years, as one of the fleet of the Atlantic Towing Company, performed the regular services of her kind until World War I. Then *Cynthia* again took up her military duty and towed merchant vessels out to sea, heading them for Europe with their cargoes of munitions. In World War II, a quarter of a century later, *Cynthia* was again drafted into war service and was kept busy nosing one merchant ship after another out into the Atlantic. First she towed out the Lend-Lease supply ships bound for England, later came those laden with ammunition, guns, tanks and airplanes for the American forces in Africa, and ultimately the craft for the invasion and conquest of France and Germany.

The service of her old age, however, was drab compared with her energetic life as a Spanish-American-War reporter. Then, as for many years afterward, *Cynthia* was under command of Captain Van Avery, who was a memorable personage along the river front. *Cynthia* saw the battle of Santiago harbor at close range, her decks crowded with eagerly watching newspapermen, and she raced back to Key West afterward with the first details of the defeat of Admiral Cervera's Spanish fleet. Captain Avery always proudly displayed certain trophies of war, two sirens from the *Almirante Oquendo* or the *Viscaya,* the Spanish cruisers which still lie beached on the Cuban coast. He and his crew boarded the enemy ship of war and bore off the sirens. They were used long afterward to make a noise for celebrations of one sort or another in Savannah. One was placed on the *Cynthia Second,* and the other on the *William F. Mc-Cauley,* another tug familiar in Savannah harbor.

As a young newspaper reporter in Savannah in 1920, I knew Captain Avery well. Often in my rounds along the waterfront I stopped to sit with him on the back portico of the Atlantic Towing Company offices overlooking the river, and listened to his tales. He was well along in years then. But he still owned *Cynthia* and one other tug. There was a time when he had owned a whole fleet. But others had come to compete with him and he was not the figure he once had been in the towing business. He was philosophical about it, however, and took his less kindly fortune gracefully.

But Captain Avery was only a legend when *Cynthia Second* signed up for her third war. The still sturdy boat was busier than ever before in her whole career. She was one of four tugs operating in and out of Savannah harbor during World War II. They handled 1,278 shiftings of oceangoing vessels in the harbor among them and participated in 586 dockings and 645 undockings. This ceaseless round of activity by the fleet of tugboats is an index to the big part that the port of Savannah played in the war. An average of well over a million tons of shipping a year went in and out during the years 1943-44-45. Of this total for the three years, a million tons of shipping was war supplies outbound to the fronts in Africa and Europe. Altogether 207 convoys were provided at Savannah while, always hovering about, were the tugboats to guide them across the bar. These little vessels were not confined entirely to the routine course in and out of the harbor, either. Often during the war they took to the open sea to assist in the rescue of vessels that had encountered difficulties, either at the hand of submarines or otherwise. They took on for those deep-sea adventures United States Navy crews skilled in such operations.

"All they had [for armaments] was the sidearms carried by the navy men," explained Commodore Frank W. Spencer, who was in charge of port operations during the war as a Coast Guard officer.

Commodore Spencer won high commendation for his services. He was a veteran at his work and knew the river intimately, having been the master pilot of the port for thirty years with a long administrative experience as general manager and treasurer of the Atlantic Towing Company as well. He literally lived on the river twenty-four hours a day during the war. In 1942 he gave up his home at "Tybee" and fixed up living quarters on Bay Street along the river and next door to his station. His eye was constantly on the river.

The war came, in truth, quite close to Savannah. Lurking outside constantly along the coast were the Nazi U-boats which, for a time, took such a toll of shipping along the entire Atlantic seaboard. During a considerable part of 1942, operations at the port of Savannah were virtually suspended, because of the submarine menace. The result was that the people of Savannah were much more aware than those of us who did not live so near the sea of how close the submarine blockade along our coast came to being a national disaster.

It was brought home tragically enough to many mothers and fathers in Savannah when the freighter *Oglethorpe*, named for the Georgia colony's founder, the first ship to slide off the ways of the Southeastern Shipbuilding Company's yards at Savannah, was sunk by a submarine on her way to Europe with war cargo. Many young men from Savannah, members of her crew, went down with her.

By this time, however, submarine activity along the coast had been almost entirely checked, and the port, once again open, did a tremendous business in 1942.

The next year it did even more. Congestion at northern ports with outgoing cargo vessels resulted in diversion of much incoming business to Savannah. Day and night the harbor was busy and a shortage of labor required the utilization of Coast Guardsmen and soldiers who worked at unloading and loading ships in their off-duty hours.

The *Oglethorpe* was the first of a succession of cargo boats —136 in all—that were constructed by the three shipbuilding companies that sprang up during the war at Savannah to make it a thriving shipbuilding center. One of these, a Liberty ship, was steaming out of the port, fully loaded with military explosives and general cargo within a week after her launching. Seeming miracles were performed here daily as elsewhere in war production.

The history of the war was written in the manifests of the cargo and the destination of the vessels that moved slowly, one after another, down the river and out to sea. In 1940 and 1941 most of the outgoing traffic was to England. In the first year all cargoes were loaded in British vessels, for that was the era of "cash and carry," before the neutrality act was repealed. War supplies had then to be paid for in cash and transported in other than American ships. We were still trying to avoid involvement. Our aim was to supply England and France in order to bolster their resistance and keep the war from reaching us.

In those early war days, in the dead of night, one might observe a strange sight on the streets of Savannah. It was a weird sort of parade, silent and eerie, trucks loaded with boxes in which were airplane wings towing the fuselages of planes behind them. Airplanes built in the United States for England or France were flown to Savannah from all parts of the country. They were then dismantled and prepared for shipment. Then came the cessation of traffic during the height of the U-boat danger. When the port was reopened, Savannah became a center for the collection and shipment of Lend-Lease supplies to England, leaving then in ever-increasing amounts. In 1944 more explosives went out of Savannah for England than from any other port. From long distances the cargos converged upon the city for shipment—steel from as far away as California; boxed trucks from Canada; synthetic rubber, tanks, armored cars, jeeps and other sorts of military vehicles from all over the map.

The coming invasion was indicated to dock workers by "alligators" and "sea mules" used later to land supplies on Utah and Omaha beaches in Normandy.

The end of the U-boat blockade was heralded by the arrival again in Tybee roads of tankers with oil to replenish dwindling and rationed supplies in the United States. Such tanker traffic had all but ceased for some time. Also there came in nitrates and sugar from South America and Cuba, and strategic materials of various kinds from faraway India.

The reopening of the seas was manifested by the partial resumption of commercial steamship service to Pacific coast ports, to Australia, and to the east coast ports of South America; all this while the German armies were being pushed across France and beyond the Rhine and the Japanese driven back slowly to their own islands.

Then, with the end of the war, the great job of rehabilitation and of reconstruction in Europe was exemplified in the cargoes that went out of Savannah—food, steel, urgently needed raw materials of all sorts.

After World War I, during which Savannah also had been quite a lively and active center, the port had sunk back into a leisurely kind of midafternoon somnolence, like the siesta hour that many of its people still observe. Covering the waterfront as a reporter in those days did not produce many news items— an occasional tramp in from the seven seas to stir the imagination, some coastwise traffic of a more normal sort, but nothing substantial enough to bear our the roseate promises of civic boosters.

But, after World War II, Savannah looked to the future much more hopefully. Many new industries came in during the war. They came to stay, and others were in prospect. The city planned confidently for continued growth and expansion in many ways. Among them was the project for state-owned modern port-terminal facilities. The legislature authorized a state port authority for construction and operation of such facilities at both Savannah and at Brunswick, the next Georgia port seventy-five miles to the south. There was a temporary setback when the state supreme court ruled against the plan to guarantee bonds for the port development by rentals from the state-owned railroad, the Western and Atlantic.

During the war there passed away a tradition of the Savannah River of many years standing. It was caused by the death in 1943 of Florence Martus, known to sailors all over the world and in local legend as "the Waving Girl"—though she had long since ceased to be a "girl."

Seamen for decades had watched for her hail and farewell as their vessels entered and left the harbor. For years she waved at every passing boat from the porch of her little house on Elba Island, seven and a half miles below Savannah. There she lived and kept house for her brother, George Washington Martus, keeper of the Tybee lights. By day she waved a handkerchief, by night a lantern. She became known for this all over the maritime world. Ships would respond to her waving with blasts of their whistles. The story was that a seaman very dear to her had sailed away down the river one day and never returned.

Her vigil, for whatever cause, ceased in 1931 when her brother was retired from the service, he having reached the age of seventy. Both moved to Thunderbolt Island to pass together their declining years. His death occurred in 1940 and she died three years later. Her brother had become keeper of the Tybee light in 1887.

They were both of the river and the sea to which it led. Their father, an army sergeant, also had been a keeper of the lights along the river. Florence Martus was born in Fort Pulaski on Cockspur Island, the locale of much history going clear back to the founding of the colony, famous as well in the American Revolution and for the Civil War defense of the city. As a girl

of thirteen—she was born in 1868—Florence learned by personal
experience of the wiles of the sea and the river. The great storm
of 1881 swept the river clear over Cockspur Island. It flooded
the parade ground and the fort. She saved herself from drown-
ing only by taking refuge on the spiral stairway of the southeastern tower of the old fort.

In 1938 there was a celebration in her honor under spon-
sorship of the Propellor Club, attended by over three thousand
people. For her there was a giant birthday cake adorned with a
replica of the home on Elba Island from which she had waved
to so many passing ships, and there were speeches in her praise,
among them one by Congressman Hugh Peterson of the Savannah District. He called her "the sweetheart of mankind." Too
moved to respond to all the oratory, she sent up a scribbled note
to Edward A. Dutton, chairman of the occasion, expressing her
pride that she was a Georgian and that she had been born at
Fort Pulaski, thanking all her friends for this celebration, and
adding:

"This is the greatest day of my life."

She was, indeed, a link with all that had gone before. As
she waved every day at the current ship parade past her island,
the very substance of living reality, she was also waving at the
mythical procession of history—the Indians who paddled by first;
the Spaniards who came later looking hungrily for gold; the
French who followed them looking for empire; and the English
who came looking for homes. But England, too, lost the dream
of an American empire because of the foolish arrogance of a
king from a German line who had never come to understand
that the English, wherever they go, love liberty more than they
love any king.

And so a new people arose, and Florence Martus waved at
the procession which, by the time she came along, revealed the
strength of a great new nation in the ships that passed her to
take its men and its wealth to the far corners of the world.

Truth indeed it was that Captain Francisco de Ejica, the Spaniard, had written far back in 1603, in the first description we have of the mouth of the Savannah River which then only led back into a wilderness. He said prophetically that "it is a very wide harbor."

$\mathcal{A}$cknowledgment

When you have taken a long time to write a book, as has been my experience with this one, and have followed a trail that wound through libraries and among people who have helped you along the way, the path becomes indistinct. Though such an experience has its frustrations, as anyone may easily realize in a task dealing with four hundred years of recorded history, it can be, as this has been, a pleasant and rewarding one because of the people encountered along the way, both in the flesh and through books, and because of the entrancing roads down which the mind and fancy are led.

My wife thought the river would never stop running, but was patient, nor did I, who have been less patient; and, as for publishers and editors—well, they have been extremely tolerant, knowing about rivers and those who write about them. Nor has the river stopped running, of course, which is what makes living with rivers so satisfying. They partake of the eternal. So that you live with all of the past and all of the future.

The people I have met, the books I have read in pursuing my river—all have become part of me and my life, something that will be with me always. And now I thank those who wrote the books, some of whom have been long gone from the earth and the river, and I thank those who counseled and guided me in person and gave me something of themselves as it was touched by the river and the country through which it flows down to the sea.

Among the latter I will call up a few who will symbolize all of them. Dr. E. Merton Coulter of the University of Georgia who advised me personally and also more than he knows through his books and articles about Georgia and the South. H. H. Mangum of the Merchants Association of Augusta, with whom I renewed a friendship that began thirty years ago at the University of Georgia. Lester J. Moody, secretary of the Augusta Chamber of Commerce, who has done so much for development of the river by promotion of the Clark's Hill project which has its part in this book. Reggie Dales of Augusta, who filled me with his feeling for the river, and is in this book. John P. Mulherin, of Augusta, who gave me the story of lumber rafting along the river. Henry Hammond, of Augusta, who introduced me to the natural history and geology of this region about which his father, Henry Hammond, once had written so movingly. Wallace G. Addison, of Augusta, who told me about the heyday of the cotton trade along the river. Erol M. Hamm, who had many a story about the exciting days of chicken fighting in this area. William H. ("Willie") Hester, of Calhoun, S. C., who entertained a delegation—Mangum, Moody, Mayor Page of Augusta and myself—on a delightful expedition to his home, and told me about the famous Hester strain of fighting cocks, and showed me where Jeff Davis had crossed the river in the flight southward that ended in his capture, and the site of old Fort Charlotte of pioneer days. William Morris, who opened up the files of the Augusta *Chronicle* for me. John Sutlive of the Savannah *Press*, my first city editor after I left college to enter the world, who assigned me to the waterfront and gave me the opportunity to wander along the river every day and learn the lore of the river and the sea, so that it became a part of me, and who provided material from his files for this book. His father, the late "Billy" Sutlive, beloved of all Savannah, who gave me the soundest advice I ever got about newspaper reporting technique in a talk the first day I arrived to work for the paper. Captain Van Avery, now long gone from the back porch of his office along the waterfront overlooking the river where I used to sit and talk with him and absorb his gentle and wise philosophy of life as a scrub newspaper reporter. Commodore Frank W. Spencer, master pilot of the port of Savannah for thirty years, who was in charge of port operations as a Coast Guard officer during World War II and told me the story of Savannah in that war. Former Mayor Thomas Gamble, of Savannah, who contributed many stories of the city and the river and whose writings were a source of information.

These I salute—and there are so many others I salute whom I saw in my adventure of research—men of the river and the life and commerce and traditions of the river; kind and helpful men and women in libraries to whom I was a stranger passing by who said he was writing a book, and who took me in and gave me their time. They all are a part of this book.

Some will not find here the things about which I asked them and about which they patiently told me; for this book is only half the book it was when I finished it, which often happens to books, and properly, no doubt. Books must be of a size and come to an end, it seems. They can't go on forever like rivers. So I had to cut and delete; but maybe someday those stories can find their way into another book.

In closing I'd like to pay a tribute to some whom I never met, to whom all of us who dig back into the past are so heavily indebted. I refer to those earnest and careful scholars who take some tiny corner of history and light it up with their painstaking study and research, and leave behind them on the shelves of libraries those monographs for which people like myself are so grateful and who give so much, far beyond their time, to the writing of history, like tributaries to the rivers. They do it for the love of the doing. They are the pure historians. They do not get great fame, nor do they seek it. A salute to them.

And, back at home among my books and my writing and all those frustrations of trying to re-create history—a salute to my wife, who knows why I wrote this book, and was sympathetic and helpful through all the tribulations connected with it.

Bibliography

ANONYMOUS. *Itinerant Observations in America*. London, 1745.

Augusta. American Guide Series. Tidwell Printing Supply Co., Augusta, 1938.

BAKER, JOHN WILLIAM. *History of Hart County*. Atlanta, 1933.

BARROW, ELFRIDA DE RENNE, and LAURA BELL. *Anchored Yesterdays*. Review Publishing and Printing Co., Savannah, Ga., 1923.

BARTRAM. *The Travels of William Bartram*. Facsimile Library. New York, 1940.

BASS, ALTHEA. *Cherokee Messenger*. University of Oklahoma Press, 1937.

BOLTON, HERBERT E. *Arredondo's Historical Proof of Spain's Title to Georgia*. University of California Press, 1925.

BOLTON, HERBERT. E., AND MARY ROSS. *The Debatable Land*. University of California Press, 1925.

BOURNE, E. G. *Spain in America. The American Nation, A History*. Edited by Albert Bushnell Hart.

BROOKS, A. M. *The Unwritten History of Old St. Augustine, copied from the Spanish Archives in Seville, Spain by Miss A. M. Brooks, and translated by Mrs. Annie Averette*. St. Augustine, 1909.

BRUCE, HENRY. *Life of General Oglethorpe.* Dodd, Mead & Co., 1890.

BURLINGAME, ROGER. *Whittling Boy. The Story of Eli Whitney.* Harcourt, Brace and Co., New York, 1941.

CARMER, CARL. *The Hudson.* Farrar & Rinehart, New York, 1939.

CATESBY, MARK. *The Natural History of Carolina, Florida and the Bahama Islands.* Vol. I. London, 1771.

CAUGHEY, JOHN WALTON. *McGillivray of the Creeks.* University of Oklahoma Press, 1938.

CORRY, JOHN PITTS. *Affairs in Georgia, 1732-36.*

COULTER, E. MERTON. *A Short History of Georgia.* University of North Carolina Press, 1933.

CRANE, VERNER W. *The Southern Frontier,* Durham, N. C., 1928.

CRANE, VERNER W. *An Historical Note on the Westo Indians.* American Anthropologist. New Series, Vol. XX.

DAVIS, JEFFERSON. *Rise and Fall of the Confederate States of America.* New York, 1881.

DAVIS, VARINA HOWELL. *Memoir of Jefferson Davis.* New York, 1890.

EVANS, LAWTON. *History of Georgia.* University Publishing Co., New York, New Orleans, 1904.

FLANDERS, RALPH BETTS. *Plantation Slavery in Georgia.* University of North Carolina Press, 1933.

FORCE, PETER. *Tracts and Other Papers.* Washington, 1836.

GABRIEL, RALPH HENRY. *Elias Boudinot, Cherokee, and His America.* University of Oklahoma Press, 1941.

GAMBLE, THOMAS. *History of Bethesda.* Savannah Morning News Print.

GAMBLE, THOMAS. *The Love Stories of John and Charles Wesley.* Savannah Morning News Print.

Georgia. A Guide to its towns and countryside. American Guide Series. University of Georgia Press, 1940.

GILMER, GEORGE R. *Sketches of the First Settlers of Upper Georgia, of the Cherokees, and the Author.* New York, 1855.

HARRIS, THADDEUS MASON, D.D. *Biographical Memorial of James Oglethorpe, Founder of the Colony of Georgia in North America;* privately printed for the author by Freeman and Bolles, Boston.

HENDRICK, BURTON J. *Statesmen of the Lost Cause.* Little, Brown & Co., Boston, 1939.

HODGE, FREDERICK WEBB (edited by). *Handbook of American Indians North of Mexico.* Bureau of American Ethnology, Bulletin 30; part I, 1907; part 2, 1910.

HUNTINGTON, ELLSWORTH. *The Red Man's Continent.* Yale University Press, 1919.

JONES, CHARLES C., JR. *The History of Georgia.* Houghton Mifflin Co., 1883.

———. *History of Savannah, Georgia.* D. Mason and Co., Syracuse, N. Y., 1890.

———. *The Dead Towns of Georgia.*

———., and DUTCHER, SALEM. *A Memorial History of Augusta, Ga.* D. Mason and Co., Syracuse, N. Y., 1890.

JOSEPHSON, MATTHEW. *The Politicos.* Harcourt, Brace and Co., New York, 1938.

KEMBLE, FANNY. *Journal of Residence on a Georgia Plantation.* Harper Brothers, New York, 1863.

KNIGHT, LUCIAN LAMAR. *A Standard History of Georgia and Georgians.* The Lewis Publishing Co., Chicago, 1917.

———. *Georgia's Landmarks, Memorials and Legends.* The Byrd Printing Co., Atlanta, Ga. 1913-1914.

———. *Reminiscences of Famous Georgians.* Franklin Tanner Co., Atlanta, Ga., 1907-1908.

LANNING, JOHN T. *Spanish Missions of Georgia.* University of North Carolina Press, 1935.

———. *The Diplomatic History of Georgia.* Little, Brown & Co., Boston, 1932.

LEWIS, LLOYD. *Sherman, The Fighting Prophet.* Harcourt, Brace and Co., New York, 1932.

LOGAN, J. H. *History of Upper South Carolina.*

LOWERY, WOODBURY. *Spanish Settlements within the Present Limits of the United States: Florida, 1562-74.* New York and London, 1905.

LYELL, CHARLES. *A Second Visit to the United States of America.* New York, 1868.

McCALL, HUGH. *History of Georgia.* Savannah, 1811.

McCRADY, EDWARD. *History of South Carolina.* Four vols. New York, 1897-1902.

McILWAINE, SHIELDS. *The Southern Poor White from Lubberland to Tobacco Road.* University of Oklahoma Press, 1939.

MILLING, CHAPMAN J. *Red Carolinians.* University of North Carolina Press, 1940.

MITCHELL, BROADUS. *William Gregg, Factory Master of the Old South.* University of North Carolina Press, 1928.

MOONEY, JAMES. *Myths of the Cherokees.* Nineteenth Annual Report of the Bureau of American Ethnology. Part I. Washington, 1900.

OLMSTED, FREDERICK LAW. *A Journey in the Seaboard Slave States.* New York, 1856.

OSKINSON, JOHN M. *Tecumseh and His Times.* G. P. Putnam's Sons. New York, 1938.

PHILLIPS, U. B. *History of Transportation in the Eastern Cotton Belt to 1860.* Columbia University Press. 1908.

———. *Life and Labor in the Old South.* Little, Brown & Co. Boston, 1929.

PINCKNEY, JOSEPHINE. *Hilton Head.* Farrar & Rinehart. New York, 1941.

RAPER, ARTHUR F. *Tenants of the Almighty.* The MacMillan Co., New York, 1943.

RICHARDSON, E. RAMSAY, *Little Aleck, A Life of Alexander H. Stephens.* Grosset and Dunlap, New York, 1932.

ROBINSON, WILLIAM MORRISON, JR. *The Confederate Privateers.* Yale University Press, 1928.

SAINT-AMAND, MARY SCOTT. *A Balcony in Charleston.* Garrett and Massie, Inc., 1941.

Savannah. American Guide Series. Review Printing Co., Savannah, 1937.

SAYE, ALBERT B. *New Viewpoints in Georgia History.* University of Georgia Press, 1943.

SHERMAN, WILLIAM TECUMSEH. *Autobiography.*

SIMKINS, FRANCIS BUTLER. *Pitchfork Ben Tillman.* Louisiana State University Press, 1944.

SIMMS, WILLIAM GILMORE. *The History of South Carolina.* Charleston, S. C., 1840.

SMITH, GEORGE G. *The Story of Georgia and the Georgia People.* Atlanta, 1900.

South Carolina, A Guide to the Palmetto State. American Guide Series. Oxford University Press, New York, 1941.

SPRUILL, JULIA CHERRY. *Women's Life and Work in the Southern Colonies.* University of North Carolina Press, 1938.

STEVENS, REV. WILLIAM BACON. *A History of Georgia from its First Discovery by Europeans.* 2 vols. I, New York, 1847; II, Philadelphia, 1859.

SWANTON, JOHN R. *Early History of the Creek Indians and Their Neighbors.* Bulletin 73 of the Bureau of American Ethnology, Smithsonian Institution, Washington, 1922.

TEMPLE, SARAH BLACKWELL GOBER. *The First Hundred Years. A Short History of Cobb County in Georgia.* Walter W. Brown Publishing Co., Atlanta, 1935.

WADE, JOHN D. *Augustus Baldwin Longstreet.* The Macmillan Co., 1924.

WALKER, ROBERT SPARKS. *Torchlight to the Cherokees.* New York, 1931.

WESLEY, JOHN. *Journal of the Rev. John Wesley, A.M.* E. P. Dutton and Co., New York, 1921.

WOODWARD, C. VANN. *Tom Watson, Agrarian Rebel.* The Macmillan Co., New York, 1938.

MISCELLANEOUS

(Newpapers, Historical Quarterlies and Bulletins, Official Records, Government Reports)

Augusta *Chronicle* and Augusta *Herald*. Newspapers.

BOLTON, HERBERT E. "Spanish Resistance to the Carolina Traders in Western Georgia," *Georgia Historical Quarterly,* IX (1925).

Bureau of American Ethnology. Washington. Annual Reports: 1883-1884; 1898; 1924-1925.

Calendar of State Papers, London, 1889.

Colonial Records of Georgia. Compiled by Allen D. Candler, 22 vols., Atlanta, 1904-1913.

COULTER, E. MERTON. "Mary Musgrove, Queen of the Creeks; A Chapter of Early Georgia Troubles," *Georgia Historical Quarterly,* XI, No. 1.

COULTER, E. MERTON. "The Great Savannah Fire of 1820," *Georgia Historical Quarterly,* XXIII, No. 1.

DUNLOP. "Journal of Captain Dunlop's Voyage to the Southward," *South Carolina Historical and Geographical Magazine,* XXX, No. 3 (July, 1929).

JOHNSTON, J. G. *The Spanish Period of Georgia and South Carolina History, 1566-1702.* Bulletin of the University of Georgia, XXIII (1923).

JONES, CHARLES C., JR. *Indian Remains of South Georgia.* An Address Before the Georgia Historical Society, 1859.

ROSS, MARY. "French Intrusions and Indian Uprisings in Georgia and South Carolina," *Georgia Historical Quarterly,* VII, No. 3.

ROSS, MARY. "The French on the Savannah, 1605," *Georgia Historical Quarterly,* VIII (1924).

Savannah *Press* and Savannah *Morning News*. Newspapers.

WILDES, HARRY EMERSON. *Anthony Wayne, Trouble Shooter of the American Revolution.* Harcourt, Brace and Company, New York, 1941.

VOIGT, GILBERT P. *The German and German-Swiss Elements in South Carolina, 1732-1752.* Bulletin of University of South Carolina, September, 1922.

Index

The dark magic of the people of the Savannah's past haunts the river today. Four hundred years ago exotically colored Indians paddled up and down its reaches. But their peaceful life was suddenly and violently disrupted by DeSoto and an army of six hundred greedy Spaniards in search of gold. The French came, and the British, under the dreamer-statesman Oglethorpe, who arrived from England with a boatload of impecunious hopefuls. Interests clashed, and blood flowed freely on the Savannah. Its shores resounded with feuding and fighting, stirred up by colorful river characters like Mary Musgrove, "Queen of the Creeks," whose lusts and feminine fireworks kept the local menfolk in an uproar for many a year.

The "Avenging Angel" Sherman, "King Cotton," Jeff Davis, "Pitchfork Ben" Tillman, and a host of other famous Southern personages, played important parts in the Savannah's great past. Mr. Stokes has told their story dramatically and with distinction.

Thomas L. Stokes, well-known author and political analyst for United Features, is the winner of Pulitzer and Raymond Clapper Reportorial awards, among others. He also has written CHIP OFF MY SHOULDER.